The Seamy Corners of American Politics

The Seamy Corners of American Politics

Current Conservative Articles on American Politics

Kevin C Caffrey

authorHOUSE®

AuthorHouse™ LLC
1663 Liberty Drive
Bloomington, IN 47403
www.authorhouse.com
Phone: 1-800-839-8640

Published by AuthorHouse   03/14/2014

ISBN: 978-1-4918-7320-5 (sc)
ISBN: 978-1-4918-7318-2 (hc)
ISBN: 978-1-4918-7319-9 (e)

Library of Congress Control Number: 2014905138

Contents

Preface

This is the book for anyone entering a college classroom for political science. If you read this book you will impress your fellow students and the professor with your knowledge and understanding of the current issues facing America today. The articles represent a lot of American history that helps to provide context and understanding for the issues being discussed. The book is great for people of all political stripes because the arguments in each article are interesting and thought provocative.

Each article is backed with knowledge about the entire subject direct and indirectly. By the time you finish the book you will truly have an understanding of the politics of the day. There are going to be just a few people that will understand as much about politics as you. This book makes a great refresher for someone who enjoys understanding current issues from a historical and political perspective. Whether young or old this book will entice and interest you.

The book operates from the conservative agenda of American politics. However, by conservative what are meant are the Tea Party conservatism and not the establishment conservatism of the Republican Party. This country needs to change. The funny thing about change is that the change this country needs is a regression to its American roots. The progressives have progressed America right out of what the Founding Fathers had in mind when writing the United States Constitution.

Instead of a country of representative government the people are being represented by a President who thinks that he is a king. The whole idea that America is a democracy is a fallacy—the United States is a Constitution-based federal republic. The President is elected by the majority of the people in a state but the presidential election is still governed by the Electoral College. The one thing that the Founding Fathers wanted to avoid is a large federal government and a president with too much power.

This book represents the politics of America from 2012 to the present. The book is based on articles from many different subject matters including: economics, education, environmentalism, immigration, American foreign policy, Affordable Care Act, presidential, progressives, and religion. All of the subjects are written from a conservative perspective and written along the lines of what is best defined by the title of Paleoconservatism.

The book represents a discussion that is based on the politics that where part of the twenty four hour news cycle from 2012 until the present. Every article written in this book was written in real time as the events unfolded and blossomed on the media scene. Every article in this book can be found on the internet and all the articles are printed by http://www.nolanchart.com/. The Nolanchart website is well known for its political discourse across the entire political spectrum from Liberals to Conservatives and everything in between.

In many cases you will learn from a perspective of American life that was lived by a person who was in their twenties during the mid-eighties. The former is important because a young person may have difficulty understanding the nuance of the articles. This is not a problem if you want to do your own research on the subject. However, you will not have to go far because all of the information that will help you learn is placed in the article by hyper-links. For older people the book is easy to understand, but it will leave a lot of questions that will stew in your mind. The articles hope to give each person a different meaning about the events that have happened in the recent past. Many of the articles take on some deep subjects while at the same time the articles can lead to laughter. Some of the articles may leave you disagreeing with my outlook on the different subject matters. This is a good thing.

Chapter One

The Elite and the Progressives

The Radicalism of the Progressives

The article discusses American progressives in light of international law and how that persuades their thinking. The Tea Party is also discussed.

Young adults need to wake up to what the progressives are doing or they will vote themselves into a new America—one unlike the America that their parents grew up in. It is the education system that needs to be blamed for the way that Americans think today. Progressives like President Obama think that the young and others are stupid and that they have fallen for the progressive line of logic. President Obama thinks that Democrats are the people that fell for the propaganda that they were taught in private and public schools around America by the liberal left.

The Affordable Care Act is a wakeup call for the so-called "Young Invincibles" because they have been taken for a ride. The worst thing about the Obamacare con job is that the "Young Invincibles" did it to themselves. Yes, young adults voted for President Obama without realizing what the consequences of that vote would mean. In fairness they trusted their professors and other liberal secularists that they met through life. It is only now that the young and others are beginning to understand that they have been lied to by the President.

Progressives represent the antithesis of liberty and the radicalism of progressives is antithetical to conservatism. Vice President Biden[1] during a speech in Virginia stated that "These guys [Tea Party] are the antithesis, the absolute antithesis, of change and progress," The problem with the thinking of the Vice President is what he means by "change and progress" because in his eyes the term means an incremental change that develops less liberty and freedom for the American people.

Progressives are levelers and the harder that a person works the more that person should expect to be taxed so that they can pay for those that do not work. The Affordable Care Act is a tax according to the United States Supreme Court even though President Obama stated in many interviews that it was not a tax. The Daily Caller [2] reminds us ". . . in 2009, the president emphatically denied George Stephanopoulos that the Affordable Care Act imposed a tax increase." Many in Congress believe that if they were told that the Affordable Care Act was a tax it would have never became law.

Progressives in America today are socialists. The entire concept of socialism is premised on "Natural Rights" the problem with the progressives in the United States is that they believe that natural rights are panoply of rights. The natural rights established by the United Nations and the Universal Declaration of Human Rights.

Russell Kirk in his book *The Conservative Mind* explains how Edmund Burke rejected both the concepts of natural rights by Hume and Bentham; "Burke, detesting both the rationalists, says that natural right is human custom conforming to divine intent" (p. 50). The whole concept of customs is developed out of tradition. Tradition and Gods natural law is what a conservative thinks about when contemplating any sort of change. A progressive is always trying to create more power for the government. The progressive creates governmental power by manipulating the majority of the American people into thinking that it is a good idea to take money from the minority of the people.

There are thirty articles of natural rights in the Universal Declaration of Human Rights.[3] Kirk argues that the rights outlined in the Universal Declaration of Human Rights are confused with desires. Those rights are developed by people in order to benefit themselves with the least amount of work being required on their part. People like to confuse rights with "Natural Law." People need to understand that 'Man's rights exist only when man obeys God's

Law" (p. 49).[4] This is an important point that a secularist cannot understand metaphysically.

The United Nations was not finished when it wrote the Universal Declaration of Human Rights because the socialists wanted to argue for even more rights. This is why in 1966 the <u>International Covenant on Economic, Social and Cultural Rights</u> was created.[5] It is in the International Covenant that we find the idea of healthcare as a human right. President Obama and the progressives get their marching orders from international law and not from the United States Constitution. This is because international rights are in many cases contradictory to the rights of citizens under the United States Constitution.

The reason why progressives like to call the Tea Party the far right is due to the fact that they are off the political scale of American politics. Progressives are socialists who are moderates when it comes to communists. The Tea Party represents constitutionalists who believe in the United States Constitution and what it represents as a blue print for American society.

The one area that the progressives and the Tea Party are the same philosophically is on the matter of free-trade. <u>Pat Buchanan argues</u> that America needs more economic nationalists and he argues for fair trade.[6] The problem with free-trade is that the progressives like to develop regulations on businesses that make it impossible to compete with foreign governments that do not have such regulations.

The inability of American men and women to compete with foreign nations with cheap labor and few regulations is what creates the large foreign trade deficits. The reason why all American politicians support free-trade is because they receive their campaign money from corporations and businesses. "<u>Thomas Jefferson wrote</u>: "Merchants have no country. The mere spot they stand on does not constitute so strong an attachment as that from which they draw their gains.""[7] It is up to the American people to demand politicians who care more about the American worker than the corporate officer.

It is time for Americans to understand that they have been lied to on many occasions by the Obama administration and that this must stop. The only way that the Democratic Party will get the message that it cannot lie to the American people is to vote them out of office in future elections. The Republicans did not shutdown the government! It was the President's refusal to face reality when it came to an extension on the implementation of the Affordable Care Act that caused the shutdown. If the President understood the word compromise perhaps he would not have to lie and talk around the American people.

The Shutdown: Democratic Progressives Working Hard to Destroy America

President Obama and his characteristics are discussed in relation with the governmental shutdown. The problem with progressives is discussed.

There is not a sign on President Obama's desk that states "The buck stops here!" like the one that was on the desk of President Truman. The trillions of debt run up by this President alone are more than all the Presidents that came before him.[8] The President has the nerve to say that the Congress has to pay the bills that it has run up. The Senate Democrats have not passed a budget since the President was elected. To correct the former President Obama did sign a budget that was started under President George Bush that was to have a budget deficit of 407 billion dollars.[9]

It is odd but the budget created by the newly elected Democratic Congress at the time ended up creating a deficit of 1.4 trillion dollars. This was the last budget to come out of the Democratic Congress and since then there has not been a budget to move out of the Democratic Senate.

The Executive Branch is the only branch that is an election by the people of the entire nation. President Obama is the leader of all Americans and not of just one state like the Senate or one district like the House of Representatives. It is up to the President to get the Congress together and have them make the compromises necessary to keep the country running.

The President should not have stated that he will not negotiate or to paraphrase the President—he will not negotiate with one small minority of one House of Congress. The President is the leader of the people in those districts too.

President Obama can careless about who gets hurt by his inability to show his leadership to the country. In fact, he enjoys the fact that people are paying a price for what he perceives as something he can play the blame game with by arguing that it is the fault of the Republicans.

The American people need to understand that it is all about the President and what he thinks is the best thing for him. The American people are nothing but the Presidents chattel that only his progressive enlightenment can help. This government shutdown will not end quickly and the President will not do a thing to stop all the bad things that he is arguing will happen.

The President states that the economy and stock market will suffer do to this government shutdown. The economy and the Presidents "New Normal" for the economy will probably fizzle out, however the economy was heading in that direction in any case—regardless if there was a shutdown or not.

In tonight's meeting (10/2/13) both the leaders of the House and the Senate met with the President and nothing happened. Why did they even bother to get together? The President already stated that he was not going to negotiate. The House of Representatives will not sign a continuing resolution without some changes with the Affordable Care Act.

The House of Representatives would like to put the Affordable Care Act on hold for one year and change some of the other parts of the law. The President will not flinch or make any changes in his mind about his plan not to negotiate. It is obvious that the country is at a standstill and that the federal government will probably be shut down until the debt ceiling fight in a couple of weeks.

The game that will be played by both parties and the President now is trying to prove to the American people that they are not at fault and that it is the other guys fault. Each party must argue that any inconveniences that may occur due to the shutdown are the fault of the other party.

Some argue that the above is not the way that a democracy should work and that the majority should get their way. This countries governmental system was built on the idea that the minority would not get trampled upon by the majority.

It was the progressives who made the election of the Senate a majority vote of the people of the state and that was not the way that the Senate was supposed to operate. It was originally up to the various states Congresses to select and send a Senate representative to Washington. Most of the states in the American Republic are in the hands of Republicans now and that would mean that the Senate would not be a Democratic Senate, but a Republican Senate today.

If the aforementioned was the case than the entire Congress would be Republican and the President would only have the power to veto any budget that was placed on his desk. To extrapolate further the Affordable Care Act was made legal by the Supreme Court due to the right of the government to tax. Taxation of the individual citizen did not become law until the progressive Woodrow Wilson manipulated the American people into thinking that only the rich would pay the tax.

The problems that America faces today are all the cause of individuals that call themselves progressive like many Democrats today and the President. The entitlement programs Social Security and Medicaid and Medicare were both developed by progressive Democratic presidents. The Affordable Care Act was created by a progressive Congress and a progressive President.

Most progressives like to argue from the perspective of the rights of the majority. The majority in American society today are looking for a government handout either from an entitlement program or a welfare program. The rights of the people who have the money to pay the taxes that feed the beast of the federal government are losing their rights of liberty and freedom to the Federal, State and Local governments of the United States of America.

America is at a very important time in its history. The Affordable Care Act will place <u>one sixth</u> of the total United States economy in the hands of the federal government.[10] In the studies of the <u>Heritage Foundation</u> it is argued that Obamacare will mean higher healthcare costs and fewer jobs for Americans as the healthcare law moves forward.[11]

Between the new type of economic recovery Americans can expect under President Obama one should wonder about the future. In the future the country will be held down by Obamacare. The United States will fall into a recession that the country is unable to recover from. The progressives or socialists will have finally won the destructive battle that they have been fighting since the late 1800's. The battle for the soul of the country will be over. This once Christian nation of freedom and liberty will become the secular socialist order that the progressives have always wanted. Is your neighbor a progressive?

Idealism and the Progressive

Progressives are the reason for the perpetual downward drop in America. The main reason for the demise of America is idealism.

The problem in America today is that Americans are filled with too much idealism. Idealism the opiate of the educated is ruining the country and if the present course continues today's infants will not understand the freedom and liberty that is enjoyed today. Yes, the young and the stupid think that they have the same freedom and liberty that Americans enjoyed since the beginning of the twentieth century. This is not true Americans have lost the freedom to choose on many different levels. The loss of choice has the effect of limiting freedom among the American people. It is the idealism taught by educators since the 1960's that is causing the loss of freedom in America today.

The rise of the liberal progressive is the cause of all the ills in American society. Liberals do not know or they do not care what their actions are going to lead to as time passes. One of the first things that the liberal progressives accomplished was to tie Americans down by the purse strings with the passage of the Sixteenth Amendment that made federal taxation legal. It is the ability to tax that gave the federal government the money that it needed to begin its expansion. The federal government has not ceased to grow in size and big government is the "New Normal" for America.

Educators have taught that the federal government is the answer for all the problems in America. However, it is the progressive liberal ideology and the federal government that has created most problems in America today. Yes, the federal government is the problem and it causes more problems that take more federal regulations to solve. The solution is always another problem and this creates a perpetual growth in the federal government. One example of a problem was the women's movement (the problem was women's rights) however; this movement caused the breakdown of America's nuclear family.

The breakdown of the American family became the reason for one parent households that paved the way for many federal programs in order to deal with the problem. Because of single families that are usually a one female household we have the need for more welfare programs, housing programs, and changes in the education system along with a laundry list of other problems. For instance, the sexual revolution has caused an entire array of problems from AIDS to children having children and young adults who are not even sure of their own sexuality.

Education was once left up to the local governments and the state governments to operate as each saw fit. It was the people who voted for the local and state representatives that made the system on a small scale work for that particular group of people. The original Dept. of Education was founded in 1867 in order to collect data on how the different schools in America taught education at all levels.[12] It was not until 1980 that Congress established the Department of Education as a cabinet level agency.

Since Charles Darwin's *Origin of the Species* secular education began to grow in the United States.[13] Secularism and progressivism have become the religion of the American education system and a consequence is the ripping of Christianity out of the school system in the United States. Students are taught that they are gods and that knowledge and science trump the moral fabric that America knew in its childhood.

Progressives are the end product of years of secular education. Progressives are taught to love big government and the idealistic concepts taught by teachers. The correlation between big government and idealism teaches students to want more government and hence, vote for the party of big government or the Democrats.

The income tax is a tool used to help limit a person's freedom and liberty. The income tax creates the funding for big government and the federal government creates government regulation and the rule of law to limit Americans freedom.

In 2013 the Tax Freedom Day fell on April 13th this is the day that each American must work until federal, state and local taxes are paid. After April 13th each citizen can then keep their own money. That is forty hours a week that a person's freedom and liberty must be admonished so that the federal government can operate.

One of the paradox's of idealism is its failure at all levels of human existence since the beginning of time. It is strange how educated people can cling to idealist philosophies like communism and socialism. The most peculiar notion being taught in schools today is that of the global citizen. The idea of a borderless world is idealism at its best. Just the idea should leave students laughing, but when explained the concept by a professor and wanting a good grade students are willing to believe anything much like the fallacy of global warming.

In the 1980's educators were teaching about the benefits of a future globalization that would help America move into the information age as the leader. For decades since the 1980's America's manufacturing base has shrunk and it continues to shrink today. It seems as if the educated in America are teaching students how to dismantle the greatest country to ever exist.

Those in government today for the most part were taught in universities that taught nothing but idealism. Idealism is the furthest thing from tradition or the conservative view of living. The United States is becoming lopsided in idealism over realism and this will prove to be the demise of America in the future. Realism takes in the human nature of man that idealism ignores and that is the problem with idealism.

There will never be a global citizen because the differences between people and groups of people will never allow for the western civilization idea of government and values. All attempts to change others into what they do not want to be will end up in war and conflict. The idealistic concept of big government leveling of citizens will fail because the differences in people that create inequality (IQ, body type, personality, etc.) will not give way to the concept of leveling because it is not a part of human nature.

The above are all examples and explanations of the problem with liberal progressives and the ideology of idealism. Idealism is the bad apple in the barrel of American society that must be removed from the mindset of the people. Students today need to be taught that they are American's and not global citizens. That America needs fair trade and not free trade in the world today. Students should reject immigration because America is only so large and resources are finite. Limited government must be a goal for America and a return to a balance budget. Americans need to change and it will take a different type of educator than the liberal progressives that are prevalent today.

The Outsiders and Their Role
in American Politics

The politics of the "far right" and the "far left" are exposed; the real problem in American politics, concerning progressivism is explored.

American politics is at a crossroads that is scary for Americans who respect the ideals that are Founding Fathers created for us. American politics was always about the founding document the United States Constitution. The United States Constitution is under attack by a political ideology that will end democracy on this planet. In order for the people to have freedom, liberty and a pursuit of happiness the United States Constitution needs to be thought of as sacred; America's founding premise must be adhered to. The premise is that America is based on equality of opportunity. This should not be confused by the idea of equality for all. America is the great republic that it is because of the aforementioned God given reality—all people have different God given abilities and skills that automatically create a hierarchy of income disparity in the United States.

The confusion that the American people have with politics is that it seems like those that are supposed to know about politics do not. The idea of a "far right" and a "far left" is ludicrous. What the people see is such a major change on the part of the progressive liberals that they are now off the American political chart. This acknowledgement allows political thinkers to go back to the original concepts of right and left in America.

What this article attempts to do is demonstrate that there is an American middle, a center that has never changed. A conservative faction of the Republican Party that is timeless in its truth, and seamless in the art of permanence that it represents. The "far right" in mainstream America does not exist. What some people now call the "far left" is in truth, an entirely different political mindset, outside of American politics. This will be explained below.

This writer likes to call the new breed of ideology and politics post–progressive because they are not progressive although they pretend to be. What the Post-progressive must do is work around the United States Constitution in order to get any of their radical ideas made law. For a better understanding of the post—progressive this article will use the term "the outsiders" because the political philosophy of outsiders is to end the American Republic. The Outsiders want to take away the citizens of America's freedom and liberty. This will be discussed later, but first let's get back to American politics.

The American middle for this article the independent can be a secularist or a religious person. They are both pro-life and some are pro-choice the one issue does not make them vote a certain way. The main concern of the independents is freedom and liberty, but they believe in recycling and do not take environmentalism much further. The economy is very important and federal taxes should not be over burdensome. The independents vary on what they think the roll of the federal government should be in their lives, but they recoil at the idea of socialism, which to them is un-American.

Liberals on the scale from the middle to the left can have any of the following attributes or beliefs. Liberal Democrats believe in big government and government intervention into the lives of people. Because of the way that they believe in environmentalism, pro-choice, and anti-gun positions they need governmental intervention into other citizen's lives. Liberals believe that they have a right to take away another person's freedom and property.

The big government mentality requires taxation at a much higher rate than the right and the middle want to pay. A liberal is secularist and idealistic so they think that government needs to help the poor not fellow Americans. Liberals are American because they love their own freedom and liberty and fight for those rights with a vengeance.

The right consists of the social conservatives who are pro-life and believe in limited government. They believe in taxation for the enumerated powers of the federal government. In some cases a social conservative will compromise their principle beliefs. This is when the choices given to them are not what they would like, but that they must stomach. The social conservative will vote for a neo-conservative if it came down to it.

A neo-conservative ideology is one of big government, deficits, and war. The neo-conservative is not a conservative at all. The very name **neo-conservative is a contradiction** because the very belief system of a conservative is the same beliefs of conservatives thousands of years ago. **There is never anything new or changing concerning a conservative**.

A majority of libertarian's are the negation of the neo-conservative. The rest of the libertarians can believe in many different things about politics, but that would take volumes to write. However, their core value is liberty and freedom and less or no government at all and this keeps them on the American charts of politics.

A conservative begins his thought from a solid foundation that God is in charge. Morality and ethics for a conservative come from the bible and the writings of those before them. Conservatives understand that they are standing on the shoulders of great men and change is something that needs—at times much thought. Conservatives understand that there will always be change but that change must move forward only after debate and reason. The conservative likes to stick with the devil that he knows.

Russell Kirk believed that conservatism is not an ideology. Conservatives have not changed beyond the reasoning of the Founding Fathers. The United States Constitution was the foundation for the United States Republic and that has and is the foundation that American conservatives have always stood on.

The Outsider would like to do away with the United States Constitution; much like the people of France who failed in their attempt of changing the governmental system by force and blood.

The French Revolution was a complete and utter failure and it took thousands of lives in the process. Let us hope that the Outsiders are not allowed to take America down the previous mentioned path.

The Outsider is sometimes considered a progressive but they are not. Progressives believed in family, religion and the concept of equality of opportunity. The idea that President Lyndon B. Johnson was a progressive is debatable because the idea of a "Great Society "crossed the line of equality of opportunity and moved towards equality for all.

The Outsider is an internationalist and a person who believes in the Constitution of the United Nations rather than the United States Constitution. Outsiders are crooks who steal for those that vote for them. The main objective of the Outsider is to create a middle class, but a middle class not like today. All Americans will end up lower class. There will not be any rich or poor.

The Outsider hates America because of its wealth and how the American people live. The idea of rich and poor as a natural outcome of capitalism is repulsive to the Outsider. The Outsiders are a revolutionary bunch bent on bringing the awesome power of the United States down to the equality of the other economic powers in the world.

In the Outsiders dreams is a one world government of equality for all. Human beings will live not in freedom of opportunity, but freedom from punishment if the rules of government are not abided by. The Outsiders understand that there will be war and the death of millions but secularists love to kill.

Americans cannot continue to be led like sheep into a world foreign from the American Dream. President Obama is an Outsider and hence, beware.

The Power Elite and American Politics

The Republican, Democratic and Tea Party represent the interests of the Power Elite. How the Power Elite control international politics

Let's start with the premise that Republicans, Democrats, and the Tea Party actually are separate units with their on missions and causes. Let us add to the idea that each one is truly different from the other. Domestically the three aforementioned parties have their differences, but they are frivolous issues or the social issues that allow the various candidates to show the constituents that they are different. Environmental, guns, abortion, gay rights, secular or religious, public and private, and now under the Obama administration we have entirely different issues: and these are capitalism or socialism—freedom, liberty and individualism or a command economy and collectivism.

One would think that these are really big issues and from the pure human sense they are important to the individual. The views of an individual are created by family, socio-economics and education. These views are personalized and they make up the individuality of each human being and how they think, or their ideology on all issues. It is the previous that make the individual believe in a certain group and group membership or regarding politics—party affiliation.

The common man is fooled into thinking that they can make a difference in America by how they vote. In politics what things that can change are at the group level. For instance: people for guns or those against guns, or people for abortion and those who are against it. Domestic politics are the items that allow people to believe that they are voting for a change. This is what makes the American voter feel validated by their vote decision.

A pollster would find it difficult to get honest answers about international issues concerning the United Nations, free-trade treaties, and other issues that are going on concerning foreign policy. Most Americans do not even know how many men and women died so far in Afghanistan. One would think that America's military projection around the world would have some sort of meaning in an average Americans life, but it does not. Sad to say most Americans are clueless about the actions taken by the United States in its self-proclaimed role as the American global leader.

It seems that money makes the establishment and without money a candidate cannot win. The Tea Party prides itself in being a grassroots organization but that is now changing. The reality of establishment politics is starting to put pressure on the Tea Party and its winning candidates. What the **Power Elite** in Washington are demonstrating is that it is their way or the inevitable highway for the candidate who does not have their stamp of approval.

Money is what greases the wheels of the political machine and the American political system. The Federal Election Committee numbers demonstrate that seven billion was spend on the 2012 election cycle. Only two billion of the seven came from the actual party committees. Super Pac's spend more than both parties put together. The Tea Party understands that it cannot win without going to the same bowl to eat as the two major parties.

The Tea Party national coordinator Jenny Beth Martin has laid down the mission of its new Super Pac called the *Tea Party Patriots Citizens*. Carl Rove has started a new Super Pac that is supposed to be capable of fighting off the Tea Party. Carl Rove figures if the establishment candidates are well funded in party primaries they will beat the Tea Party candidates. Carl Roves new Super Pac is called *The Conservative Victory Group*. The name of Carl Roves Super Pac is an insult to true conservatives.

It is interesting to see that American politics has an Us and Them mentality when it comes to the media hype created between the old media and Fox News. This US and Them mentality trickles down to the viewers and like magic the media has created political groups that are all financed by the establishment or the Power Elite interests. Money makes the world go round and that is why the Power Elite must control the international global economic community.

The United States after World War II had complete control over the free market system in the world. It was gold that backed the dollar and the dollar became the international currency of the world. The dollar is still the international currency of the world, but if the United States continues on its deficit projections this will change.

After the fall of the Soviet Union the United States took on the task of being the only super power in the world. The American economy and military dominance left the Power Elite thinking that the United States was in for a glorious ride of world power, dominance, and making money for the international community.

If the above is true then the American people really do not matter in the scheme of things; what matters is that the Power Elite continue to control American politics. By controlling American politics the Power Elite control the world. This is why what we are seeing is a Tea Party moving away from its grassroots and moving towards the Power Elite. It will be interesting to observe how politics are argued and who is winning and who is losing within the Republican Party.

The establishment will win either way whether the Tea Party or the Neoconservatives win the battle for the helm of the Republican Party. The Democrats are the Power Elite party of the year in 2013. International politics will not change and America will continue in the same direction that it has been moving towards since the first Bush took office. It does not matter which party is in charge when it comes to international politics and economics.

Americans need to become aware of the fact that there is a Power Elite that have an allegiance not to the United States, but to the world. This is why Americans are right when they say that their children will not be better off in America than them. The establishment is about making the world equal in living standards and in order to accomplish that Americans will be squeezed dry. The awareness of what is happening in America may help the American people to wage a political war against the establishment.

The Tea Party needs to get away from the idea of using Super Pac's and get back to the grassroots that gives them the power they have politically. The neo-cons need to go back to the Democratic Party from which they came and the Tea Party and conservative and libertarian wings of the Republican Party should join forces. If the American people understand the establishment then they can find and vote for candidates that do not belong to the establishment. Perhaps the American people can take back America.

The Problem with Progressive Teachers

Progressives look at America through their own lens and that is different than traditional Americans. Progressive education and its problems in America.

What will America be like when tradition and morality are no longer a part of the American culture? American culture will disappear if the progressives have their way with American society as a whole. The secular religion taught in public schools represents a new belief system for many young people today. The young are taught a liberal education of "eat, drink, and be merry because tomorrow you may die." It is ironic that that quote comes from Ecclesiastics VIII 15 the King James Version because it is a representation of Christianity. Christianity is the one thing that progressives are trying hard to rid America of. The progressives from the 1960's forward by using the education system of America have dismantled the foundation of goodness, morality, and ethics which were once taught in the Judeo-Christian society called the United States of America.

History from the 1960's forward has been manipulated and rewritten discarding many of the facts about this great country while adding historical exaggerations and complete falsehoods. A conservative student must dig deep in order to find accurate American history books, books that still rely on primary sources and first-hand accounts about the true American History of this country. A student cannot depend on teachers to teach the truth in American history classes.

It seems that liberal teachers are too busy teaching students about "white guilt" and how as a white person the student must repent for their sins of being a white American.[14] It was the Spanish who killed a majority of the American Indians and more white blood was spilled to free the slaves than in all the wars America has fought in since the Civil War. Do not be ashamed of being white!

In schools students are not given the complete truth and facts about American government. The Constitution is a one day class because progressives cannot stand the American Constitution and consider it a nuisance. However, progressive teachers will spend five days on a segment of multi-culturalism about one minority group or another. Students are taught statistical falsehoods in order for a liberal teacher to expound upon their own ideological way of thinking. The latest falsehoods are taught about the amounts of spending that went into the Iraq War and the War in Afghanistan in order to justify more welfare spending in America.

The real numbers for war are miniscule compared to the money spend on some eighty plus overlapping welfare programs that are in place in America. In 2011 the Congressional Research Service (CRS) figured that the total money spend for the federal welfare programs after adding the amount that states are forced to pay equaled 1.3 trillion dollars for just one year.[15] The total cost of eight years of war in Iraq had a price tag of 3 trillion dollars.[16]

To place the 1.3 trillion dollar price tag into a better perspective look at it this way—the total cost in 2011 for Social Security was 725 billion, Medicare 480 billion and non-war defense spending was 540 billion. Since 2008 the cost of welfare programs has skyrocketed and is up 32 percent.[17] This is not due to a bad economy as many liberals would want the American citizen to believe. The main reason is a relaxing of welfare standards and requirements to receive welfare. The progressives have taught young people in the secondary education setting that due to the Republican Party people are cold, starving, and homeless on the streets.

The fall from morality and American grace is due completely to the education system in America. The liberal progressives do not teach morals and ethics in the classroom and if they try to teach their perspective it is morality and ethics on dope. For instance, the whole issue of gay marriage is sickening in many ways, but worst of all it represents just another way for progressives to rip away another foundational piece of Western Civilization. And for what reason do progressives hope to tear away at Western Civilization—it is because they hate themselves and the good society.

The good society was America before the 1960's. The riots and radical display's by misfits foisting nonsense on the American Christian society changed America. It is the progressive teachers who have American youth biting at the forbidden fruit. What did the Women's Rights Movement doe for America accept to cause high divorce rates and one parent family homes. The movement also forced both men and women into the work force. The doubling of people in the work force meant that the employers could bid down the price of wage labor. This is why many couples are forced to rely on a two income family in order to make ends meet.

Progressive teachers create problems and then attempt to solve the problems they created by making more problems. Hence, the problems that progressives create in the first place are then perpetuated into further problems for American society.

One example of the backwardness of progressive thinkers is first of all trying to take religion out of the public realm. This caused a good part of young people to grow up in a one parent home while allowing Hollywood to create a bunch of trash for kids' to fill their minds with. The aforementioned societal back steps occur because Christian morality is taken out of the school and replaced by liberal ideological paganism.

For instance, teaching elementary school children sex education and giving children contraceptives and pills without their parent's knowledge. This policy raises further problems and is a catalyst for young people to have sex. This is because school children are taught how to have sex without consequences.

And if a young girl gets pregnant than they can always abort the fetus and that is another problem which has left over fifty billion children unborn and killed by the progressives. It is the secular religion taught in the American school system that teaches it is perfectly fine to kill an unborn baby.

The progressive teachers have a remedy for abortion as well. It is to teach young people the benefits of same sex coupling. Yes, have all the sex that you want without the fear of ever having a child. The union or the making of one whole in regards to same sex couples in marriage is not even appropriate to imagine without feeling ill. The polls on any liberal agenda item are always for the change of something rather than holding to the traditions that helped the American system to survive as long as it has under freedom and representative democracy.

The above as a whole outlines some of the problems America faces due to the education unions and the teachers that belong to them. It is as if the enemy was allowed into a guarded fortress and understands everything that is going on inside and outside. Most teachers grew up in America and where educated in the liberal halls of academia to not think for themselves.

Like students today the current teachers were taught through liberal progressive group think. This new age teaching made popular students the ones that parroted and agreed with the teacher while the unpopular kids who thought for themselves and argued became outcasts. Most students choose to be on the inside or the liberal ideological side of political social and economic issues. The young adults of today taught in liberal progressivism and secular enlightenment will pay for their voting mistakes. Yes, the middle aged of tomorrow will have to pay the bills for those that they voted for while they still lived at home with mommy or just a daddy. Most of the kids with two parent homes have their own values and think for themselves and many are morally steep in religion.

The Secular "New Elite" and President Obama Working Together

The article discusses the "New Elite" and their thinking on Obama politics, society, and morals in light of socialism, religion and WASPs.

The problem with the Ivy towers of America, the universities that are admired by society is that they have changed drastically. The best universities with supposedly the best academic Doctors in the world seem to teach from the international perspective, they are global professors. In grades K thru 12 the teachers were taught by the above professors. The conclusion must be that the students in K thru 12 because of their teachers are also schooled in the philosophy of the Ivy League professors. Since the early 1960s, and K thru 12 starting in the 1970s, all teachers are wrapped around a western international idealist ideology perpetuated by groupthink. Groupthink is rewarded within the group and by the group it is this circular process that develops its own hypothesis, theories and rules of learning.[18] The system of the 'New Elite" has in the process mastered the art of meritocracy, or of giving the teacher what the teacher expects and more.[19] Hence, everyone begins to think with the same social liberal underlying ideology. The thought process of the entire meritocracy is today intertwined in the United States political fabric.

The professors of education from the 1960s onward seem to have from decade to decade dismantled the belief system of the United States. The God and country philosophy that the WASP's taught in public schools and in the general public is no longer pertinent.[20] The truth about America's Christian heritage is ridiculed, mocked and attacked by the left wing supporters in the last few decades; it is easy for a centrist or conservative American to believe the worst from the federal government. The next step will come from the Homeland Security it will start the <u>arresting of patriotic groups</u> in America.[21] The last premise is not farfetched it is something that Homeland Security is practicing and preparing to do if needed. In 2012 a child is sometimes sent home from school for expressing their love for God. And a t-shirt that states, 'Jesus loves you" will in some areas of the United States earn a child suspension for a week or more.

A student today is more likely to receive a lessor grade on a paper if the writing expresses anything good about America; while the student next to them is given an 'A' paper for America bashing. Children today have a similar mindset with their parents, but an education that is radical to that of their grandparents. It is sad. Americans do not even recognize the change that has moved through the country in the last fifty years. The high levels of divorce and the two working parent family creates less quality time for a family. The Christian family is the key to a great nation and that key is lost in America currently. American society at all levels economically and socially is much worse today than it was prior to the 1960s.

It seems like the gap between Americans is growing and the middle class is being crushed. The evidence is in how President Obama is operating his campaign in order to win the 2012 election. The Presidents election is not about America. To listen to President Obama this 2012 election is about one group against another. President Obama has all Americans pointing a gun at the other, group against group, but we are all in a circle firing at each other. The American people are mostly going to lose: money, freedom, liberty and dignity, if President Obama is re-elected. The only winners will be the *new elite* and President Obama. Another four years of President Obama will make the new elite rich. Obama will get a chance to put America in a deficit hole that it may never recover from.

President Obama calls the aforementioned "Fairness." [Rawls] calls his theory—aimed at formulating a conception of the basic structure of society in accordance with social justice—**justice as fairness**."[22] Republican conservatives call the type of **fairness** mentioned above nothing but what it is—the economic leveling of a society.[23] The new elite believe in globalization for personal profits without a sense of nationalism or patriotism towards their home country, the United States. The rich in America prefer to have their assets funneled off by free-trade globalization.

The United Nations will end up a large winner, because of international taxation that is already in the works. In many cases the money will end up in Africa because the people are suffering more in Africa than the poor in the United States. It is only **fair** to take from the nations with more and to give it to the poorer nations. Therefore, America will not need to worry about class warfare. America will end up as a two class system of rich and poor with a military between the two in order to maintain the "Rule of Law."

According to liberal secularists or leftist Democrats nationalism is a sin. Because of the rate that this nation is assaulted by fringe leftist democratic terrorist groups like the '99 percent' the working Christian family is threatened. There are many liberal groups attacking all American symbolism, religious and nationalistic. This is forcibly accomplished through litigation in order to have the former American symbolism removed by the courts. It will not be long until in the name of democracy, a world majority vote will nullify the American flag and Old Glory will no longer be flown in the United States. America will end up under a United Nations flag. America will not be a sovereign nation, but a political and economic area that belongs to the "International Order" like President Obama told the cadets' at West Point in 2010.[24]

The old elite David Brooks points out were the White Anglo Saxon Protestants (WASP's) or the old protestant establishment.[25] The WASP's sat atop of the country and controlled the universities, the politics, the law, the finances and the entire world for that matter. But they have relinquished their power and a 'New Elite" has taken over, David Brooks believes that this *new elite* stinks.[26] The big question now is why did the old elite WASP's relinquish power? The protestant WASP believed in the United States Constitution and its

Founding Fathers. The Founding Fathers did not want an aristocracy in America.

The WASP's for love of country, its Constitution, and God allowed the *new elite* to take over the positions of power in the United States. In other words, the WASP's moved back and let the *new elite* enter into the <u>American establishment</u>.[27] A perfect example is the Supreme Court, it took until 1916 for the first Jew to be appointed to the court. The rest of the court since the nation's birth was White Protestant. Today in 2012 the court is made up of seven Catholics and two Jews, and not one White Protestant.

The <u>New Elite of America</u> have no understanding about America or the American Dream. They are deists, theists and atheists, they are not Christian.[28] *New elites* are mostly part of the <u>secular religion</u> and this writer, like others consider the previous blasphemies, but yet a religion.[29] The *new elite* understand only what they have seen, and what they are taught. What they have seen is the degradation and downhill slide of American culture and morals.

The *new elite* were not born when everyone learned English, saluted the American flag, and loved America, The days when neighbors cared and helped each other. <u>Movsesian</u> explains that there were days when an American was an American regardless of religion—it was the days of unity in America: whether Irish, English, German, Scottish, or Jewish. Religion was free to practice and people respected each other's separate beliefs.[30] Before 1962 and John F. Kennedy's assassination America was a different country than it is today.

The problem with the exit of the WASPs and the entrance of the "<u>New Elite</u>" is in the character, values and political beliefs of the two.[31] The WASPs supported the United States Constitution, its foundation of God, and the belief that America, and the people that came to America through providence, had the <u>Manifest Destiny</u> to control all of North America. <u>Walter Russell Mead</u> argues that the <u>New Elite</u> are all different in terms of creation theory.[32] <u>Deists</u>, Theists or Atheists are best a description for political use and that is that they are <u>secular idealists</u>. The *new elite* have one major ideological belief and that is: "The meritocratic social ideal is that there should be an open competition ['open meritocracy'] to determine who is best."[33] That the smartest should lead. Besides the latter in order of importance: money, internationalism, Multi and International Corporations, NGOs and IGOs along with a domestic policy of big government and spending. The morals of the *new elite* are that they have no morals; everything is permissible. In morals and ethics the *new elite* are just like a Libertarian.

Despite the new elites learning and living their lives in the top niches of American society the new elite are lacking in common sense in the writer's opinion. The world that the *new elite* created and operate is an oligarchy and nothing like a democracy. The new elites have developed what Robert Michel's calls the "Iron Law of Oligarchy" the Law of Oligarchy at its root definition is simply the organization.[34] How a corporation or and widget is organized and how that organization changes and making it better is what the new elite do best. In the new elites mind the smartest individuals should be able to maximize life for others because of the control over the organization. The *new elite* operate mostly as technocrats.

There are two principles to the Law of Oligarchy, the first is the principle of differences or the idea that there are vast differences among human beings and hence, a natural hierarchy.[35] It follows that being the smartest of the smart means that that person leads and so on. The second principle is a lot like the reasoning of the WASPs and that is that there must be mobility. That those at the bottom can move to the top and those at the top can move in other directions. The whole organization continues to grow and change. Hayes seems to think that the new elite should be feared, because they are Social Darwinists.[36] The new elite believe in survival to the fittest (smartest) and they do not think that people are equal. The Protestant WASP believes that everyone is equal, because everyone is equal in God. This is the main difference the concept of equality, because it is equality that breeds' freedom and liberty.

Democrats Thrive on Inequality

The Democrats believe that the American people will support them if they continue with the Robin Hood routine.

President Obama does not want a better economy he loves the "New Normal" economy. The "New Normal" economy is good for liberals. Yes, liberals thrive on a bad economy because a bad economy means that people are hurting. People that are hurting are good business for Democrats—it helps them get elected. Inequality is the new gem for the Democratic Party. The Democrats like to pit the different economic classes against each other. When the Democrats are in the majority that is the time when more redistribution takes place. Tax the rich. The Democratic Party is the Robin Hood of America.

The reason why the federal government has the right to tax individuals in the first place is due to the <u>Sixteenth Amendment</u> that was voted on by the people. The people were sold on the idea of the Sixteenth Amendment by the politicians at the time who said that the new tax was for corporations and the rich only. All humans love things that are free. The politicians argued that they would take from the rich to help the poor. The people were all for it. The Democratic Party plays the same game today. Tax the rich.

The problem with the tax the rich concept is that there is not enough revenue for the government by taxing the rich. In fact, the government could take every penny from the rich and still not cover a year's worth of the federal deficit. John Stossel in a <u>Forbes</u> magazine article argues: "If the IRS grabbed 100 percent of income over $1 million, the take would be just $616 billion. That's only a third of this year's deficit."[38] It should be obvious that when the Democrats are asking for taxes they really want the money from the middle class.

The best example of one of the ways that the Democrats operate is the Affordable Care Act. The American people where lied to in many ways and not just the President's lie about being able to keep your insurance if you like your insurance. But the original lie that the Affordable Care Act was not a tax and taxes were not going to go up. In order for the Affordable Care Act to get passed the Supreme Court—the Supreme Court declared the law a tax. Many people thought that the Affordable Care Act would not affect them; however the act taxes everyone more. The people that have company insurance will also pay more.

John Hayward of Human Events wrote an entire article called: "Here Comes the Obamacare Tax Avalanche." In the article all of the new taxes for the Affordable Care Act are discussed. Hayward argues that Obamacare is ". . . the largest tax increase in a generation, much of it levied against the middle class." [39] And the American people thought that President Obama and the Democratic Party were looking out for the middle class.

How will a person pay a tax for Obamacare when they get their insurance from their employer? First, there is a two percent tax levy on all insurance policies that will affect everyone. Secondly, there is the two dollar fee per policy to pay for the new Medical Research Trust Fund. And of course lastly, but not least there is the tax on insurance providers who must pay a three and one half percent fee just to sell insurance on the Obamacare exchange. This tax will naturally get passed onto the consumer. These are only some of the new taxes that the Obama administration and the Democratic Party have foisted on the American people. To learn more the reader should read the Obamacare Tax Avalanche article.[40]

The "Young Invincibles" are expected to pay the most for the new Democratic Parties redistribution system called Obamacare. This is because they are forced to pay for the old and the sick. The "Young Invincibles" not only have to pay for the Affordable Care

Act, but they must also pay taxes for Social Security and Medicare. It seems that the teacher unions that created the mindset of today's liberals deserve more government money for education. After all it is the teacher unions that taught the "Young Invincibles" of America how to vote only for the Democratic Party and to read the New York Times and watch MSNBC.

How else will the Democratic Party try to usher votes for their plans on the redistribution of the American people's money? One of the plans of the Democratic Party is to raise the minimum wage. The Democrats are already explaining to the American people that it is the Republican Party that is against raising the minimum wage to help the poor. The minimum wage issue is another scam developed by the Democratic Party for redistribution. One group of Americans may benefit from a rise in the minimum wage, but this will be at the expense of the working poor and unemployed.

Businesses will have no choice but to raise prices in order to pay workers and still make a profit. This means that the working poor who already make ten dollars an hour will probably not see a wage increase, but they will have to pay more money for goods and services. This means that the dollar that the working poor make will not go as far or one can say the people are paying a tax. The tax is because of a weaker dollar due to a government policy that makes the dollar weak by creating artificial wage requirements for all Americans.

The unemployed will not be able to get a job. The fact is that companies will not hire as many workers due to the new minimum wage law. Less work for Americans means that more Americans will end up on the welfare rolls. Putting people on welfare is a win–win for the Democratic Party, because it makes automatic votes for the Democratic Party. Hence, the people who get a pay raise because of the minimum wage increase will vote Democratic. The people who end up on welfare because of the new minimum wage law will also vote Democratic. The working poor and the middle class will end up having to pay more for goods and services due to the new minimum wage. The aforementioned developments are just another way that the Democratic Party can redistribute wealth in America.

The above will go on and on in different ways until all Americans are socioeconomically the same. Everyone will be relatively poor. It is the Democratic Parties communist dream. Just when the American people think that they can go no lower the Democratic Party—and its one world order—will bring them down even further. The only way out of the Democrats "race to the bottom" is to vote them all out of office.

Democrats Think Equality is
a Government Program

The Democratic Party thinks that the only way that the American people can achieve equality is through government intervention.

It is hard to imagine that Americans can be as stupid as the Democratic Party makes them out to be. President Obama spent his first two years making sure that his healthcare bill was passed. The President did not seem to care about the tragic state of the American economy. The Congress passed the American Recovery and Reinvestment Act (ARRA) worth a total of 787 billion dollars in February of 2009.[41] A month after the President took office. The President should have put all of his efforts into the American economy and left healthcare alone. It seems President Obama did not care about the American economy. The President was more interested in passing his legacy legislation the Affordable Care Act (ACA).

In a _National Review_ article Harvard economist Alberto Alensina argues that government stimulus spending does little to spur GDP growth in the economy.[42] Another interesting point that economist Alberto Alensina makes is that increased taxes actually depress the economy. Hence, President Obama's stimulus failed; and by raising taxes the President actually hindered America's economic growth.

There are many ways to look at the ARRA. The liberals will have you look at it one way—as a winner. The conservatives will show statistics that make it look like a loser. The main point is that a lot of money was spent and the American people were ripped off. A perfect example is from the <u>American Enterprise Institute</u> on how the United States spent some of the stimulus money: "seven households in Montana for whom taxpayers just spent $7 million each to extend broadband access probably don't even want it."[43] The Harvard economist is right just spending money does not spur the economy.

In 2014 what America is seeing is the faulty beginning of the ACA and its pending failure. The American people have now learned that the President lied to them when it came to his comment "That you can keep your insurance if you want to." The President also lied about his comment that Obamacare is not a tax. The Supreme Court made the point that the ACA is a tax.

More Americans will lose their health insurance and many will end up paying more money for health insurance. Some Americans may get free health insurance, but that will come at the cost of the Presidents lackey's the "Young Invincibles." It is the "Young Invincibles" that in the years to come—because of the debt and taxes that President Obama is creating—are going to end up under government serfdom.

The main argument of the aforementioned paragraphs above is that the President did not make the economy his first priority. The President made healthcare his number one priority on taking office. The President squandered the stimulus money and did not create the jobs that the Democratic Party promised that the stimulus money would create. Because healthcare is the Presidents priority it should have run smoothly, but instead upon implementation the program is nothing but problems. The inherent contradictions within Obamacare have not yet begun to affect Americans. Hence, the President has not accomplished anything for the American people economically or with his healthcare program. In fact, the Affordable Care Act will further affect the American economy in a negative way according to many scholars.

How do the Democrats plan on running campaigns in 2014? The Democrats are going to run on inequality and how they can fix inequality. This is pathetic, because the Democrats have not done a thing to help Americans. The Democrats should have worked on developing a vibrant economy and not creating a welfare state.

A strong economy would have forced companies to pay people more money. The poor economy is causing the American people to ask for a higher minimum wage. A higher minimum wage will hurt the American economy. The Democrats are all for making the economy worse. A bad economy makes for more Democratic voters. It is all about getting the votes of the uneducated Americans. Many Americans do not realize how a higher minimum wage can hurt them in the long run.

Thanks to President Obama people will suffer from further inequality as soon as companies decide to stop offering health insurance to its employees. Yes, Obamacare will end up being one of the only healthcare choices for the American people. This will cause the American people to pay for their own health insurance out of their own paycheck. Companies will not pay employees more money after they take insurance away from them. This will cause further inequality for the American people.

The Democrats want to go into the 2014 election as the party of equality for the American people. The problem is that the Democratic Parties policies are what are causing the inequality in America.

The main purpose behind this article is to demonstrate how ludicrous it is for the Democrats to campaign on inequality. Inequality is a problem the Democrats have created. If the American people want to know why the rich are getting richer it is due to the 85 billion dollars a month that the Federal Reserve is pumping into the economy. Banks and businesses do not have anywhere to invest the money because the Obama administration's policies make them fearful. What the banks and businesses are doing is taking the money from the Federal Reserve for investment and putting it into the stock market. It is President Obama that is helping the rich get richer.

If the Democrats do not take major loses in the 2014 elections it is due to poor messaging by the Republicans. There is not a reason for the Democrats to win any seats in the 2014 elections. There are only two reasons why the Democrats may win in 2014. The first is the American people are as stupid as the Democrats think that they are. Secondly, the rich will pour tons of money into the Democrats campaigns. This is so that President Obama and his new Federal Reserve chairwoman continue to pump 85 billion a month into the economy. It should be noted that the "Young Invincibles" at home with mom and dad are going to have to pay back the 85 billion dollars a month in the future. Living home will cost the "Young Invincibles" a lot of money in the future.

The Democrats will try to blame the Republican Party for inequality. It is federal regulation and taxes that create inequality. It is the welfare state that the Democratic Party tries to uphold that causes inequality. It is a poor economy that lowers wages. It is the federal mandatory healthcare apparatus that will cause more inequality. The only equality that the progressive Democrats will stop at is complete and utter poverty for all Americans. The policies of the Democratic Party do not live up to the American way of life—less government, hard work, and charity for your neighbors—because it is the moral thing to do. Democrats respect handouts and morality as long as it comes at the expense of someone else's dime.

Chapter Two

Immigration and Affirmative Action

Illegal Aliens Make all Americans Suffer

In competing for jobs the illegal immigrants make it so the poor in America must work for less. Illegal Aliens cost the nation a lot in social welfare programs.

The irony of American politics is best represented by the idea of immigration reform legislation. There are so many different ways to deal with the problem because there are so many different positions on the subject of illegal immigrants. Some think that just ignoring the problem and not upholding the law is a good policy. Others think that we should reward illegal aliens by giving them amnesty and afterwards uphold the laws that already exist. The policy of President Obama is to ignore federal immigration law to begin with. Today the President wants to pass more immigration legislation by Executive Order. This President is not in a position to change the laws of this country unilaterally although he thinks that he is.

Many people who have done the right thing and followed the law concerning immigrating to America are affected in a bad way by illegal aliens. Americans who have come to the country legally are forced to work for less. This is because a business owner can hire illegals to do a job much cheaper than an American will do the job for. Americans that want more money should not be clamoring about increasing the minimum wage. The people that make minimum wage should be shouting from the roof tops to get the illegals out of the country so that businesses would have to pay more.

Politicians believe that all Latino's think that amnesty is the answer. Politicians believe that if they are soft on immigration then the Latino's will vote for them. This is not true. A better part of the majority of Latino's would rather not have the illegals in the country. Especially the Latino's who work in the construction and service industries in America. The illegals are actually hurting the Latino's who are in the country legally. It is not only the working Latino's who are paying the price for illegal immigrants. All Americans from the middle class down to the dirt poor suffer from the many different problems that illegal aliens produce.

First, let's take a closer look at the children of Latino's that are legally in the United States. It is the children that are affected by the illegal aliens in this country the most. The children of American Latino's are getting short changed in education by the <u>states allowing illegal children</u> into the school system.[1] Many of the illegal children do not speak English and come from a home that does not speak English. In school the illegal students take up the time of the teachers and dumb the entire class of students down. This has broad negative effects on how all Latino's measure on state and federal education tests.

The largest problem with progressives is that they have no understanding of how one event can affect other things. For instance, a lack of immigration law enforcement affects the education and general welfare of all legal Americans. Do the progressives (by progressives it is also meant establishment Republicans) care about the general welfare of the American people? It is hard to argue that progressives care about the American people because if they did they would uphold the laws of America in relation to illegal immigration.

There are many ways to look at the issue of general welfare and it must be looked at in the terms of the welfare safety net. The welfare system that provides money, housing, food, and healthcare is inundated by illegals. Illegals should not be able to receive any welfare benefits in America. It is a lack of law enforcement that is the cause of welfare benefits ending up in the hands of illegals— because of this all welfare recipients must suffer. In fact, American war veterans lost six billion dollars over the next ten years because the Democrats in Congress did not want to close a <u>loophole that gave IRS tax credits</u> to illegal aliens.[2]

Everyone suffers because of illegal aliens in the United States. At the federal, state and local levels law agencies are not doing their job of upholding immigration law. It is this lack of law enforcement that makes it more convincing for an illegal to make the move to the United States. A person from Mexico with nothing begins to think about coming to America. The reason being is that there are all kinds of free stuff that are given away in the United States. If the person is smart they will decide to cross the border and make it into the United States.

The illegal will justify the move by rationalizing the idea that America does not uphold its own immigration laws. America is the place to be—because a person can get more from welfare than they can make on a minimum wage job. The American government will provide everything. The federal government makes illegal border crossing a no brainer.

The Democrats talk about inequality and it is because of the Democrats that America has more inequality. The Democrats receive the Latino vote because they are perceived as helping the Latino's more than the Republican Party. The Democrats are hurting the hardworking Americans in this country by making them compete for jobs against illegal workers. Some argue that the illegals do the jobs that Americans will not do. If an American is paid a fair wage for an honest day's wage they will work. There are more than enough Americans in this economy looking for jobs than there are jobs. It is the rich and American businesses that love illegals because they keep wages down for Americans.

Studies show that most of the congressional members that are for amnesty and immigration reform are from districts with a large Latino population. Other congressional members are getting bank rolled by the many businesses that thrive on the labor of illegals. It is the establishment Republicans and the Democrats that are in support of immigration reform that allows for amnesty. The aforementioned are the same politicians who support the United Nations, globalization, and NAFTA. In many cases Americans are forced to vote for people who do not have their interests at heart. President Obama argues that Congress is doing nothing about immigration and it is his job to pass immigration law by Executive fiat.

Illegal immigration has nothing to do with race and everything to do with economics. Money is colorblind and it speaks every language. Corporations love cheap labor because it means higher profits. Americans do not dislike illegal aliens because of any race issue it is purely an economic issue that affects the middle class and the poor in the United States. Illegal aliens affect the education of America's children to a detriment. Illegals perpetuate the movement of illegal drugs into the county. The only immigration reform that will work is strict adherence to American immigration laws that are on the books. It takes a President who cares about the American people and not special interests to think realistically about immigration reform. President Obama cares more about the illegals in this country than he respects the people that voted for him.

The Founding Fathers Never Envisioned American Multi-Culturalism

The history of American immigration and the failure of the present day politicians to do anything about the problem are discussed.

The problem with American political leaders is that they were taught at universities by either socialist or communist professors. They were professors that filled students' heads with a bunch of garbage that had nothing to do with the true history of America. President Eisenhower knew that something had to be done about the Mexican problem. Mexicans were running wild throughout the western border states of America. President Eisenhower removed by force the Mexicans that were in the country illegally. The President was responsible for the deportation of 1.3 million Mexicans back to Mexico. President Eisenhower did not just move the Mexicans across the Mexican border. In many cases the illegal aliens were moved by bus or train over five hundred miles into Mexico. Other illegals were put on ships and brought from Port Isabel Texas to Vera Cruz Mexico.

The Eisenhower policy started on June 17, 1954 and it was called "Operation Wetback."[3] The person in charge of Operation Wetback was General Swing who was an old army buddy of President Eisenhower from his WestPoint days. General Swing was made the director of Immigration and Naturalization Services (INS). General Swing had about 750 agents and the agents began rounding up close to 100,000 illegals each day. This went on for months and expanded too many states including: California, Arizona, Texas, Utah, Nevada, and Idaho. The illegal Mexicans who did not get caught were said to have fled the United States and went back to Mexico; "General Swing's fast-moving campaign soon secured America's borders— an accomplishment no other president has since equaled.[4] Illegal migration had dropped 95 percent by the late 1950s." Keep in mind that the states mentioned above were once American territories. It is important for Americans to remember that the majority of states that petitioned and voted for statehood did so when only white males were eligible to vote in America. Hence, a state in America did not become a state until it had established a majority white threshold.

The most ludicrous argument by politicians is that this country is a country of immigrants. The progressive President Theodore Roosevelt warned America about allowing the wrong type of person the ability to immigrate to the United States: ""Americanization" was a favorite theme of Roosevelt's during his later years, when he railed repeatedly against "hyphenated Americans" and the prospect of a nation "brought to ruins" by a "tangle of squabbling nationalities."[5] The American Congress was very particular on who was allowed into the United States of America. The term immigrant before 1880 was more or less semantics. Congress in the early twentieth century allowed immigration by specific numbers and by European country of origin.

It was in 1875 that the United States Supreme Court made immigration the sole responsibility of the federal government rather than the states. In 1880 the United States had its large influx of immigration into the Country. Congress needed to address the situation and get immigration under control. "The government introduced the National Origins Quota Act in 1921.[6] The quota limited the number of legal immigrants to 3% of their current ethnic makeup in the United States. This immigration quota system was altered three years later and the percentage was lowered to 2%." In 1924 the Comprehensive Immigration Law was passed which eliminated almost all immigration, except for the college educated and those with other needed skills.[7]

In 1927 the "2 percent Rule" was established and immigration was capped at 150,000 individuals annually.[8] This meant that from 1927 until the Immigration Act of 1965 Americans had about forty years to develop an American identity. A new type of American was established after World War II and that was an American character steep in the development of an American moral code and value structure that was based on a Christion Code of Ethics.[9] Americans in 1965 had a strong sense of what an American was. This created Americans that were patriotic and proud of their American heritage.

The death of John F. Kennedy marks the beginning of the decline of America. President Lyndon B. Johnson and his "Great Society" idealism paved the way for the Immigration and Nationality Act of 1965 (Hart-Cellar Act).[10] This created a globalization of immigration in America. People from around the world were allowed to immigrate to the United States. President Johnsons Immigration Act did away with all discriminatory quotas on immigration.[11] Many argue that President Johnson's policy was an extension of the Civil Rights legislation of 1964. Johnson's "War on Poverty" meant: "American liberalism was at high tide under President Johnson."

Between 1965 until the present the United States has averaged over one million immigrants a year and this includes over three hundred thousand illegals. From 1980 to 1993 over eighty percent of those immigrating to America were from Latin America and Asia.[12] In November of 1986 President Reagan signed the Immigration Reform and Control Act (IRCA) this act gave amnesty to over three million illegal immigrants.[13] The act was supposed to end the illegal immigration problem in America permanently.

The Bi-partisan Congressional Bill IRCA ". . . required all persons to show authorization to work in the U.S., increased border enforcement, and created a legalization program for undocumented immigrants who met eligibility requirements." Critics of the bill argued and their arguments are still relevant today that the federal government seems unable to secure or control America's borders. Congress has passed seven amnesties for illegal immigrants since President Reagans Immigration Reform and Control Act.[14] Illegal immigrants continue to pour over are borders and the federal government does absolutely nothing to stop it.

The Humane thing to do for the American people are to control American borders and President Obama should be doing all that is possible to make that happen. The Office of Homeland Security is a governmental agency that was created because of the 9/11 tragedy in the United States. President Obama's amnesty for illegal immigrants is a crime and sadistic for many law abiding Americans. Amnesty for illegals is a lot like water boarding the American people. Homeland Security was created because of America's porous borders and terrorism. The main reasons why the 9/11 hijackers were in this country to begin with was because of weak border control. President Obama's Homeland Security amnesty was worked out in October of 2011.

Homeland Security argues that the cost of removing illegal immigrants is too high and another solution should be worked out by Congress. If the borders are secure illegals are not going to get into the United States to begin with. The rich in America think that it is unfair to deport illegal aliens. Who are the rich and what gives them the right to discuss fairness? What the American rich do not understand is that by supporting illegals they are pitting underclass against underclass for jobs. This makes a terrible situation in America even worse. Many of the illegals in America benefit from government programs. The American nanny state is going to be the end of America. America needs another forty years for "Americanization" without immigration and the borders must be secured. If not, America is on its way to the ash heap of history.

Neocon Champ Senator Marco Rubio on Immigration

Senator Rubio has walked away from his Tea Party roots in order to win the favor of the Republican Establishment and the Neoconservatives.

After winning his Senate seat in 2010 Senator Marco Rubio <u>did not even thank</u> the Tea Party organization for his victory during his acceptance speech.[15] In fact, when asked questions about the Tea Party Senator Rubio tries to distance himself from the Tea Party. Senator Rubio this February said that he backs Carl <u>Rove's Conservative Victory Project PAC</u> as something worthwhile in order to get more mainstream Republicans elected in districts that a Tea Party candidate would lose during a general election.[16] Why would a person reject the group of people that were most responsible for their senate victory?

A Self-centered man like Senator Rubio with his eyes on a much larger role for himself in American politics must think of himself as a visionary. Perhaps the presidency is on Senator Rubio's mind and this requires much more than small government conservatives like those in the Tea Party. **Senator Rubio must become a Republican Establishment man** and this means that he must be many things to many different people.

Money is very important when it comes to presidential politics. The Tea Party has nowhere near the money that a candidate Marco Rubio would need to win the Republican primaries and then go on to win the White House. This kind of money can only come from the establishment and who understands the establishment better than the neoconservatives.

It did not take long for the neoconservatives to pass the torch to Senator Rubio. James Kitfield wrote an article called *The Neocon Torch: Marco Rubio*; Kitfield argues how at a retirement party for Senator Joe Lieberman Senator Rubio laid out his ideals about American global leadership, freedom fighters, and America's quest against evil around the world.[17] This was hardly a speech that someone would hear from traditional conservatives like Pat Buchanan or Russell Kirk. The neoconservatives believe that it is America's mission to spread democracy around the world. The amount of American blood and treasure is of little importance to the neoconservative internationalist.

Many people are not aware of what exactly a neoconservative is and what they stand for it is important to solve that problem here. Neoconservatives had a home in the Democratic Party and they did not start coming over to the Republican Party until the days of the Rockefeller Republicans. The neoconservatives are interested in big government and international institutions with America at the helm. Hence, for the neoconservative it is the job of every American president to rid the world of evil and to help the downtrodden.

What confuses people about the neoconservative is that during the Cold War traditional conservatives felt that it was necessary to approach the Soviet Union with a containment strategy. This containment strategy brought America into wars like the Korean War and the Vietnam Conflict, but these wars where in order to stop communist aggression. The neoconservatives saw the end of the Cold War as a time of peace but also as a time of great opportunity to bring democracy to the world.

The big difference between Cold War presidents and neoconservatives is that conservatives acted out of national interests; and the neoconservative presidents fought wars for reasons that do not reflect America's national interest. The best example is the most recent Iraq War and the idea that America did not have a national interest at stake. Hence, America should probably have avoided the war altogether.

Neoconservatives are big government and big spending politicians that do not really care much about a balanced budget approach to American politics.[18] Conservatives and the Tea Party are interested in limited government and balanced federal budgets. The neoconservatives are globalists who believe in handing American sovereignty over to international institutions. Conservatives believe in looking out for the best interests of the American people. The aforementioned paragraphs discussing neoconservatives explains the confusion when a person hears the term conservative because the term is loaded with many different meanings in today's political realm.

When the term neoconservative is used for Senator Marco Rubio then the reader must understand what political philosophy is being discussed and what Senator Rubio stands for. With this in mind let's turn attention to the "Gang of Eight" and the Senator's role in immigration reform.

The immigration bill being proposed by the "Gang of Eight' does not have the American peoples best interest in mind. Every President since President Reagan has wanted to get some sort of immigration bill passed. It should be noted that Bush, Clinton, Bush, and Obama are all globalist leaning Presidents who all wanted or want immigration reform. Immigration is good for big business, commercial farmers and all other businesses that benefit from unskilled labor. There is nothing good that can come from the immigration bill being presented by the "Gang of Eight" for the American working class.

The President of the Heritage Foundation Jim DeMint argues that over the next fifty years the legalization of eleven million illegal aliens will cost the American people 6.3 trillion dollars. DeMint argues that the Rubio family immigrated to the United States in the 1950's before the big social welfare changes of President Johnson's "Great Society" and today's Patient Protection Affordable Care Act (PPACA) passed by the Obama Administration. DeMint argues that the welfare state that exists in America today is detrimental for the

American people because the low skilled immigrants that will receive amnesty will cost the American people more than they pay in taxes.

The <u>844 page bill</u> created by the "Gang of Eight" is difficult to understand and some think the bill will have many repercussions that the bill does not account for.[19] For instance, many think the border should be secured before any forward movement or talks about amnesty are on the table for discussion. For many traditional conservatives the new immigration bill looks like what was seen under President Reagans amnesty plan. The bill promised enforcement and yet in the end we have millions of illegals in the country again and the problem is even worse now than it was during the Reagan era.

In Florida there are Tea Party activists that are picketing outside some of Senator Rubio's offices about the immigration bill. The protesters are saying "no to amnesty" and the immigration bill that Senator Rubio is trying to rush through Congress. Apparently Senator Rubio is listening because he sent a letter to the protesters promising that he was not going to try to rush anything through the Congress that does not fix the border problem. Paraphrasing the letter from Senator Rubio he thinks that he is doing what the Tea Party sent him to Washington to do and that is tackling the big problems in Washington.

Can Senator Marco Rubio be trusted as a man for the American people? Is Senator Rubio a man that stands for the ideals of America first, limited government, secure borders, constitutionalism and balanced budgets? This article has pointed out that Senator Rubio is a neoconservative and not a real member of the Tea Party. It is easy to believe that the best interests of Senator Rubio are whatever benefits Senator Rubio and his aspirations.

The Internationalists on Immigration and America

The article discusses immigration from the perspective of the internationalist and the motivations of immigration for the protectionist view

Attorney General Eric Holder is responsible for the laws of the United States of America and the United States Constitution not the Universal Declaration of Human Rights (<u>UDHR</u>).[20] Apparently in a speech in front of ". . . <u>the Mexican American</u> Legal Defense and Educational Fund, Attorney General Eric Holder said that creating a "pathway to earned citizenship" was a "civil right.""[21] The United Nations and international law are what the Obama Administration hold as the law of the land in America. America our land and our sea rights are little more than one state of the many nation-states—according to President Obama—that make up this world. The Obama administration is filled with people that believe in a one world government. Attorney General Eric Holder does not adhere to or have any respect for America's sovereignty, borders, or law unless it is in alignment with the International Court of Justice (<u>ICJ or the world court</u>) and the Universal Declaration of Human Rights.[22]

In Attorney General Eric Holders view the illegal immigrants in America should be treated under international law and the United Nations Human Rights Council (<u>UNHRC</u>).[23] The Bush presidency removed the United States from membership in the (UNHRC) and the Obama administration renewed the United States membership in the United Nations Human Rights Council. The aforementioned remark by Attorney General Eric Holder regarding the civil rights of illegal immigrants represents one of the many international law positions that the Obama administration and our Attorney General believe in.

In fact, the Obama administration treats the American people under the philosophy found in the International Covenant on Economic, Social and Cultural Rights (ICESCR).[24] The ICESCR was developed and enforced in 1976 and it is an addition to the United Nation Charter (UNC).[25] The UNC created the United Nations in San Francisco in 1945. What needs to be addressed is the fact that the ICESCR has never been ratified by the United States Senate. The reason why is the ICESCR is not about liberty for all Americans, but rather it outlines a communist philosophy of the Marxist variety.

The progressives that support President Obama are consistently discussing the ICESCR when they discuss the rights of people to health, shelter, food, education, employment, social security and anything else that a person wants. The problem is that in order to give all Americans these 'wants' the federal government must consider the previous list of need and wants—rights. This philosophy is a far cry from what our Founding Fathers considered as the natural rights of man granted by God. Hence, the American life, liberty and the pursuit of happiness takes on an entirely new meaning through the ideological lens of the Obama administration.

Implementing the ICESCR fully will create an America without social status due to the leveling aspects that the federal government puts in place through taxation in order to keep many Americans down while lifting other Americans up. In this way America's elected secular leaders like the President and his administration believe that they can play god. It is this idealism that hurts all American citizens, but helps those that are in this country illegally. It is apparent that President Obama likes helping illegals at the expense of the American people. The Department of Homeland Security is supposed to protect American sovereignty from this influx of illegal people into the United States.

The Obama administration has done everything in its power to hinder the laws that the federal government is supposed to uphold regarding the American border. The Presidents amnesty of the "Dreamers" and his end around Congress that failed to pass the "Dream Act" three times demonstrates the President's contempt for Congress and American law.[26] President Obama believes that as the President of the Executive Branch of American government he may override laws that are contrary to the ICESCR and the United Nations. President Obama's de facto amnesty that he gave to the 'Dreamers" is one example of the Presidents contempt for American law.

There are two other examples discussed here concerning President Obama and his utilization of the Department of Homeland Security (DHS). For instance, DHS has directed U.S. Immigration and Customs Enforcement (ICE) agents that they must enforce President Obama's "non-deportation policy."[27] that goes against the 1996 law that requires ICE agents to place illegal aliens into deportation proceedings. There are ten ICE agents that have sued the President for his non-deportation policies. The ten ICE agents state that by refusing to acknowledge the Obama administrations new deportation laws that their superiors are punishing them and that is wrong.

The second example is the release of detainees from deportation facilities: "This week ICE revealed that in preparation for budget cuts as a result of the sequester they have started to release detainees."[28] Who gave ICE the green light to release the detainees? It seems obvious that because of President Obama's hatred of the sequestration ICE became an easy target. President Obama through his channels had ICE begin to release illegals. The President did not even care if the illegals held for deportation had broken other laws.

The American people can see the President and his administrations motivation and thinking when looking at Obamacare. Obamacare represents a perfect example of the health aspect of the ICESCR. Obamacare is another example of the American people loosing liberty because they are forced to buy healthcare that they may not want to buy. The entire packages of welfare reform under President

Obama including food stamps are examples of the implementation of the ICESCR here in America. The crux of the problem with the ICESCR and the "American Dream" is that the two are incompatible.

The Obamacare victory for the President was one that is great for the illegal residents in this country. It is believed that the costs of Obamacare will grow exponentially with the amount of low income people in the United States. Many of these low income people will come from two sources. The legal American citizens who will end up making less money because of competition with illegals that are given a pathway to citizenship or amnesty. And secondly even without an immigration bill the President will just continue business as usual. The President's business as usual approach will further punish the American people because there will be a larger flow of illegals across the border. The large flow of illegals will come from the promise of amnesty in the air and the understanding that President Obama is on the illegals side.

Congress needs to act in a manner that will strengthen the American border. This is the United States of America and not one nation-state under the United Nations. President Obama thinks that opening America to further immigration is a good thing for the United States. The United States federal debt demonstrates that this country cannot be all things to all the people of the world. America needs to retreat into a protectionist and anti-internationalist posture until the country is healthy and strong again. It is only then that America once again can be the leader of freedom in the world and a country of liberty. The Europeans are internationalists and look at the problems that they are having. America should not go down the same path.

Immigration and a Caveat about the Immigration Process

The article discusses how immigration since 1954 has changed the American culture.

Why did people vote for President Obama? This writer blames it on American immigration. President Obama is going to ruin this country over the next four years. The Republican Party will not stop him. The House cannot do anything without the Senate; hence the House Republicans are in what would seem like a locked cage. The President has already told the country and Republicans what the next four years will be like. President Obama has the nation on pace to run trillion dollar deficits for the next four years

President Obama will continue to grow government. The rights of citizens will erode due to the stupidity of the last four generations of new Americans. In 1892 Ellis Island was opened and for over forty years more than 12 million people came to America. The 'Era of Restriction' occurred from 1917 to 1954 when immigration to the United States was brought to a drip, and it was a very slow drip of new immigrants to the United States.

In 1964 America started the 'Era of Liberation' and this liberation has brought America away from its original American culture that existed prior to1964. This 'Era of Liberation' created an influx of immigrants both legal and illegal. The population growth in America amounted to an increase of at least fifty million people under the new 'Era of Liberation.' This is more than the entire immigration to the

United States since the Spanish landed in 1564. This writer argues that America has had too much immigration both legal and illegal since 1964. This period of immigrants understands nothing but the goodness of big government. The immigrants to the United States have a different American mindset concerning America. What the immigrants think is that America is a forward movement towards the former President Johnson's "Great Society."

The Democratic Party of former presidents: John F. Kennedy, Lyndon B. Johnson, Jimmy Carter and Bill Clinton make an interesting comparison in one way with each other. The first three presidents just mentioned are Cold War realist presidents. The foreign policy of America was the same for all the Presidents since former President Harry Truman and George Kennan's containment theory. President Carter was an American anomaly. President Clinton began to demonstrate American foreign power in an offensive manner under the guise of humanitarianism. The policy and use of American military power are rooted in the war factions of both the Republican and Democratic Parties.

The Internationalist is a president with an ideology that reflects the thought that it is America's job as the only superpower to bring conflict on this planet to a halt. Internationalists believe that the United States is the leader of a movement towards one world government. The Internationalists are peaceful and socialist in nature domestically. However both parties have a war faction, the neo-cons for the sake of Israel and treasure, and the Democratic Party war faction that is grounded in nation building. Neo-cons have attached themselves to any president with an international perspective. For instance, President Bush the elder and the son are both internationalists and this allowed them to get involved with the neo-cons—the neo-cons caused war for both the Bushes. Both the Bushes were all for easy immigration law and amnesty during their presidencies. The whole reason for this discussion about internationalists is to demonstrate that all the Presidents in the last fifty years have been for immigration reform and open borders.

Internationalists like former President Clinton had his hands full with the Republican Congress. The Republican Party at the time was made up of constitutionalists that created a wedge in order to stop the forward movement of socialism in America. The two presidents that are not mentioned and who round off all the Presidents since World War II are former President Nixon and President Reagan. Both Nixon and Reagan were realists concerning foreign policy and both where constitutionalists. Nixon and Reagan were against easy immigration, but President Reagan was fooled into signing an immigration bill that allowed for amnesty. In the eyes of President Reagan the immigration bill was supposed to end the American immigration problem forever.

President Reagan signed into law the largest illegal immigration policy law since 1964. The Immigration Reform and Control Act of 1986 granted amnesty to about three million illegal immigrants and gave them legal status in America. This was supposed to be met with strict immigration laws. Strict laws on employers and new enhanced border control, neither of the two ended up getting enforced. President Obama without the consent of Congress and armed with the power of the Executive Order gave over 10 million illegals amnesty. It is easy to argue that President Obama won the presidential election of 2012 because of his Executive Order on amnesty for the children of illegals.

President Obama is an internationalist and socialist. President Obama will get his way in the next two years, but then the Democrats will get crushed in the 2014 elections by the Republicans. The reason why the Republicans will crush the Democrats in the Senate and House races will be the result of President Obama. President Obama who cares only about himself and his agenda will show the Democratic Party as unyielding and the true obstructionists over the next two years. Secondly, the economy will not grow at a rate of three percent a year. The economy may decline further over the presidency of President Obama. This writer blames new taxes and more taxes in the future which will leave America with anemic growth throughout the Obama Presidency. The Affordable Care Act will be another disaster for the President and a drag on the economy.

The 'Era of Liberation' brought about massive legal immigration along with a large influx of illegal immigrants. The generations since 1964 have been seduced by secularism, sex and an anything goes mentality because of the American education system. The immigrants that have come to this country are used to being told what to do by government. The American people are now more susceptible than ever to a big government mentality. The Republicans had no chance of winning the presidential election due to the mentality of a large sector of the American people who have no understanding of federal debt or American government. In the people's minds government problems are meaningless all that matters is that President Obama is giving the people free stuff.

In conclusion each President since World War II has had a different set of circumstances that needed to be dealt with in America. The reason why immigration was slowed to a drip from 1917 to 1964 was due to the fact that the immigrants needed to be Americanized. American assimilation has not materialized in the same way as the immigrants prior to 1917. From the twenties until 1964 the United States government put a basic hold on all immigration so that the people could assimilate. America needs to halt all immigration now so that the people we have in the nation are given the time to adapt to the American culture. A culture of individualism and a love of the concepts imbedded in the United States Constitution—the Constitution that progressives wish never existed.

Immigration Policy Today will Change the Future of America

The article looks to past immigration bill attempts and the history behind border control between the United States and Mexico.

Immigration reform could be the end of America as it is known today. The eleven million illegal immigrants and if given amnesty another four family members for each individual adds up. America was once famous for its brain drain of other nations around the world that helped to develop the sciences and technology that America leads the world in now. However, many of the illegals in this country and those that would come are mostly uneducated and Spanish speaking individuals that are in many cases in allegiance with Mexico and the Democratic Party.

The President by Executive Order made it clear that children of undocumented illegals in the United States should not be arrested or deported. The President and those that favor immigration want the American people to believe that the children of illegals are educated and ready to go to college. This is far from the truth. Only one in six of the so-called educated illegals who were raised in America are educated. Most do not have a legitimate High School Diploma level of education and most are not ready for the academics at a university. Not everyone who graduates from a high school deserves it and many that have could not pass through a Ninth grade achievement test.

With the above said let's look at some of the history of illegal Mexican immigration to America and how the problem was dealt with in the past. It is important because the **Gang of Eight** who are selling immigration today are trying to sell the same bill of goods that has already been tried in America. In fact, the immigration problem would not exist today if Congress had lived up to the obligations developed during the Reagan administration.

Ever since the Mexican and American War of 1846 the United States has had nothing but problems with the Mexican people. Many Mexicans believe that a third of the United States from Texas to California and up into parts of Colorado were taken from them during the two year war. Today it is the belief of many Mexicans undocumented in the United States that this territory is rightfully theirs. This is what is known as the Chicano Movement that was on fire during the protest era of the 1960s.

What American immigration policy should be today is the same policy that worked in the 1950's. In the early 1950's President Eisenhower introduced the immigration policy called "Operation Wetback"[29] and millions of Mexicans where sent back across the Rio Grande River which was the border between the United States and Mexico. This operation was not pretty and the policy went against the civil rights of the illegals and violated international standards. President Eisenhower was worried about the invasion taking place on are border and he dealt with it using military means.

During Operation Wetback President Eisenhower put the good of **America first**. This is another reason why America needs to reject the United Nations and the progressive ideas of putting international law over American law. Many of the progressives today do not care about what is best for the country. The progressives have never cared about traditional America. The progressives have always put idealism in front of realism and it is the progressive philosophy that will destroy America.

What we are seeing today on the immigration debate is a *déjà vu* of President Reagans Immigration Reform and Control Act of 1986. At that time amnesty was given to about three million undocumented Mexicans living in the United States.[30] The bill was supposed to secure the border and make it illegal to hire illegal immigrants in the United States. The border was discussed and stricter measures and money was to go to the implementation of a security system on the border that would work. This was never accomplished and the problem has ballooned into what we see today.

The President will not lift a finger to secure the border as long as Homeland Security is running the show. The Immigration and Naturalization Department has been swallowed up by the Homeland Security bureaucratic machine. This is why we see immigration workers suing the federal government. The ICE agents are suing because they cannot perform their jobs due to the orders given to them by the Homeland Security Office.[31]

Homeland Security Secretary Janet Napolitano is playing politics by not allowing the 10 ICE agents to do their job of containing illegals for exportation back to Mexico by the federal law. The agents think that the politics of the President's Executive Order is against the laws created by Congress. Preston and Cushman argue that hundreds of thousands of illegal Mexican's will be allowed to stay in the country if they have been here since childhood. President Obama stated in a speech discussing his decision; "[32]They are Americans in their heart, in their minds, in every single way but one: on paper . . ." Many would tend to believe the President is wrong on his assertion.

In 2006 hundreds of thousands of Mexicans marched for American rights and citizenship while carrying the Mexican flag.[33] Why carry a Mexican flag for a protest for American citizenship? The answer is simple it goes back to the Chicano Movement of the 1960s. Many Mexicans give their allegiance to Mexico even though they live in America. It is the Mexican enemy within the United States.

Living underground as illegals being paid slave labor wages and trying to get by in an America that wants you out is not easy to forget. The hardships of the illegal Mexicans are passed on from generation to generation and they write home about how the people of America treat them as third rate citizens. Why is it that the Mexican people who came to this country legally are willing to suffer the consequences of an increased labor force with less jobs? It is a mentality among the Mexican and other Hispanics that they will control American politics and hence the country in the near future.

Immigration Reform in its given form is especially dangerous to the Republican Party. This is because as we have seen seventy percent of the Hispanic vote went to the Democratic Party in 2012. This same phenomenon will continue to happen within the Mexican population if they are given citizenship. This country needs to remove all illegals from the nation including the children of illegals. America needs an immigration policy that lets people into the United States that are needed and that can be assimilated to the traditional American philosophy of freedom, liberty, God and country.

The lack of education and the deindustrialization of America will put the lower classes of all of America in tight competition. The whole concept of multi-culturalism instead of nationalism is going to turn the poor against the poor down racial lines and this will be a large problem in America's future. However, the greatest threat to America is what Americans cherish the most and that is freedom and liberty through a representative democracy.

American immigration policy as a whole and the problem with illegals in the nation at the moment must be dealt with. It is in the best interest of America to expel all illegals at any cost or the cost will be a loss of the American way of life in the future for all Americans.

Governor Christie Supports
Illegals and Amnesty

Governor Christie can careless about American immigration law. In fact he throws it in the face of the people in his state by making them pay for illegals education.

President Nixon was less of a criminal than Governor Chris Christie who the <u>Star-Ledger</u> reports signed into law ceremonially the "Dream Act" for illegals in the State of New Jersey at the Colin Powell Elementary School in Union City, New Jersey.[34] The Governors message to the unemployed in New Jersey is that he wants to help illegals to get an education and give them jobs. The <u>351,767 or 7.8%</u> of the unemployed in New Jersey were out in the cold searching for work in the State of New Jersey while the Governor took applause from the illegals in Colin Powell Elementary School.[35] The message from Governor Christie to the Red Border States in the South is the people in the Blue State of New Jersey can careless about the illegal border crossings in Red States.

The Democrats seem to love Governor Chris Christie along with the Republicans in Name Only (Rinos'). The Rinos' are all over the idea of a run for the presidency by either Rino Chris Christie or Jeb Bush. The Democrats are salivating like Pavlov's dogs for Governor Christie to run for president. For instance, the <u>Washington Examiner</u> argues: "Lots of people love New Jersey Gov. Chris Christie, but few pundits have as great an attraction to him as MSNBC's Joe Scarborough and the "Morning Joe" crew."[36] If Morning Joe would love to see him run against the coveted Hillary Clinton then it is obvious that the Democrats understand that Governor Christie is a loser.

From what is seen in American politics today it is the American people who do not really have a choice for which candidate they get to vote for as president. The big money business interests and special interest groups have already decided who will run for the Democrats and who will run for the Republicans. The elite are just hedging their bet by making sure that no matter who wins the presidency it will be business as usual in the United States. Business as usual means sticking it to the middleclass.

The job of the American public is to consume. It is nonsensical for the American people to have serious input on how much they pay for what they consume—that is left up to the globalists. All of the President's since the end of the Spanish American War which brought the United States into the game of imperialism have been globalists. It is only from the first Bush administration until today that the Presidents have worked against the American economic system and the American people for the sake of the economic interests of the world.

Governor Chris Christie is a person who will play by the rules of the people who put him in office—the globalists. Globalists are the people who run world trade—the transnational (TNC) and multinational corporations (MNC) that are run by the rich and powerful around the globe. America does not have a monopoly on globalism ask the United Nations, World Trade Organization (WTO) or the International Monetary Fund (IMF). In America keeping the flow of cheap labor coming into the nation is the reason why the border has not been secured. Low labor costs facilitate business activity in the United States and increase profits.

A serious effort to secure the American border has not been seen since President Eisenhower told the head of Immigration and Naturalization General Joseph Swing to do something about the undocumented aliens in America. Operation Wetback from 1950 to 1955 was a program that amounted to the expulsion of some 3.8

million Mexicans back to Mexico. The program was also meant to create a good reason for some illegals to leave voluntarily.

The Secretary of the Homeland Security Department thinks that it is not cost-effective to remove illegals from the United States. It is difficult for the Department of Homeland Security to operate in the states and cities that are protecting illegals from deportation. Governors like Chris Christie are what make deportation less cost effective. However, can there be such a thing as cost effective after looking at the cost of illegals below?

The cost of deportation is high after the illegal immigrants have made it to sanctuary cities around America: "Sanctuary policies—official or otherwise, result in safe havens (or safer havens) for illegal aliens involved in a variety of criminal enterprises . . . Sanctuary policies also provide an environment helpful to Latin American drug cartels, gangs, and terrorist cells—since their activities are less likely to be detected by law enforcement."[37] Apparently Governor Chris Christie cares more about illegals than he does for the innocent citizens of his state and country.

The American Thinker has an article about sanctuary cities and the states that promote them. The article is very disconcerting.[38] Apparently over the last twenty five years the ability for illegals to gain sanctuary in various cities around the country has actually created a lower standard of living by keeping the cost of labor down. In regards to education a Mexican family has an average of 3.5 children; this makes the cost of education to the state per family an average of sixty to eighty five thousand dollars a year depending on the city that the illegal family lives in.

If Governor Chris Christie was elected president he would be the first to sign a bill for amnesty for all illegals like he has already done in his own state. The cost of amnesty for illegals is incredibly high: "The Heritage Foundation estimate the cost of amnesty is at $6.3 trillion and that is accurate for the entire country."[39] The above statistics alone demonstrate how bad a choice for the Republican Party a person like Governor Chris Christie can be.

The Republican Party has to look very closely at what the establishment RINO's are trying to pimp the real conservatives of the

Republican Party. It is time for the Republican Party to work from the grassroots like what is seen in the Tea Party. It is time for America's new "Silent Majority" to stand up for itself in the politics of this great nation.[40] A "Silent Majority" of not just middle America, but of the "Young Invincibles" that are tired of the two party establishment system putting today's costs of the nation on their backs.

This country wants higher wages—well the people are not going to get higher wages by putting an additional twenty million illegals into the workforce. The cost of Obamacare is not going to go down when a majority of the twenty million illegals sign up for Medicaid. Nothing good can come from legalizing people who have no respect for the laws of America.[41] Illegals who think of America as not the land of opportunity—but a country like that advertised by the Democratic Party—a land of free stuff. Governor Chris Christie in short is nothing more than a coconspirator helping illegals break American law.

Just Say No to Affirmative Action in Redistricting

Discussed is how it is wrong for the Justice Department to continue to control some southern states and how they redistrict themselves.

Between affirmative action and laws that protect every American except the white male one would think that the majority of the American population would be happy. However, the majority of the population continues to remind white males of how they expect more. This continuation is hurting the country. The problem of individuals thinking in terms of their group rather than as an American has gone on for way too long. The groupings of socio-economics and race have been exasperated by the last election and the manner in which President Obama ran his campaign. Now that the election is over one would think that the pitting of groups against each other would begin to dissipate, but this is not the case under the Obama presidency. In this nation called the United States of America all of the people should consider themselves an American first.

While reading an article by Patrick Buchanan he asked a question: "What is [America's] guiding light now that the philosophical, cultural, religious and political roots of the old republic are being systematically severed?"[42] The question deserves some contemplation and discussion in the newest version of progressivism. Many could say that what President Obama, and others on the left call progressive, is in reality the dismantling of all the items mentioned above by Pat

Buchanan. The differences between Americans need to be put aside for the sake of America as a whole. America has its own bad political roots but that needs to be forgotten for the good of the nation.

The problem pointed out in the last paragraph is not unique to twenty first century America. During the last great influxes of immigrants President Theodore Roosevelt contemplated the same problem of people associative with groups rather than as everyone being American. Americans must ask can America stand as the country decay's. Theodore Roosevelt warned America: ". . . for we intend to see that the crucible turns our people out as Americans, of American nationality, and not as dwellers in a polyglot boarding house; and we have room for but one soul loyalty, and that is loyalty to the American people."[43] Nationalism is a good thing for the United States because it bonds people together under the American flag. It lets the individual no that he may be of any race, but that we are all equal in opportunity in America.

The job of President Obama should be to unite the people and this is not the case. For instance, the President is still promoting race tensions in America. Vice President Biden marched in Selma with civil rights activists on Sunday as a commemorative display of respect for the March 7, 1965 "Bloody Sunday" march that took place in Selma, Alabama.[44] In that march over fifty blacks were beaten and tear gassed by the Alabama police as they tried to cross the Edmund Pettus Bridge.[45] Is this something that needs to be promoted by the Vice President?

The Supreme Court is hearing a case now that questions Section Five of the 1965 Voters Rights Act. Paraphrasing the Bloody Sunday article it appears that Chief Justice Roberts and the court question the "coverage formula." In Section five the coverage formula forces the southern states of Alabama, Arizona, Georgia, Louisiana, Mississippi, South Carolina, Texas and parts of Virginia, other states, and counties to get authorization from the Justice Department before any changes can be made in the redistricting of each given state.

The Shelby County case in front of the Supreme Court is about the equal protection of the states rather than an argument about equal protection of the people.[46] Should all the states be treated equally or should the Southern states be treated differently than the rest of the country. The real issues that need addressing are how far the United States has evolved from the Jim Crow days before the Voting Rights Act. And how far has America come from the days after the Voting Rights Act?

Justice Antonin <u>Scalia questioned</u> Section five as allowing for what he called "racial entitlements."[47] This left many in the media and the black community up in arms. It appears that after four decades it is the states mentioned above that are being discriminated against by the federal government. Is it fair to treat a handful of states differently for voting problems that occurred over forty years ago?

If a state cannot make its own decisions concerning redistricting the entire congressional system is undermined. In fact, the legitimate makeup of the House of Representatives changes because of the Justice Departments interference with the operation of a states redistricting. This is due to the fact that there are members in the House of Representatives that do not belong there. It should not be the job of the Justice Department to invalidate districts voting results. It is the states' rights that need to prevail.

In the Shelby Case in front of the Supreme Court what is in question is changing a district that was overwhelmingly black and because of redistricting the demographics changed. Under the new redistricting formula the district ended up with more whites. The black candidate lost his re-election bid because of the change. It was because of that loss that the Justice Department entered the arena of politics by invalidating election results.

Redistricting is supposed to be left up to the state. The politics of redistricting for most of the country leaves redistricting up to the individual state. Because of population changes the state decides the method it uses to redistrict its portion of federal representatives. Redistricting always means change. Race should not be a card in the mix of how districts are rearranged. The aforementioned is what this writer thinks that Justice Scalia meant by "racial entitlement."

The Southern states that are affected by Section 5 of the 1965 Voters Rights Act creates implications for the entire country. If race is determinate of how redistricting occurs that means that more Blacks and Latino's are elected to the House of Representatives than should be. It is wrong for the Justice Department to decide how Americans will end up being represented in American government. Each state needs to be allowed to redistrict using the states normal method for realignment or else injustices for all will occur.

Inevitably the House of Representatives will end up having a disproportionate amount Black and Latino representatives than are reflected by the populations of each state. This would be due to gerrymandering by the Justice Department rather than the state legislators and both would be wrong. If the Justice Department stays out of the affairs of the states then districts will realign more in tune with population changes rather than race or political affiliations. This is the crux of the case in front of the Supreme Court and why it is so important.

In conclusion this writer is not trying to abdicate that it would be a bad thing to have more minorities in the Congress of the United States. The power politics of American representation in Congress should not be delegated like some sort of affirmative action plan. If there is one place that merit rather than any other factor needs to be upheld as virtuous it is in the election of political representatives for the American people. The Justice Department should have absolutely no jurisdiction or authority about how a state redistricts.

Affirmative Action is Obsolete for America

Affirmative action and whether it is needed in America today. Has the white male paid enough yet after 50 years of Affirmative action?

American society is filled with many different ethnic and religious groups today. America has reached a new voting threshold in that not one group can control the electorate. This was illustrated by the last presidential election. If equality has been achieved in America then should we do away with Affirmative Action? Paraphrasing the former President Johnson we cannot send blacks, women and other minorities up to the starting line of life with crutches and expect them to run an equal race with the white male. This may have been true in 1965, but affirmative action has run its course in America one would think. After all it is close to fifty years and in many cases four generations since Affirmative Action was established.

The term "Fairness" means in the Merriam dictionary: "Marked by impartiality and honesty: free from self-interest, prejudice or favoritism." Quoting the President if "fairness" is what America is truly striving for, then let America start with equality for all. America has come a long way from the days of 1965 when Affirmative Action was developed and implemented into American society.

In 1961 President Kennedy created Executive Order 10925 which was the beginning of the American government's commitment to the equality for all. Executive order 10925 was then superseded in 1965 by President Johnson who enhanced on what President

Kennedy had started.[48] Later in 1967 President Johnson amended the Executive Order to include all women and minorities. These federal requirements for Affirmative Action quickly made its way to the states and like a plague Affirmative Action spread to all aspects of American society.

The office of Equal Opportunity and Diversity (OEOD) points out that the Supreme Court allowed to stand the State of California's ballot initiative 209 in 1997 for a new amendment to the California Constitution called the California Civil Rights Act.[49] The California Civil Rights Act decimated Affirmative Action policy; however the case still held that equal opportunity for all was required. This was met accordingly with a strict Federal guideline that essentially makes Affirmative Action in California the easier and softer way to do business.

It seems that Universities are the leading group in court cases that make it to the Supreme Court. In 2003 there was a University of Michigan Affirmative Action case that upheld the right of the school to apply affirmative action to the admissions standards of the school.[50] However, the 2003 case was decided by the swing vote of Sandra Day O'Conner who has left the Supreme Court. The new Supreme Court in 2012 some argue is a more conservative Supreme Court.

Bill Frezza has written a Forbes article that questions whether the Affirmative Action policy has become a new entitlement for minorities and women.[51] Is Affirmative Action the new post-progressive vogue, a contraction in terms that argues equality and fairness for all—except if you're a white male? Frezza argues that the 2012 Supreme Court case Fisher v. University of Texas could put the final nail in the coffin of Affirmative Action.

There are two sides to the argument for and against Affirmative Action and that seems odd to me in 2012. The presidential election screams the forward leaning of minorities and women in prominent political rolls that were a result of President Obama's election victory. In the news one can watch and listen to how well minorities and women have moved forward in the last fifty years with Affirmative Action.

All the Supreme Court needs to do is look at its own bench and how it is represented along the lines of Affirmative Action. The past Presidents have made sure that today the Supreme Court looks like the poster child for Affirmative Action with women, Jew, Black, and Hispanic justices that represent the make-up of the Supreme Court. The <u>Fisher case</u> seems to be turning into a watershed case.[52] It will take the Fisher side winning the argument in the Supreme Court case to dismantle the federal, state, and local government's affirmative action policies.

If President Obama would issue an Executive order to eliminate Affirmative Action the Holy Grail and savior of women and minorities, then the United States would begin to regain its competitiveness in business, education, and politics. America once again can be the envy of the world. It is all about the results. Keep in mind the President does not have another election to worry about why not do the humane things for America and unchain the white male. The act would have great ironic virtue.

The Founding Fathers believed in equality of opportunity knowing full well that the country would have various economic segments and levels. The idea of equality of opportunity meant that a person that worked hard could become President of the United States. Social fairness the Founding Fathers left up to the morals of the people. The Founding Fathers took for granted that America the Christian nation could take care of itself through the morals taught in the bible.

Women and minorities should be offended by Affirmative Action because it implies that a lessor group needs an artificial advantage in order to have fairness in the United States. When Affirmative Action is elevated then women and minorities could feel that they truly are equal in all ways. Should government policy support the idea of minorities and women punishing white males? If no then in the year 2012 Affirmative Action should be done away with.

If Affirmative Action was elevated it will take ten years for the work place and universities to get back to normal. There will need to be an adjustment to the reality of more white males in positions of power. College students will need to adjust to the increase in numbers of white males in better quality universities where their skills would demand admission. The last statement is rhetorical because in good conscious all Americans without physical or mental handicaps are equal and the universities and work place should not change when Affirmative Action is done away with.

If America was still a Christian nation rather than the secular nation in this day and age there would not be a need for government involvement in social fairness. All social fairness and welfare in the eyes of the Founding Fathers would be eliminated because of the moral backbone of the American people. The Founding Fathers did not create an income tax it was done by Former President Wilson who fooled the American people into thinking the tax would be just for the rich. There is no fairness or liberty when the majority of the people vote for candidates that are going to give them "free stuff" and amnesty.

This nation needs to get off the road to socialism before we end up like the European Union. America can do anything if we stick to the proper values and morals that made this country great. It is time to unleash the individuals tied down and hurt by Affirmative action so that this country can get back to the business of business. If the people hope to strengthen the American economy and how other nations look towards America, then dismantling Affirmative Action will create instant respect in the world and calm in financial institutions international and national. It is time to unleash the people of America responsible for its past success so that once again America can 'Lean Forward.'[53]

Chapter Three

Economics the Obama Way

President Obama the Big Spending and Regulating President

This is a discussion on President Obama's use of regulatory law as it is developed by administrative agencies under his control. There is a concentration on the environmental issues.

Rand Paul decides to have an old fashion filibuster for the sole purpose of principle. Principle is the new hallmark of Congress. Congress has already given away the farm. The creation and growth of agencies given to presidents in the past and handed over by Congress is remarkable. President Obama needed only to extend upon the power he was handed by past Congresses and with his creation of Obamacare the President enjoys regulatory law ad-infinitum. President Obama has already won in many ways. The President's agenda is moving forward untouched by Congress and unseen by many in Congress or the people of this nation.

The Founding Fathers created a Constitution on principle and what the American government is now are founders would not recognize. In dreams and fantasy the Founding Fathers could never imagine the power that Congress has given the President of the United States through the Administrative branch. Add to the Administrative branch of government the President's unlimited spending ability, the Executive Order privilege, and all Americans have a king not a president.

The Tea Party is all about the United States Constitution and that is good, but the Constitution does not take into account such a large bureaucracy like the federal government of the 21st century. Sequestration is a minor inconvenience for the President because he has raised taxes. The Presidents threat to raise taxes further is just a ploy and a powerful tool in the President's tool box. Eighty five billion dollars in cuts is nothing but a short-term announce for the President. The debt ceiling is his big prize; because the President must feed the beast mentioned earlier—the Administrative branch. And Congress will relinquish the funds to President Obama. Hence, the Power of the Purse is irrelevant, especially since America has not seen a budget since 2009.

The War on Terror and the need for Homeland Security to protect Americans is debatable because it gives ultimate power of domestic and foreign problems to the President. For example, the Presidents amnesty for millions of illegals in the United States without going to Congress is a perfect example of the power Homeland Security allows the President. The President gets to act like king by Executive Order. Congress was furious about what the President had done, but Homeland Security was ready: "the House Homeland Security Committee, like the forgotten redheaded step child of Congress, was eager to assert authority over their border security jurisdiction."[1] The Secretary of Homeland Security Janet Napolitano was right there in order to back her boss (President Obama) on his amnesty for illegals.

The President now has Secretary Napolitano of Homeland Security releasing illegals from jails using the excuse of the sequester cuts.[2] **President Obama has all the power he needs to do whatever he sees fit to do without any consultation with Congress**. Another example of the Presidents power is in the latest incident by the Justice Department charging Osama bin Laden's son-in-law in New York for crimes and he awaits a trial.[3] The CIA and the White House refuse to comment. Representative Mike Rogers the Republican Chairman of the House Select Intelligence Committee stated that anyone captured on the battlefield should be sent straight to Guantanamo. The "President's Men" had one thing to say figuratively and that was 'Hey Congress, Talk to the hand.'[4]

The above is just the ice breaker to a much larger role that the President plays throughout the country using the Administrative branch. Through regulations the President's agencies make new laws. It will take either the Supreme Court or a majority of Congress if necessary to override a President's veto. President Obama knows the Republicans do not have the votes to override a veto of any congressional law that attempts to stymie his plan for America. President Obama's legacy will play out in the seamy underworld of government regulations, Obamacare, and massive deficits that will change America forever.

Senator James Inhofe (R-Okla) wrote a letter to the President because he was concerned about the government's legal requirement to publish the semi-annual regulatory agenda's.[5] It seemed that the government had failed to do so since the fall of 2011. Senator Inhofe wrote the letter in November before the presidential election. Since President Obama's reelection there has been a mountain of new regulations from all the various agencies that affect business, commerce, health and just about all other aspects of American society.

Senator Inhofe wrote to the Environment and Public Works Committee about his outrage over not hearing anything back from the Whitehouse.[6] Senator Inhofe seemed to think that if the American people knew about what regulations President Obama had waiting for the American people he would not get reelected. Senator Inhofe found that; ". . . the Office of Information and Regulatory Affairs (OIRA) just waiting for the election to be over. According to OIRA, there are 151 major regulations (those having an impact of $100 million or more) awaiting review, with 118 of them more than 90 days old." This paragraph is only the beginning of a much more serious plague that President Obama is unleashing on America.

Steve Goreham in his article *Lisa Jackson leaving EPA and path of economic destruction* discusses how Lisa Jackson left the EPA on a pathway to destruction that had not been seen in the last forty years.[7] Goreham argues that if things do not turn around at the EPA the American people will end up paying while at the same time dealing with heavy job losses and economic stagnation. One is left wondering if the prices that American citizens are paying at the pump have more to do with the actions of the EPA rather than OPEC.

President Obama would like to end the use of fossil fuels in the United States and he is doing everything that he can to make sure that that happens. Eighty percent of the electricity in Ohio comes from coal and the EPA is forcing coal generated power plants to close and jobs are being lost in Ohio. This is not to mention the amount of money consumers are paying for the added cost of electricity. The new regulations that are being passed are all hidden taxes that the American people have to pay just to survive.

The aforementioned is just the tip of a much larger regulatory America that President Obama is creating. This article does not even delve into Health and Human Services and the regulations that they have only just begun to unleash on the American people. The contraception problem and the Churches is a good example of just one of the problems that regulations are causing. Congress would never pass a law that forced churches to do something against their religious conscious, but the Department of Health and Human Services did it with the stroke of a regulatory pen.

The President's principles are not the same as the American peoples. There are seven hundred places in the law of Obamacare with the word "shall," two hundred places where it states "may" and a 139 times where it says "the Secretary determines."[8] Hence, one person appointed by the President of the United States will have the health of 310 million people in their hands. This is the way that President Obama thinks that the American governmental system should be run. The American people do not think that that is democracy Mr. President!

Making Money and Debt
the President's way

Discusses the end around President Obama has used to add debt to the country without Congresses approval. A brief history on progressivism

The post-progressives are the new 21ˢᵗ century anti-federalists in America. The real progressives and past Presidents: Theodore Roosevelt, Woodrow Wilson, Franklin Delano Roosevelt and Lyndon B. Johnson all disliked the idea of the American republic and the checks and balances found in the United States Constitution. Russell Kirk would say that traditional conservatives believe that they stand on the shoulders of great men under God.[9] The traditional progressives aforementioned are small men who believed that they should have complete control over the federal government much like the post-progressive President Obama.

President Theodore Roosevelt was the trust-buster an enemy of the big corporations and a believer in the American people and democracy for America. President Woodrow Wilson in his memoirs was influenced by Walter Bagehot's who believed that the United States Constitution was pre-modern and cumbersome.[10] President Franklin D. Roosevelt wanted to pack the Supreme Court with his own appointees in order to pass many of the programs developed in the "New Deal."[11] President Johnson was the master of the Senate who manipulated the Congress and used the death of President Kennedy, still fresh in the people's minds to pass the Civil Rights Act and develop his "Great Society."[12] The aforementioned represent the small minds who laid the foundation for America's demise. President Obama and his big government Affordable Care Act will put the nail in the coffin of American prosperity, freedom and liberty.

The above paragraphs are the backdrop of the need for Congress to neuter the President and place him in a vice in order to stop his imperial tendencies. The issue at hand is the attempt of Congress to stop the Federal Reserve Chairman Ben Bernanke from his "Dual Mandate" of both controlling inflation and trying to keep unemployment down. Kevin Brady has introduced into Congress "The Sound Dollar Act of 2012" this act would take away the fiscal policy responsibility that is used by the federal government in order to reduce spending or to increase spending during an economic downturn.

Congressman Brady's main objective is to take away the monetary experimentation since 1977: "Congress should give the Federal Reserve a single mandate for price stability, and the Federal Reserve should return to a rules-based system of inflation targeting to achieve that mandate."[13] The Federal Reserve is a self-funded entity and hence, it is not under the control of Congress or especially it is not subject to the House of Representatives "power of the purse."[14] Without getting into a deep understanding of the Federal Reserve let us just say that it involves the Federal Open Economic Market Committee (FOMC) which is a twelve member board, representing the twelve different Federal Reserve Banks around the country, which was put in place in 1913.

The problem is found in the details; the United States Senate and the President must confirm all the FOMC members and the President picks the Chairman who is known today as Ben Bernanke. The "Dual Mandate" that the Federal Reserve is responsible for creates broad powers that allows the President, Chairman Ben Bernanke, and the United States Treasury Secretary Tim Geithner to join forces.

In joining forces Forbes magazine explains how President Obama and the Federal Reserve are making money by quantitative easing; "The Federal Reserve acquired most of this US debt by simply creating dollars."[15] The last quote is the free money that the post-progressive left want more of—making money, funny money and federal debt are two things that President Obama has mastered.

United States Treasury Secretary Tim Geithner may not be serving a second term and President Obama will probably have a whole new team of economic advisors in order to squeeze money out of Congress.[16] One would assume that the current quantitative easing policies will stay in place in order to give President Obama access to cash that he is denied by Congress. The President is in a spot right now, because he wishes to work independent of Congress and he wants things his way. The President understands that more stimulus funds from Congress will not come. What can the President do?

The one thing that the President and his band of happy money makers have decided to do is pump Forty Five Billion into the economy every month through 2013 in order to stimulate the economy.[17] The Federal Reserve has announced that it will buy United States Treasury Bonds and place the money back into the economy. This will make the market happy and perhaps business will respond and start investing so that they can increase profits by increasing production. The new business will in theory create jobs for the American people.

In theory the United States Treasury bonds which the Federal Reserve is buying must pay interest. The Federal Reserve has also decided to buy forty billion dollars in mortgage backed securities in order to keep interest rates at zero through hopefully the middle of 2015. In total this means the Federal Reserve is going to pump another eighty five billion dollars into the economy for months and hope that the economy begins to grow faster.

The purpose of this entire article is to point out that the President, Federal Reserve, and the Treasury is creating money and American debt without permission of Congress. Essentially, once again the President has found a way to create federal debt that the American people owe without the sanction of the United States Congress. This situation is very problematic and demonstrates the length that President Obama will go to in order to get things done his own way.

Sequestration is the only Road Forward for the Republicans

President Obama will not stop until he gets everything that he wants. It is up to the Republicans to stop him. The sequestration is a must.

In reality the President could care less about the forthcoming sequestration on March 1, 2013. The President did not care about the American people during the fiscal cliff problem and he does not care now. President Obama does not even care about the American economy and he gives the economy last bidding it seems. In his first four years it was all about Obamacare and getting that passed. Now at the beginning of his second term the President seems to want to concentrate on gun control, immigration, and gay rights. The American economy for the President is to spend money, have the treasury make money (literally), and place America's future into hoc.

The Republicans are dealing with a President that understands only tax and spend. President Obama is not concerned about the budget deficit. In the President's mind he will force the Republicans into giving him more tax increases for little in spending cuts. The President honored one of his pledges and that was to tax the rich. Now the President must honor his second pledge and give the people all of the free stuff he promised.

It is this writer's opinion that the country should brace itself for the 1.2 trillion dollars in across the board sequester cuts.[18] The brunt of the cost of the sequestration is going to be paid for by the same people who voted for President Obama. The people will pay for the sequestration by receiving less in general fund dollars. Why should the Republicans care? The Republicans future vote loss is going to be slim to none concerning the people who are most affected by the sequestration. It is not that the Republicans do not care, but the future is at stake and this President is willing to throw his constituents under the bus.

If this President thinks that the Republicans are going to continue on the road towards American bankruptcy he will have another thing coming. The people who voted for President Obama will suffer the most because of the cuts in social programs brought on by the sequester. The President thinks that the Republicans are not going to allow the cuts to defense to occur. That is why the President believes he is holding all the cards in regards to the sequestration.

The sequestration is the only thing that can be done to stop President Obama from running up another 4.4 trillion in debt before he leaves office.[19] To rephrase that it is the only option that the President is giving the Republicans. The President is betting that he will get all of the revenue he needs along with more tax increases. The President is a spending junky, worse than any President in the history of the United States.

In a speech given by the outgoing Secretary of Defense Leon Panetta he warned: ". . ." pattern of constant partisanship and gridlock and recrimination" in Washington would gravely threaten America's national security, economy, and military readiness."[20] The threats that Leon Panetta discusses are certainly worth taking a look at. The American military is the strongest force by far in the world. The United States Military can work through the cuts required by the sequestration.

The military would have to cut new programs and make sure that what military equipment there is stay's in top running order. Things will have to be cut and the Republican Congress should suggest cutting all of the green energy initiatives slated for the military. For instance, the Navy ships those that are to run on ethanol only. The American people will suffer from higher food costs. The President thinks it would be a good idea to use corn to create ethanol for the Navy ships at five times the cost per gallon. The livestock and chickens need corn grain to produce meat products and an increase in the price of corn means higher food costs for the consumer. This is just another hidden Obama cost and the price of gas is yet another.

Many Senators will not like the cuts to the military in their states, but it is for the good of the country. This economic war that President Obama has unleashed like germ warfare on the American people it is worse than the Afghanistan War. America cannot allow Obama economic policies to continue.

President Obama wants to walk America down the road that the European Countries are already walking down. One look at the European Union should be enough for all Americans. America should not want to repeat the problems that the Europeans are facing in Europe today.

The defense cuts do not have to last; because once the President realizes he is 'human' he will take a different path towards persuasion with Congress. If the Republicans allow it to happen the sequestration would be a wakeup call for the President. Hello, Mr. President we do not like the direction that you are taking this country. The President does not have a mandate with the American people!

The main concern would be the economy and America falling back into a recession. A recession is just about the same as the Presidents "New Normal" for the economy.[21] Grover Norquist argues that America's two percent growth a year is the same growth that France has had for the last twenty years.[22] Norquist points out that the American economy has even shrunk in the fourth quarter of 2012. The entire Obama recovery has been a joke! Unemployment is speculated not to move below 6.5 percent anytime in the next few years.

The obvious thing that needs to be learned by the Obama economic policy of spend, spend, and spend is that although close to a trillion dollars was spent in stimulus money alone America did not receive the bang for the buck that was expected. Wall Street is doing great while Main Street is still in the dumps. The reason for the previous is the increasing interconnectedness of globalization. Keynesian economics are about the sovereign state economy. America due to the new global market is not a sovereign, but one widget amongst many.

The Multiplier Effect for the United States is minimized in a global economy when it comes to stimulus money. It seems that every dollar that the United States Federal Reserve put into the United States economy had a limited return. This is because the item bought by the American consumer was not going back into the United States economy. The many goods American consumers bought with their money went to China and elsewhere. The American stimulus package was more about President Obama's payback to his Wall Street interests. Wall Street invested a lot of money in the Obama campaign for the President in 2008. In fact, President <u>Obama received more money</u> from Wall Street than anyone running for President in the last twenty years.[23]

The Republicans should force the President into the sequestration for the overall betterment of the country in the long run. The sequestration is the only way to get spending cuts out of President Obama without tax increases. It is up to the House of Representatives to stop the President Obama onslaught against America's future. America's freedom and liberty depends on how much of the Obama agenda is put into an early grave.

A Different View of the Fiscal Cliff

Different ways to look at the problems America faces because of the fiscal cliff. The Presidents discussion about sequestration in the third presidential debate is classic.

How can anyone think that a sequestration is going to happen? Doesn't anyone remember the President's comments in the third and final debate? Why <u>the President</u> made it quite clear: "The sequester is not something that I proposed," Obama said, of the $1.2 trillion in automatic budget cuts set to kick in on Jan. 2. **It's something that Congress has proposed. It will not happen**."[24] If an American citizen takes the President at his word then all Americans can sleep well, because the President has promised that the sequestration will never happen. On Monday there must be a bill that the President is willing to sign. How can anyone in Congress think that President Obama lied to the American people in his final debate for re-election?

Whose fault will it be after we do go over the "fiscal cliff?" The <u>2.1 million</u> people who have lost their unemployment benefits as of December 29th are already barely scraping by as it is.[25] This may cause more home foreclosures and some people may even end up on the streets. The money that the 2.1 million people receive is put right back into the economy. The money is spent as soon as they get it for food, gas, rent, and all the other bills that go along with living a normal life in America. Are homelessness, ruining people's credit, and self-respect also part of the Obama economic "<u>New Normal</u>?"[26] This loss of unemployment benefits will have a ripple effect through the economy. This action alone will mean more lost jobs for the people who benefit from the spending of unemployment checks like the local grocery store, gas stations, and the list goes on.

It is the incredible ego of the President that is causing much of the problem in Congress. The President looks at one deal and rejects it; and then the President comes back with a 1.6 trillion dollar deal that is twice the amount of the deal before it.[27] President Obama from the beginning has placed obstacles in the way of progress on a solution to the fiscal cliff. It is obvious what an ego the President possesses. To go on television and make it look like Congress is a bunch of idiots and then remark on how he should have something on his desk to sign just shows his audacious and cocksure attitude towards Congress and the American people.

President Obama is at the end of his rope. House Speaker Boehner can decide not to make a deal and refuse what the Senate offers the House of Representatives. Hopefully, the President whose fault it will be if a deal is not made can carry the weight and the burden that going over the cliff will bring. The fiscal cliff is more of a financial nightmare and economy staller than those on Capitol Hill make it out to be.

The problem for the Republicans is that they will take the political beating just to avoid the fiscal cliff. President Obama understands the Republicans love America and its people. Most people realize that President Obama does not really care about the American people. The President is willing to sacrifice Americans on the altar for his "New World Order."[28] A multipolar world is redeveloping and the United States is not looking all that powerful in the future due to the seventeen trillion plus in debt that the country owes. In President Obama's eyes the United States needs to come down a few notches' in order to blend in with the rest of the economic powers.

Sanger in the *New York Times* writes that the projected deficits over the next ten years will cause a great deal of difficulty and after the ten years the deficits will go up another five percent.[29] The numbers are very shaky because the United States has never gone ten years without going into an economic slowdown. Without money to stimulate a slowdown in the American economy a recession will hurt more. America's failure to obtain loans will cause grave danger for the United States. President Obama's "New Normal" will end up putting America into the ash heap with the rest of the imperialist nations before us.

The time to act is now and it seems the President is not worried about the future of the American people. The President is not worried because he would like America's standard of living to be equal with that of the rest of the world. It seems that the youth vote for Obama in the future will look like the worst decision the youth that voted for President Obama could have made. The most ironic thing is that the have-nots who voted for handouts now will have absolutely nothing in the near future. This represents a civil unrest problem brewing for America in the near future. Good thing that most Republicans own guns!

Dennis Gallagher writes that Obamacare alone represents a takeover of one sixth of the country's economy at a cost of 1.7 trillion dollars a year.[30] Gallagher argues that President Obama is trampling all over the First Amendment Rights of the Catholic Church and other religious institutions with the regulations and laws of Obamacare. The peoples "Right to Conscience" is something that no government should tread upon.[31] President Obama has decided to pounce and beat down the ideas of those that do not adhere to a secular agenda.

Charles Krauthammer argues that President Obama is in essence asking the Republicans to sign on to an unconditional surrender to the President's way or over the cliff America will go.[32]President Obama's tax the rich scam is just that a scam. If the President was to take every penny that Warren Buffett has it would only pay for about five days of government.

The money that going over the cliff will bring in by the Sequester amounts to a drop in the Obama budget bucket. The money will barely cover the new costs of welfare programs that the Obama administration has encouraged over the last four years. America will still run a deficit after taking close to three thousand dollars from most middle class families. Money is no object to President Obama if Congress fails to give him money he will just make it.

The 2.1 million American unemployed will have to fend for themselves. The new Obamacare taxes will begin to kick in. Inflation on gas, food and other essentials will rise four percent in 2013. It will take a lot of praying and the will of God to pull America from the fire that President Obama is moving the country closer too.

Free Money and Free Stuff is
not the American Dream

The article discusses the fiscal cliff and why it may be better if Congress lets us go over it. Obama money as it can be called instead of a dollar is explained.

Throw President Obama and his constituency over the "fiscal cliff." The fiscal cliff affects all Americans and that is not good. It is time that America understands what Obama's four year strings of trillion dollar deficits are doing. President Obama expects four more years of the same regarding yearly federal debt and that will cost all Americans. The post-progressives are going to be happy since the American people will have developed into a nation with social equality. However, the rub for the American people is that social equality will mean that everyone will have an equally low standard of living.

One way to wake the majority of the population up is to punish them even if it means punishing <u>ninety percent of the American people</u>.[33] Yes, punish and an imperial president or a majority Congress because of big government can manipulate and control the American people. Therefore, through taxation each of the aforementioned can punish and regulate more and more of the lives of the American people. As Obamacare and other agencies regulations kick in people will wish that they had voted differently.

America stands at the cross roads. President Obama won reelection and all that is left between him, and his socialist agenda is the United States House of Representatives. The "fiscal cliff" is real and those who are calling it a mere slope are absolutely wrong.[34] Without a budget deal America will proceed over the fiscal cliff and that will affect everyone: the poor, the married, the middle class, the federal employees, college students, small and large businesses, and the world. Middle class families will see taxes go up three thousand five hundred dollars.[35]

The most ironic thing about the fiscal cliff is all it means is that the countries federal deficit will raise by only five hundred billion, instead of a trillion or more. The American people in 2013 will end up after paying all the extra taxes—still billions of dollars in yearly debt.

The recession that America will fall into will actually help the American people with the federal deficit.[36] The federal deficit already consumes six percent of the United States yearly budget. The reason why a recession is good is that it will keep interest rates down; and that means less interest will accumulate on the United States outstanding 17 trillion dollar deficit. One percentage point up on interest amounts to more government programs that will need to be cut in the future.

The States in America will receive less federal funding along with the cities in the United States.[37] That makes it hard to understand why the Democrats ask the states to except Obamacare and the money at no cost to the state; **that the federal government is going to pay for everything!** The problem with this is that the treasury is only printing forty five billion dollars of Obama money or what is called the free money a month.

The treasury because of "Operation twist" is printing 45 billion in Obama money each month. The Obama money; "The Fed is funding the mortgage purchases with money it effectively creates itself when it credits the accounts of bond dealers with funds in exchange for the securities."[38] The yearly debt of the federal government is still 500 billion for 2013. How is the federal government going to get the money for the states and the cities? How can the federal government in good faith promise the people of America and their states and cities healthcare when the federal government can't pay what it has already committed to pay? The answer to that question is just creating more federal debt.

At this point a person can see how the reader may be confused, **especially when the government has all this "free stuff" for the American people.** Perhaps, those that voted for President Obama can tell the American people how they expect the federal government to give them all of the free stuff that they want.

Sarah Palin was right when she stated that the American people have a "choice between free stuff or freedom" and the American people voted for free stuff.[39] True Americans will keep moving forward because the stakes are just too high. The key is to cut the heads off of government which are the ever growing agencies in the Administrative branch. The Administrative branch just keeps growing. Congress created and pays for the agencies so it is Congress that can create limited government in America again. Congress can do so by not funding the federal agencies to the extent that they are being funded. Essentially Congress must starve the agencies through money into submission.

The Ryan Budget is nothing but a Republican Fantasy

Representative Paul Ryan created a budget that can never get passed in Congress or get signed into law by the President.

Rep. Paul Ryan is completely unreasonable by offering up a budget that is dead on arrival. Rep. Paul Ryan doesn't even try to accommodate the Senate and the President with anything reasonable as a position to start from concerning a federal budget. Chris Wallace of Fox News Sunday was absolutely correct when he stated: "Well, That is not going to happen." when Rep. Paul Ryan stated that his budget required the appealing of Obamacare. At least let the Senate work from something plausible in order to reach some kind of a budget agreement. Most people are excited about the idea of the Senate even proposing a budget never mind trying to pass one. After all it has been years since the United States has had a budget.

Otto Von Bismarck stated: "Politics is the art of the possible, the attainable—the art of the next best."[40] The establishment Republicans should understand that they have already ran a ticket that they thought could beat Obama; and that was the "Romney and Ryan" ticket that lost the election. As a realist conservative the best thing that the Republican Party can hope for is to stop the bleeding. Curbing the trillion dollars a year projected Obama federal deficits, and the President's projected national debt of twenty trillion in 2016 is a great beginning for the Republican House. This should be the main objective in developing a budget for Rep. Ryan. Forbes magazine on

Christmas day of 2012 wrote an article *President Obama's Legacy: 20 Trillion in debt for 2016 Victor* speaks for itself.[41] Keeping the national debt from increasing would be a great step forward for the Congress and especially for the Republican Party.

Bob Adelmann thinks that Rep. Paul Ryan is out of touch with reality. Adelmann argues that Ryan's unreasonable budget is evident in the fact that the 112th Congress voted 33 times to repeal PPACA [Obamacare] and failed. Adelmann goes on to say that the 113th Congress has two less Senate seats and ten less House seats. The more a person looks into Rep. Paul Ryan's budget called "Pathway to Prosperity" the more one can see the 2012 presidential race all over again.[42] It is time to face the reality that the Republican Party lost the election.

Most Republicans think that the 2012 presidential loss is something that America will not be able to recover from and that perhaps the country is on the democratic pathway to socialism. However, the previous should not be the argument at this juncture in American politics. Good men and women get up and back into the saddle again while being undaunted by a loss and that is the attitude that Republicans need today. It will take strong Americans to look into the reality of what America is facing economically.

Who can have faith in a budget ten years out judging from an American economic recovery that is unlike any recovery since the Great Depression? America's recovery from the Great Depression was mostly due to World War II.[43] The government programs initiated by President Franklin D. Roosevelt had very little to do with getting the United States out of the Great Depression. America is crawling out of a second war since the beginning of the Great Recession so the option of a war is off the table. And for the record the Afghanistan War like the Iraq War does not have a peace dividend because both wars are financed by debt.

It is hard to believe that the American economy making its way through a recovery as anemic as the one in progress can live up to the statistical projections cited in order to create the accurate numbers for deficit reduction. The Ryan budget plan would cut spending by 4.6 trillion by 2023 and that is by doing away with programs like

Obamacare discussed above. Hence, right from the beginning the numbers are skewed.[44] The Democrats were all over the Ryan budget before it was even out of the gate. This fairs poorly for the majority of Republicans in the House and is beneficial to the President.

Senator Reed stated that it was the same old Republican arguments that American's have been hearing about for years. The Bush Presidency was filled with spending and the Obama administration has taken debt to an entirely new level. Both Republicans and Democrats are to blame for the 17 trillion dollars of Federal debt even though it is the Obama Administration that is the cause of most of it.

The nineties are gone. Throughout all of American history the years from 1991 to 2001 represent the longest period without an economic recession. Looking at projections based on American history the United States from 2013 to 2023 will go through at least two recessions. This is true when a study of the history of recessions in America is looked at.[45] Any recession is going to be worse because the United States will not have any money to spend itself out of another recession. In other words, America cannot have another American Recovery and Reinvestment Act of 2009 (ARRA) of 831 billion dollars for a Keynesian macroeconomic recovery.[46] This is due to the fact that America according to the numbers projected by today's politicians are not accounting for a future recession. The reason why is that today's politicians are too busy formulating ten year projections because, they as politicians for the most part—will not be in politics ten years from now.

The President's budget is going to be about two months past due if he releases it by April 8th as promised by White House Press Secretary Jay Carney. This seems odd since the government runs out of money March 27, 2013.[47] The President is going to spend a lot of time on Capitol Hill the next few days trying to get a feel for the pulse of Congress in order to do something about the deficit. Some people argue that the President is on Capitol Hill in order to show the American people that it will not be his fault if both Houses of Congress do not come up with a budget. And naturally it will be the Republicans that will take most of the blame that is why the Ryan budget is so upsetting. The Ryan budget gives the President a lot to complain about in a logical manner.

The <u>Senate Budget</u> Committee Chairwomen Patty Murray released the Democratic Senates budget proposal hours after the Ryan budget was released.[48] It seems natural that since the Senate Democrats haven't produced a budget in four years it needed to be filled with a trillion dollars in new taxes. The Senate Democrats budget does not even try to balance the budget in ten years. If the sequester is turned off the Senate budget will cut the deficit about 800 billion over a ten year period using the congressional budget baseline. Therefore, it seems that the Senate Budget is just about as worthless as that proposed by the Republican House.

It is hard to believe that with the Presidents help Congress cannot come together with any sort of a budget that can get signed into law by the President. It just seems farfetched from everything written in the news that any real deficit reduction is going to take place. This is even if some sort of agreement is met by the President and Congress concerning a budget. It seems that some sort of a "Grand Bargain" on deficits is something that will not happen under the second term of the Obama administration unless the Democrats take over both Houses of Congress in 2014. The only grand bargain at that point will be more taxes and more deficit spending for most Americans and handouts for the rest of America.

A Higher Minimum Wage Hurts America

Changing the minimum wage in a traumatic way will cause inflation and higher costs for the poor and middle-class when it comes to disposable income for goods and services.

How does increasing the minimum wage affect America in regards to the "race to the bottom?" There are many different ways to look at the problem of the American economy and its stagnation and the so-called "New Normal" economy that America is living with.[49] A "New Normal" for the American economy that embellishes a constant or permanent mild depression. Economist Paul Krugman wrote an article for the *New York Times* called "A Permanent Slump" that discusses a good portion of what the American economy is suffering from.[50] This idea of a new sluggish economy according to Paul Krugman is not going to last for years, but for the decades to come.

The short term feel good rise in the minimum wage for the least skilled workers in America will only exasperate the exodus of multinational corporations from what little business that they still manufacture in the United States. It is not an exodus of corporations that America needs, but an increase in the amount of manufacturing companies that want to set up shop in the United States.

The first problem is that the United States represents one of the worst places for a corporation to start a business. It is not only the cost of labor that a business needs to be concerned with. Any business that hopes to operate in the United States must deal with all of the environmental and other regulations that add cost to the product hoped to be produced. The elephant in the room for the United States is the American push towards free markets. The push tore corporations from America and sent them overseas for cheaper labor and less governmental regulations on the part of business.

A person can look at the world and all of the sovereign nations of the world as a competition against each other in order to lure business to their particular nation-state. In order to grasp the extent of the competitive nature of the international system one only has to go as far as the United States and the Federalist System that exists in this country.

States compete with each other in order to get business to move to a specific state. This competition among the states forces the states to sweeten the pot more and more for businesses. This competition on steroids weakens all states and benefits business greatly at the expense of the local citizens and the citizens of the state.

How are the citizens of a specific state affected by the lax state corporate taxation and free lands in some cases that are relinquished in order to lure business to the state? Well first of all it is the citizens that will have to pay to pave the roads and bridges and plow the roads for these businesses at the cost of the citizens. In fact, all local and state benefits will get paid by the citizens of the local and state governments. The bottom line is that the business can earn profit without that profit being taxed and the people are footing the entire bill for the corporation.

One can argue that in the long run the added jobs and the corporate multiplier effect will outweigh all of the costs that the business is saving. However, what if the company that now has no taxes and every business advantage that a state can provide is still not enough for the business to move to a state. One would ask how this could be. It is the cost of labor in that state. When push comes to shove a business when all else is equal will move to a state that is a right to work state, rather than move to a state that is unionized. Labor costs and benefit costs and regulation costs are all items that do matter to a corporation's bottom line.

To extrapolate the aforementioned to the national and international level who is going to want to move business to the United States when the minimum cost of labor is in many cases three times the cost of labor in other countries. President Obama is one of the biggest regulating President's to ever govern over the United States.

Diane Katz of the Heritage Foundation in an article titled "Obama's Regulatory Agenda: Calm before the Superstorm" argues that President Obama's regulations will cost over ninety billion dollars a year and a potential loss of millions of American jobs. It needs to be noted that the jobs being lost are in the coal industry and electric industry that pay a good wage.

The entire liberal agenda is to level the American economy to its lowest common denominator in the future. A higher minimum wage will only hurt the United States in its competitiveness around the world. The Chinese and other foreign companies will keep the wages in their nations the same while raising the cost of products being sold to the United States in order to increase their bottom line. The excuse of the multinational corporations will be that the American dollar is not worth as much as it once was. The higher minimum wage will lessen the buying power of each dollar as the entire market system redistributes costs around the added cost of doing business because of the higher minimum wage.

Some may argue that mass production requires mass consumption that may be true. However, in this article the underlying argument is that the mass production will occur in foreign countries that have lower labor costs whose goods are shipped to the United States for consumption. The mass consumption in the United States will produce higher trade deficits that will in the end force the federal government to borrow more money and run higher national debt.

America will have accomplished nothing from a higher minimum wage accept for a short term fix like that of a drug addict. In the long run the American economy will collapse under its own artificial market system of elevated wages, over regulation, huge foreign trade deficits and an inflationary dollar.

The Americans that will suffer most are the Americans who work hard and have kept a job for years that make more than the minimum wage. The previous Americans will suffer because they will not get a raise because most businesses are operating on a minimum profit margin that will not allow them to pay the middle income workers in this nation more money.

The only people that will benefit from a higher minimum wage are the people who do not deserve more money—because if they did—the company would pay them more money. If there is anyone to blame for inequality in America it is the lying teachers who taught for the last thirty years that globalization was a good thing for America. Globalization created the inequality in America and this "New Normal" economy in America. It is the "New Elite" who fooled the American people into thinking that the cheap foreign goods were a good thing.[51] That was until the cheap foreign goods forced a particular American worker out of their job.

Ghetto Housing and Senator Rand's Economic Freedom Zones

Urban Revitalization has been tried in the past. In many cases there are city success stories, but they are never success for the poor.

U.S. Senator Rand Paul is getting a lot of attention for his idea of using "Economic Freedom Zones" around the United States. This idea has been tried before under different names we have seen Urban Revitalization and Urban Enterprise Zones going back to the 1970s. However, in this instance, U.S. Senator Rand Paul argues that his plan is ". . . <u>enterprise zones on steroids</u>."[52] The Senator wants to try his specific system of "Economic Freedom Zones" (EFZ) in Detroit Michigan and in other depressed cities and counties across the nation.

The term Urban Enterprise Zones were used in the 1990s and were introduced by Republican Jack Kemp. The ideas about enterprise zones came from the concepts inherent in supply-side economics. Jack Kemp believed in supply-side economics and ". . . <u>the assumption</u> of employer's will respond positively to tax incentives and reduced government regulation."[53] This is the crux of the Rand Paul's argument concerning Detroit.

The <u>newspapers are all talking</u> about how Senator Rand Paul is hoping to run for president in 2016 and how this is just another platform for him.[54] The 2016 election argument cannot be further from the truth. Senator Paul is a realist and his proposal is simple and that is that business and employees know what is best for them.

By leaving more money in the pockets of businesses and employee's the multiplier effect will generate a robust economy in the city and its surrounding areas. At least the aforementioned is how the argument is presented.

Senator Rand Paul's position allows that migrants are offered 50,000 dollars to move into specific EFZ cities.[55] Entrepreneurs would also be welcomed through tax incentives for moving to the EFZ city. The whole idea is to bring people back to the cities that will have a positive effect on the rebuilding of the infrastructure of the city and its streets. The approach is analogous to the idea of Urban Revitalization.

Some argue that Urban Revitalization or what is more commonly called gentrification does not actually help the poor in cities. In fact, in many instances the poor are just placed somewhere else. This is seen in New York and in many other cities where liberals claim the prize for the revitalization of a city. A building contractor with a small amount of capital and some good credit is able to rebuild an entire street from boarded up houses into beautiful condominiums for a new group of young urbanites. The poor are forced out of their homes to make more room for the rich. Conceptually and in many cities what is seen is a city that springs to life with all new buildings and rents that are incredibly high.

The poor in a city that has gone through gentrification have had their homes torn down and the poor are forced to move elsewhere. Many argue that this type of urban revitalization makes contractors rich. It also creates a new real estate market that is very beneficial for the people who make the move to the city. In other words people with money are making plenty of money. The city receives a great tax increase and all of the new urbanites are happy.

What happens to the poor? In many instances they are moved to new low income housing that is developed using federal and state dollars. This is seen as helping the poor by putting them all together in a ghetto complex far on the outskirts of the city. In many instances this makes it much more difficult to find work. In many cases a bad transportation system to and from the new housing complex area hurts the poor.

The distance back to the city for work is very discouraging to the people. In many cases individuals get fed up and once again are in the cycle of government welfare and poor housing. The new schools that are built get filled with low achievers and this creates a new education problem for the poor. It is proven a low achieving school perpetuates low achievement for many of the students.

In essence nothing good has happened for the poor through the entire EFZ transformation. The rich have all made out in a new city for the rich that pay's all the cities bills. The New Elite can feel good about building a new ghetto housing project; and for feeding and clothing the poor whose homes were destroyed to make way for the gentrification. Senator Rand Paul should wait and put the new GOP headquarters for Detroit right smack in the center of the new ghetto housing. That will get the Republicans a lot of votes.

The entire argument for the reintroduction of EFZ's is to create jobs. A job for the least amount of cost and this is done by providing the tax incentives per job. The Obama Stimulus package was said to have cost 400,000 dollars for each job that was created. This is beyond ridiculous and should have been a crime. Many individuals deserve jail time for such mismanagement of the federal monies. It is estimated and some economists think it is still expensive that a job can be produced using EFZ's at a <u>cost of 5,000 dollars per job</u>.[56] Hence, it appears that leaving the money in the hands of the businesses and the people rather than sending the money to Washington and then back to Detroit is a no brainer.

The problem with the plan outlined by U.S. Senator Rand Paul is in the details of how the program is developed. The new Economic Freedom Zones or EFZ's from the history of such programs tells a story that urban revitalization and enterprise zones are not all about freedom especially for the poor.

The Senator wants to start up EFZ's in cities and counties with an unemployment rate of one and one half times the unemployment rate. The Senator also expects to enact the following policies: "<u>a reduction in individual</u> and corporate income tax to a single, flat rate of 5 percent, a reduction in the payroll tax, the providing of child education tax credits to parents, a suspension of Environmental Protection Agency

(EPA) non-attainment designations, and a suspension of the Davis-Bacon wage requirements."[57] What the Senator is proposing seems like a lot of benefits for the city of Detroit, but the city of Detroit is bankrupt and many people are hurting.

Something needs to be done to help areas that are suffering from the loss of manufacturing and other industries due to globalization and outsourcing. The two generations represented in Washington now are all from the school that taught that globalization is a good thing for America. It turns out that in some cases globalization is hurting the people of the United States through no fault of their own. It is a matter of the profit margin for business and not about the American people. Government should stay out of the free market system.

The idea of Economic Freedom Zones is a much better way to try and help Americans to help themselves by creating business incentives that promote jobs and employment. What needs to happen is that the poor are not minimalized and pushed aside. It is a good thing to revitalize a city. However, it is a terrible thing to create incentives for one class of people that helps to diminish another class of people in American society. The proposals that move forward concerning the Economic Freedom Zones must take the poor into account.

The Republicans must lose
the Debt Ceiling Fight

The Republicans need to give the Democrats what they want in the debt ceiling fight. This is in order to fight another day. Getting rid of Obamacare can wait until the 2016 elections. The economy is the most important thing in America now.

Is there a reason for President Obama to deal with the Republicans over the debt ceiling? The Republicans have already argued that the last thing they want to do is shutdown the government. What does the President have to worry about? President Obama is in a win–win situation over the federal budget. First, if the economy goes into a tailspin the President and the Democrats can blame it on the government shutdown. Secondly, in the 1995-1996[58] government shutdown although President Clinton took a hit in the polls to begin with after the shutdown ended President Clinton's approval rating went through the roof.

When one looks at the American economy the statistics do not look very good. The main concern is the fact that the unemployment rate is 7.3 percent.[60] This creates a lower demand for all consumer goods; including housing and housing construction that normally play a large role in an economic recovery.

Another reason for consumers not spending their money is the fact that their wages are stagnating and this makes for less surplus income and demand for goods weak. The Affordable Care Act and its implementation are not helping the domestic economy at all from what is seen already. The above are problems that President Obama would like to blame the Republicans on exclusively as the economy begins to tank because of a government shutdown.

It is inconceivable that anything good will come from <u>Fridays' vote</u> to strip the funding of the Affordable Care Act on the floor of the House of Representatives by a vote that passed exclusively along party lines.[60] It is ten days until a bill must pass the Congress on the federal budget. The Senate Majority Leader Harry Reid states that he will not get the bill back to the House of Representatives until a day before the deadline and this gives the House only one day to vote before shutting down the government.

President Obama has argued that the debt ceiling problem is more of a <u>personal attack</u> on him than anything else.[61] This is our President it seems that everything is about him! Forget about the fact that the Affordable Care Act was passed by the Congress in 2009 and upheld by the Supreme Court. The Congress voted for the Affordable Care Act and the Supreme Court upheld the bill as law. However, President Obama believes the Republicans are out to get him personally.

It is hard to believe that the Congress will pass a budget before September 30th especially one that puts Obamacare on hold for one more year. The whole idea of putting the Affordable Care Act on hold for a year is a political one, but it is hard to figure out who would gain the most from the Affordable Care Act being placed on hold until the 2014 elections.

It seems that the Democrats would like to see the Affordable Care Act go away because it will not help them in their re-election bids for Congress. The question is what is better for the Democrats? A one year extension on the Affordable Care Act or allowing Obamacare to go into effect so that people can see it in action before the 2014 elections.

It is probably best for the Democrats to allow the Republicans to choke on their own missteps. The Democrats should allow the government to go bankrupt and then President Obama and the Democrats can blame the failure of the economy and of Obamacare on the Republican Party.

The Democrats would love to blame the economies failure in 2014 on any government shutdown that takes place during the debt ceiling fight. President Obama will blame all the problems that occur for the implementation of Obamacare on the Republicans.

If the Democratic Party can blame the Republican Party for the problems that arise because of Obamacare this will help the Democrats in the 2014 mid-term elections. In other words a government shutdown is the last thing that the Republicans need and President Obama is aware of that.

If the House GOP is hoping for the Senate and the main event Senator Cruz to make something happen they are misguided for sure. In fact, Senator Ted Cruz (R-Texas) has back peddled on himself about what he can provide for a bill that can be sent back to the House of Representatives. Even if Senator Ted Cruz does filibuster the Senate—all that will do is slow the process of getting a bill back to the House that can be supported.[62] All it takes for Senator Harry Reid to remove the defunding of the Affordable Care Act from the House bill is a simple majority vote that he will have no problem getting.

The Republicans have painted themselves into the corner by developing a no win situation for the party. The Senate will pass a bill that the Democrats have been pushing for from the beginning. There will not be a one year extension on Obamacare and the Affordable Care Act will get its funding. There is nothing that the Republicans can do except sign what the Senate gives them with a twenty four hour grace period before the government is forced to shut down.

President Obama will have his debt ceiling increase and that will be the end of it. The only thing that the Republicans can hope for is a complete failure of Obamacare and a lot of angry Americans. The Republicans may have to lose the debt ceiling battle to win the war on the Affordable Care Act and the future deficit. Hence, the Republicans need to sign whatever comes out of the Senate and then let it ride until the Affordable Care Act crashes and burns.

The above paragraph can occur when the Republican Party cleans the clock on the Democratic Party in the 2014 election. The Republicans may then have control of both the House and the Senate.

The President will be all alone. President Obama's complaints about being picked on by Congress will have some validity.

The Republicans will be able to blame any problems with the economy after the 2014 elections on Obamacare. The President can veto any defunding of Obamacare all he likes and the people will end up putting his presidential approval rating in the teens.

The election of 2016 will be a mandate against Obamacare and all the Democrats who are the cause of the American people's problems. Perhaps, as in 2008 when the Democrats controlled the Executive and the Congress the Republicans can do the same in 2016. However, this is wishful thinking unless the Affordable Care Act ends up being the nightmare it is shaping up to.

Democrats Agree Spend Billions More on Infrastructure

One train wreck and the Democrats are coming out in full force for more big government spending on infrastructure.

All it takes is one tragedy for the Democratic Party to start up the argument that Americans need more government to fix the problem. This weekend a <u>commuter train</u> derailed that resulted in the death of four individuals and sixty others were injured.[64] The first thing that the Democrats started to argue was the need for more infrastructure spending. The train was going at a rate of eighty two miles an hour into a curve with a speed limit of only 30 miles per hour.

The conductor argues that the brakes would not work and he was unable to slow down. This is something that the people will learn more about as the investigation moves forward. The American people have seen this knee-jerk reaction in the past with the gun control issue. It seems that after each tragic isolated killing by guns the Democrats cry for more gun control. How much traction will the Democratic Party get on this new crusade for more infrastructure spending?

This Monday on MSNBC Morning Joe the program started with the Metro North train disaster and moved directly to a long discussion on America's infrastructure problem. Former Secretary of Transportation Ray LaHood argued that: "<u>Of the $800 billion</u> in the economic recovery plan, we got $48 billion. We spent $48 billion in two years; we put 65,000 people to work on 15,000 projects . . ."

President Obama's token Republican former Secretary LaHood went on to say that the Department of Transportation (DOT) should have been given 480 billion.[64] The bottom line is that MSNBC went from a disastrous train wreck to the federal government needing more money for infrastructure.

Paraphrasing Emily Goff of the Heritage Foundation—the Department of Transportation can take two different paths. At the moment the federal government collects 18.1 cents for every gallon of gas that is bought by Americans; this money goes into the Highway Trust Fund (HTF). At the moment the DOT is spending about fifty three billion dollars a year. In six years this will end up amounting to 320 billion dollars. However, the (HTF) will bring in only a projected 240 billion dollars; this leaves an eighty billion dollar shortfall.[65] This means that Congress will have to come up with the extra money from the general fund. The question is should the federal government expand the DOT or should Congress begin to turn the DOT over to the states?

Some argue that the federal government put to many regulations on how the transportation money must be distributed over the two year period that the money was to be spent. The stimulus money was supposed to be for shovel ready jobs, but that is not what happened. The stimulus money ended up developing far less jobs than was projected. It is argued that instead of all the regulations placed on the states the federal government should have supplied block grants. In the case of block grants the states could have decided what projects would have created the most jobs and also, which jobs are the most efficient for the state's transportation needs.

Other economists believe that the federal government is just too large of a bureaucratic maze and that makes it unable to respond quickly to complicated matters in the fifty markets of the states. In other words, it is too difficult for the federal government to try and spread money like peanut butter across the American landscape. It is argued that the multiplier effect of thirty thousand jobs for every one billion in stimulus money did not even come close. The Heritage Foundation did its own study and came to the conclusion that: ". . . many lawmakers claim that every $1 billion in highway stimulus can create 47,576 [transportation] new construction jobs. But Congress must first borrow that $1 billion from the private economy, which will then lose at least as many jobs."[66] From the aforementioned argument if stimulus at the federal level does not work can it work at the state level?

Each state has its own gas tax on a gallon of gas. Some states charge more than other states in 2013 Connecticut charged a state gas tax of forty five cents, California—forty nine cents and the average for the fifty states is twenty five cents.[67] It may not be plausible to close the Department of Transportation. However, can the functions that the DOT performs be handed over to the states? The money that the federal government collects per gallon could be cut in half and that half added to the state's gas tax. This would give the states much more money to fund their own infrastructure problems.

A system could get set up where the states can petition the federal government to provide the funding out of the money that the federal government takes in from the Highway Trust Fund (HTF). However, the money used would have to fix only the federal roads within each state. Both Republicans and Democrats who are reelected by getting money for their states could get together and pass a transportation bill based on the compromises that the representatives come up with. In this manner each state would benefit from the bill. This system would prioritize federal transportation projects within each state instead of money going to build bridges to nowhere.

The smaller DOT would only have to deal with the maintenance of federal transportation needs and not developing new projects. All new projects would be left up to the specific state to build themselves. This may lead to more private roadways with tolls being built, but this can be a good thing. Bringing private enterprise into the building of infrastructure around the country will be much more efficient and less costly. This is due to the fact that private enterprise building roads can get away with non-union labor and this would bring about substantial savings for the state. The state would have the infrastructure without the budget outlays. This would create funds to invest in other areas of the state economy.

The federal government needs to get out of the Transportation business. As described above the federal government must either raise taxes or borrow the money for transportation over the next six years. The argument here is that the federal government should defer the established tax in a percentage back to the states. The states should be in charge of their own infrastructure needs. The states if they are smart will give block grants to the local governments. This will bring transportation to the lowest levels of government where the people understand the most about that specific area.

It is not up to the federal government to decide what is best for a state when it comes to a particular states infrastructure. It should be left up to the state to decide. America may need to work on infrastructure, but it should be the states and not the federal government that is doing the job. The less big government is involved the better off the states and local governments will be when it comes to infrastructure. The Democrats can't expect the federal government to solve all of the people's problems.

Chapter Four

The Affordable Care Act and its Problems

All Americans Should be Exempt from Obamacare

The article is a letter to President Obama about Obamacare. The Politico article about congressional exemptions for Obamacare is discussed.

Dear Mr. President, not even the lawmakers in Congress and their aides want anything to do with Obamacare. Over half of the American states do not want to set up your healthcare exchanges for Obamacare. The projected costs of Obamacare continue to rise. There is not one study that shows that Obamacare will cost what it was promised to cost the American people. President Obama what is disgusting are the lies that have come about because of your signature federal healthcare program the Affordable Care Act.

Mr. President you spoke eloquently to the American people about how Obamacare is not a tax and how the American people that have insurance will be able to keep the companies that already represent them. The <u>Patient Protection and Affordable Care Act</u> (PPACA) or Obamacare went all the way to the Supreme Court.[1] It seemed that the American people did not think that the government had the right to force people to buy something—in this case it was healthcare that they did not want to buy.

Mr. President you made it clear to the American people that taxes were not going to go up due to PPACA or Obamacare. However, the Supreme Court in order to make Obamacare legal had to call the penalty for not having health insurance a tax. Chief Justice Roberts in a five to four ruling stated that Obamacare was legal only because the penalty was in essence a tax. Mr. President the whole healthcare bill (PPACA) was a lie regarding what you said about no new taxes.

In an <u>interview with George Stephanopoulos</u> on ABC News Mr. President you stated: "No. That's not true, George. The—for us to say that you've got to take a responsibility to get health insurance is **absolutely not a tax increase**. What its saying is, that we're not going to have other people carrying your burdens for you anymore than the fact that right now everybody in America, just about, has to get auto insurance."[2] George Stephanopoulos asked the question like a statement and he thought that the Affordable Care Act was a tax. The quote above is how Mr. President you answered the question. Is what you said a lie or not a lie? Chief Justice Roberts would have to say, if it is not a lie, then President Obama you are not one of our brightest presidents. The long and short of it is that Obamacare is a middle-class tax increase and one of the largest in the history of the United States.

Back in September <u>Lizette Alvarez of the *New York Times*</u> wrote that over half the states governors where refusing to set up insurance exchanges for Obamacare.[3] An insurance exchange is like online shopping for a product in this case individuals would shop their states healthcare exchange for the best health insurance and rate that they can find. The governors of the states are refusing to set up exchanges. The governors think that in the end each state will pay more for the Obamacare exchanges than they already must pay under the various state Medicaid programs. In other words the governors think that the Obamacare funding is front loaded and although the money is good to begin with in the future the state would have to pay much more.

Mr. President why do some state governors think that your pick for the Department of Health and Human Services, Secretary Kathleen Sebelius would try to lie and cheat the states? Secretary Kathleen Sebelius is in charge of taking Congresses general law concerning Obamacare and turning it into her own interpretation of Obamacare by creating her own new regulatory law. The best example of a regulatory law she wrote was making religious institutions and Christian business leaders pay for birth control and abortion for their workers. Mr. President, Secretary Kathleen Sebelius could care less about a person's "Religious Conscious." A law like the one Secretary Kathleen Sebelius created by regulations would never see the light of day in Congress.

It is a good thing that many judges in the various state courts are finding Secretary Kathleen Sebelius secular ideals and regulations regarding those ideals unconstitutional. For instance, Joe Wolverton of The New American argues that on April 19, Judge Joy Flowers Conti of the U.S. District Court for the Western District of Pennsylvania found in favor of the Heplers: "As indicated in the judge's order, the particular provision of Obamacare at issue in this case is the mandate that forces business to provide employee health insurance plans that include compensation for birth control and so-called "morning after pills." [4]This ruling must be a shock for someone as progressive and secular as Kathleen Sebelius. It must be a shock to you as well Mr. President.

Mr. President are the new costs projected for Obamacare a shock to you or did you know that your projected costs where a lie? Merrill Matthews argues in a *Forbes magazine article* called "I'm Shocked! Obamacare Costs more than Promised" that the cost of Obamacare will sky rocket. The Congressional Budget Office has changed its projected cost for Obamacare from 938 billion dollars in 2010 to 1.76 trillion dollars in 2012 for a ten year projected period.[5] The change in cost Matthews argues is chump change because the rise in cost equals only three months of your yearly deficits—Mr. President. However, that chump change will be a drain on the future generations that have to pay the bills that Mr. President seem to be mounting up.

Mr. President the above is just the beginning and it is hard to believe what this writer read in Politico today. It seems that the entire Congress is now starting to conspire against the Obamacare bill that they were dumb enough to pass into law. Apparently lawmakers and their aids are looking at ways to get an exemption from the Obamacare exchanges that are being set up.[6] This is hard to swallow that our elected officials pass laws against the will of the majority of the American people and now hope to pass into law an exemption for themselves. Everyone on Capitol Hill wants to be exempt from your signature legislation Mr. President.

The American people are going to have to pay the taxes and penalties that Obamacare will cost and a majority of Americans did not want it begin with. The story goes that Congress will all stand together hand and hand and attach the exemption bill to a mandatory legislative bill. Mr. President the bill will be one that must get passed and one that you must sign. President Obama you should help Congress get rid of (PPACA) for all Americans. If Obamacare moves forward along with your deficit spending then your legacy is going to be as the worst President to ever hold the Office of President of the United States.

Medicaid Expansion is a Federal Trap

The Affordable Care Act and Medicaid expansion are methods for the federal government to gain control over the sovereignty of the states.

Medicaid expansion is just another hook for the federal government to reel the states in. When you look at Europe and the European Commission what is seen is that each country has one vote. It is easy to understand why many of the larger European countries are contemplating leaving the European Union, but that is an entirely different subject. What is important here is that each member of the European Commission are not supposed to vote or act in the interests of their own country but in the interest of the European Union as a whole.

Medicaid expansion is an attempt to usurp state power through the purse of the federal government. Many liberals argue—why don't the states want the "free pot of money?" The progressives on the left cannot comprehend the reality that there is no such thing as free money. The Medicaid expansion is just another way for the federal government to gain control over the states. A person needs to look as far as the Department of Education to see how the federal government can control how a state allocates its education funding. The federal government dictates how each state must spend education funding.

The states from the beginning of the Department of Education until now have had to fall in line with the federal government requirements in order for the state to receive federal money. This means that the control of education is not in the hands of the state and local education systems. States have taken education and placed the power of education into the hands of the federal government. Now the federal government wants to do the same thing with healthcare.

Medicaid expansion has an end game it is to take power away the states and limit each state's sovereignty. As a child this writer would get a wooden box and a stick and place a piece of string around the stick and prop-up the wooden box. Then the writer would place bread outside of the box and inside the box and grab one end of the string and hide from any birds that may come to feed.

The smart birds would not go into the box, but some birds would get greedy and enter the box and at that time the writer would pull the string and trap the bird. The aforementioned concept is exactly what that "free pot of money" is supposed to do. The "free money" is for the purpose of trapping the states and placing them under the control of the federal government.

Remember that healthcare is one sixth of the American economy. Healthcare will end up as one more apparatus of the federal government that continues to grow. Government growth is illustrated best by the growth seen in the Administrative branch of the federal government. The federal bureaucracy continues to grow from President to President. In the Bush era Homeland Security was created and that became the largest government agency in the history of the United States. Now the biggest segment of the federal government is the federal healthcare system which is so big it falls underneath the scope of several federal agencies.

The 25 states that are not under the control of the federal government because they opted out of Medicaid expansion are in trouble. The first example of the power of the federal government is the Virginia governor's race where the Democrat that won campaigned on the promise to bring the state in line with the Affordable Care Act. This will place the state of Virginia under the Medicaid expansion proposal of the federal government. One can argue that the people who voted for more entitlement spending won the Virginia state governor's race.

In states where the Medicaid expansion has not taken place the Virginia results have set precedence. The Democratic Party nominee for a governor's position in a red state can now use the Medicaid expansion issue to defeat Republicans running for governor. In the future all states will end up being run by progressive Democratic governors who get their marching orders from the federal government.

The "free money pot" is the bread that the entitlement voter will grasp at in the federal box that will unknowingly trap the state and place it under the control of the federal government. This may take years—but it will happen—if the Democratic Party can continue to run up federal deficits and gain power over the states with the lure of the "free money pot."

The American Congress may end up like the European Commission and all the members of Congress may vote for the good of the federal government rather than each individual state. This will happen because the federal government will have gained enough power to make the states completely depended on the federal government.

Each person in Congress will vote for the federal interest because the federal interest is the same as the state interest. The only difference is that under the American system some states will receive more money than some of the other states. Hence, the blue states with a greater population and more representatives will in the end get a majority of the funds that go into the federal coffers.

The country will truly be a majority rules system from the federal government in control downward over the states and local governments. The country will be an entitlement nation well on its way to communism.

The entitlement programs if they go unchecked will go into bankruptcy in two decades at the most. The healthcare program will cost more than all the federal discretionary programs combined. There will not be funds that can be transferred and the dollar will lose its creditability around the world. The federal government cannot just continue to print money. Foreign nations will not want to lend the United States more money. The country will be broke and the illusion of the "free money pot." will bury the country in turmoil. America will not be the land of the free at the end of the revolution.

The President's "Baby" will Devastate the Democrats in 2014

The Affordable Care Act and its need for the "Young Invincibles" will backfire. The President will get nothing accomplished on immigration.

The Democratic Party is talking about how they beat down the Republican Party in the last government shut-down and debt ceiling crises. This is true for the moment but politics are fickle and time heals all wounds in American politics. <u>President Clinton</u> went from the House of Representatives impeaching him to a leader of the Democratic Party in the 2012 election.[7] The saving grace for the Republican Party is the President's baby the Affordable Care Act. The shut-down was because of the President's unwillingness to delay the implementation of Obamacare for one year and the steadfastness of the President left the Republicans between a rock and a hard place.

The debt ceiling fight and the eventual giving in by the Republican Party was due to a variable concerning the President, that the Republicans did not take into account; and that is the President's ego and aloofness are greater than his love of country. It was the Republicans that love this country and are willing to die for it. The Republicans decided to fall on the sword no matter what the political consequences at the moment may cause. This is way the country is back in business and the debt ceiling fight is going to be dealt with at a later time.

The President after his proclaimed victory over the Republicans stated that he wanted to forge forward, first of all—on <u>immigration reform</u>.[8] This new Presidential positioning in regards to moving forward on immigration is going to be a mute issue. First of all the President already supplied millions of illegals with de facto amnesty months before the November 2012 presidential election. The President's actions implemented most of what was considered the "Dream Act" for children of illegals who had been in the country for years. It is important to note that the "<u>Dream Act</u>" was rejected by Congress about thirty times and the President decided to implement it by executive fiat.[9]

It is outrageous that the President thinks that he will get anything done at all in the remainder of his Presidency. Mr. President you will get nothing! Yes, the President will not get the money that he wants in taxation, because the people are going to feel the effects of the Affordable Care Act on their wallets. Especially the young that the Obama administration has renamed the "Young Invincibles" they are the ones that voted for the President. The "Young Invincibles" might as well be called the "Young Suckers."

Chief Justice John Roberts and the ruling of the Supreme Court stated that the Affordable Care Act and its "<u>individual mandate is a tax</u>."[10] After the dust settled and various organizations began to investigate what the tax of the Affordable Care Act will cost the American people, well it is the largest tax increase across the board in American history.

In an article by the American Action Forum called the *Impending Premium Spiral* that discusses the 2013 premium rates the "Young Invincibles" are going to pay for insurance it is apparent that they are in for a rude awakening.[11] A complete and utter sticker shock for the 'Young Suckers" that voted for the President even for the cheapest Affordable Care Act insurance called the bronze insurance.

The above article explains how the <u>U.S. Government Accountability Office</u> (GAO) reports that 44 states will see premium increases: "Pre-ACA premiums average $62.00 monthly, while post-ACA premiums average $187.08 per month, a $125.08, or 202 percent, increase. The average percent change between 2013 and 2014 minimum level plan monthly premiums is 260 percent, reflecting a nearly 3 to 1 ratio between the two sets of premiums."[12] When a person because of the individual mandate is forced to pay these prices there is something wrong in America. The Affordable Care Act is in need of the young who voted for the President's re-election.

Americans are already seeing the poor ability of the federal government to even create a website. Yes, a government website that forces people to pay a mandatory tax if they do not have health insurance. The ironic thing about the Democrats Affordable Care Act is the only thing that seems to be working is the increase of the age that a child can stay on their parent's health insurance.

The aforementioned is ironic because poor parents do not have insurance and their eighteen to twenty six year old children will have to pay outrageous premiums for health insurance on the money that they make part-time at McDonald's because working full-time would require the McDonald's to pay health insurance. Hence, the people that health insurance is supposed to help will only shift the cost from the poor parents to the young healthy and working children. The poor children who are forced to buy insurance (individual mandate) at triple the premium if they decide to buy insurance at all.

Most healthy young adults in past generations have decided to forgo health insurance when a company was not offering health insurance for a minimal allowance out of their paycheck. However, the increases in health insurance costs have made insurance scarce for many people in new jobs. Health insurance in the future at the company level probably will be nonexistent with the role out of the Affordable Care Act. Hence, what is going to be on the minds of the "Young Suckers" when in anger they go to the polls in order to get rid of the dreaded Obamacare in the 2014 elections?

The President's baby the Affordable Care Act will suffer major kickback when the "Young Invincibles" decide to pay the mandatory penalty for not having insurance rather than buying insurance at an outrageous cost. This noncompliance by the "Young Invincibles" will have repercussions throughout the entire Affordable Care Act apparatus that will have devastating effects on how the American people feel about the Democratic Party.

It is the reality of money coming out of the pockets of the young that will finally change the idealism they learned in public education into the realism of life in America under a socialist President. It is this realism of the young and the rest of America that will leave the American people begging for not the Obama "New Normal," but just the America of the pre-Obama era.

Obamacare Needs More Than a Patch

The entire Affordable Care Act is in a lot of trouble and it is the working Americans that will end up paying the bills for the progressives.

It is only in the mind of a progressive that the government can do all things for all people. The magic of the progressive is to have government money for everything even if the government does not have any money. In fact, the federal debt is over seventeen trillion dollars. This writer scratches his head when ever more money continues to flow from the magic progressive money pot.

In 2010 the cost of the Affordable Care Act was projected by the CBO to cost 930 billion.[13] In 2012 the projected cost by the CBO has gone up to 1.7 trillion dollars.[14] It is this writers estimate that the Affordable Care Act will add over four trillion dollars to the national debt by the time President Obama serves his last day in office.

The health care website does not work so the federal government will spend millions more to fix it. The federal government has already paid 634 million dollars for the healthcare website and it does not work.[15] Keep in mind that the previous price is seven times the original cost of 93 million dollars. Any business that was run like the aforementioned would go bankrupt. In business on the open market of the free enterprise system such a miscalculation would not take place. Probably the last time that a mistake of this magnitude and cost occurred was in the days of the old planned economy of the Soviet Union.

The President's health care patch for people who have received cancellation notices from insurance companies <u>will not work</u>.[16] Once a company that works on a profit margin makes a decision and puts it into operation it is very difficult to put the brakes on. The President understands that most of the people that have lost their insurance will not get that insurance back at the same price that they have previously paid.

The entire speech and so-called fix is a feel good approach to politics. The President's speech was to publicly demonstrate one thing and that is—the President is sorry—and that he tried to make the situation right. It does not matter if the patch works or not. In fact, the Affordable Care Act is better off if the insurance companies decide not to allow the customers to receive the policies that have been cancelled. After all what is the sense of all that work to create a policy that only has a one year shelf life?

The reason why the insurance companies will not accept the President's idea is due to the fact that they will lose money. The President added strings to the insurance companies by stipulating that they must tell the customer what is in the policy and what other policies exist. It is not the job of insurance companies to teach the consumer.

Each consumer needs to do their own research and understand what they are buying before they buy it. The whole idea of American business operates on caveat emptor or let the buyers beware. Only in the minds of the leaders of a progressive nanny state are the people too stupid to make their own decisions.

The idea of government subsidies is mind boggling because the concept is sold once again as "free money." It seems that the cost scale for insurance under the Affordable Care Act goes from free—to major subsidies, some subsidies, and then there is no subsidy at all. However, for the people who work hard and earn a good living, well they are forced to pay more money, and more money, and some even more money for health insurance.

One would think that in America a person would have a choice on what they want to do with their money. For instance, for someone that is young and healthy why would that person decide to pay more money for health insurance just because they make a lot of money? The Affordable Care Act takes away an individual's right of liberty in making a decision on whether or not to buy health insurance. A person must have health insurance or pay a mandatory fine to the IRS.

The above is the progressive's idea of what is best for the whole society; the progressive is so bright that they think that it is their right to make decisions about your liberty and freedom through laws, taxes, and regulations. It is the idealist progressive who believes that they are better than the rest of the public and that it is their job to orchestrate how individuals need to live.

The whole idea of the progressive is to fool the people into thinking that the federal government is everything for everyone and that every individual should want to give all that they have to the good of the federal government. The states are taught that all money that comes from the federal government is free money. The smart states or the states with Republican governors understand that there is no such thing as free money; this is why they have decided not to take the federal governments money for Medicaid.

The websites in the states that have accepted the federal government's money for Medicaid have in total signed up <u>396 thousand</u> people for Medicaid and these are all people who are getting health insurance for nothing.[17] The total amount of people that have signed up for health insurance through the federal and state websites is <u>106,185 thousand</u> people.[18] More than three times as many people have signed up for the free Medicaid insurance and the jury is still out on the amount of subsidies that the other 106,185 people are going to receive from the federal government.

The numbers are adding up and one can only say that the United States is lucky that the country has so much free money that can be printed. It makes a person wonder why they should even bother working. The federal government will provide a person with everything that they need to live a very comfortable life in the United States. It is a good thing for secular progressives that there are still individuals in this country who live by a moral code of conduct and believe in the American work ethic or no one in America would work.

"Young Invincibles" are Paying the Price for America's Future

Because of the national debt that the young must pay off in the future and the tax that must be paid under the Affordable Care Act the "Young Invincibles" better get to work.

It is getting closer to the magic time when idealism meets reality. The Affordable Care Act is a wonderful lofty concept for healthcare. The best of the best from all the highest ranked universities are at work on making sure that Obamacare works. The Congress past and present are all once again from the best of the best. It is how the members of Congress get elected. It is by proving that their ideas are the best thing for their constituency. It is Congress that continues to run up the federal debt. There is a nasty problem with the best of the best and the idealism that they learned about and emulate. It is that when the rubber hits the road idealism gets stuck in the mud of reality.

That is why the country continues to run up trillion dollar debt each year. It is why the Affordable Care Act is failing. Idealism is nothing more than a floating abstraction that in the history of man has never developed a good governmental system for the people.

It is from the end of the Cold War until now that idealism was supposed to triumph over the old school of realism. In today's world idealism has the country marred in national debt. Most of the American citizens are trapped by a governmental healthcare system that will not work. Today the American people need to realize that idealism and its "<u>free money</u>" is going to run out.[19]

President Obama and Congress have it out for the so-called "<u>Young Invincibles</u>" that age group from 18 to 34.[20] The President and Democrats in Congress expect the Young Invincibles to pay by mandate five hundred dollars a year or more for health insurance. The federal mandate requiring all Americans to have health insurance is a tax in the eyes of the Supreme Court. The bottom line is that the Young Invincibles are expected to pay the tax for a health insurance policy that ninety percent of them will not even use. In an idealistic world the Young Invincibles would pay for Obamacare, but this is a world of realistic thinking and human action so they are not.

In order to add insult to injury the Congress is about to pass a federal budget that will keep the national debt climbing. By the time President Obama leaves office it is projected that the national debt will be well over <u>twenty trillion dollars</u>.[21] The Young Invincibles are the ones that are going to be expected to pay the debt and all of the interest on that debt that is racked up in the future. In the mind of young adults will they think that this is fair treatment? Of course not the young adults are more than just upset.

The new Ryan-Murray federal budget will not stop the national debt from increasing. It is hard to understand how the budget is supposed to cut the deficit by twenty three billion dollars. George will has said "Well, first of all, <u>$23 billion is a rounding error</u>.[22] It's a rounding error on the budget. It's a rounding error on the debt. It's a rounding error on the deficit. It's a rounding error on the economy. It's trivial." The Federal Reserve is printing and pumping <u>eighty five billion</u> dollars or close to a trillion dollars a year into the economic market place and Representative Ryan wants to talk about twenty three billion dollars.[23]

It is true Americans would like to believe that the Congress can balance the budget ten years out. There is no way of knowing at the moment how much debt the Affordable Care Act is going to cost the American people. The <u>price tag</u> has already gone up by 621 billion dollars and this will add to healthcare alone an additional 7,450 dollars for a family of four.[24] The Democrats understand this reality, but in their vision and under President Obama they feel taxes need to be raised even further. That is a doubling down on idealism unfortunately the people betting do not have to pay the bill.

All one needs to know in order to make an educated guess about the future cost of the Affordable Care Act is to look at the numbers that are coming in from the sample. On MSNBC news at the end of November over 800,000 people have been given Medicaid for free; and only 364,682 people have enrolled for the Affordable Care Act. Regardless, if the site is operational or not, the statistics are illustrating that the Young Invincibles are not as stupid as President Obama thinks. They are deciding to pay the $95.00 fine that they must pay under the healthcare mandate.

The age groups of 18 to 34 year olds will have to deal with: debt problems, healthcare problems, education problems, and economic problems that are beyond comprehension. The Young Invincibles are going to be forced by the elders and leaders of the country to pay the bills for what the elders are so freely spending now. It is up to the young adults to get realistic about the future of America. At this juncture in American history idealism should be dead.

The 18 to 34 year olds in America are stuck between two things. First, they must take care of the mess that they are being left with from the two generations before them: Social Security, Medicare and Medicaid, the Affordable Care Act, and the national debt. Secondly, even if this group can pull the country out of the mess that the older Americans will have racked up; they still must worry about how they set America up for their children. It is time for the young adults to ask the educators in this country to teach about realism and the evil inherent in <u>secular humanism</u>. Kids today need to get real.

Yes, if the Young Invincibles turn out to be true Americans they will want to leave this nation in better shape for their children than they are inheriting. This is the first generation of Americans that are inheriting a country where they are worse off. It is even more disturbing that at this moment it looks even worse for their children. It will be a tribute to the Young Invincibles if they decide to shed their Democratic Party ties and vote Republican in order to do away with the Affordable Care Act. In the process the Young Invincibles can vote for leaders that want to reign in the entitlement disaster in Washington and get a true grip on the national debt.

Between the national debt and the impending disaster of the Affordable Care Act the young adults of this country do not have the luxury to think in idealistic terms. It is realism that the young adults need to follow in domestic policy in order to get the nation in order. Realism is also the foreign policy that America needs to get back to for our own security and the security of the world. The idealism of President Obama is the straw that has broken this great countries' back. The Young Invincibles will have to live up to the expectations bestowed upon them. It is realistic thinking that is needed in American government today. America it is time to grow up!

President Obama and Obamacare
are not for College Students

The cost of Obamacare is going to go up from 940 billion to 1.7 trillion dollars. Americans need to worry about the hidden costs in Obamacare like the Wedding Tax, mandatory programs, and death panels

College students are finally waking up to the fact that ObamaCare is going to hurt them and treat them unfairly. Wouldn't it be nice if the college students who voted for President Obama had done their homework about the candidate instead of listening to peer pressure and their left wing socialist professors? The most ironic advantage for older Americans who did not vote for President Obama and the Affordable Care Act is that they are going to reap the benefits of Obamacare. This is right the strong and young will pick up the bill for older Americans and others that have pre-existing conditions.

Another ironic addition to Obamacare is the "Wedding Tax" that is foisted on individuals because the Affordable Care Act penalizes young couples who marry instead of just deciding to live together.[25] That is what kids in school are taught in any case that marriage is a structural inconvenience that is no longer a requirement for a society as secular and progressive as the United States. One may ask how bad the Wedding Tax can actually be for young people getting married. The President's Wedding Tax will have a profound effect on the cost of healthcare for young married couples in comparison with their cohorts who just decide to live together.

The <u>Heritage Foundation argues</u> that the Wedding Tax could cost newlywed couples up to ten thousand dollars a year compared to couples that cohabitate.[26] This is due to the fact that a married couple's income is looked at as one sum rather than two separate sums. Hence, for a married couple each individual making twenty five thousand will get a governmental subsidy for the higher amount or the fifty thousand dollars.

Conversely a couple that cohabitates will get their subsidies based on twenty five thousand dollars separately, which means that the two that cohabitate will get more of a governmental subsidy and payless in premiums. Hence, it is government policy to penalize marriage and family since the two are taxed. Whereas the couple who has children out of wedlock and decide to cohabitate will receive greater benefits and less taxes from the federal government.

It is not a problem to live together and not have children or family because Obamacare health policies have free abortion. Even if a person does not want an abortion policy the federal government has decided that Americans must pay for additional abortion health benefits. This does not mean that a person has to use the abortion benefits but they will pay for people who do want them. This is due to the fact that in many states a person can only buy insurance from a federal provider because many states have opted out of setting up insurance exchanges in their states.

Many pro-life affiliates have warned about the many anti-life measures that have been put in place by the federal government for people who have absolutely no choice but to buy their health insurance from a federal exchange. Yes, some Americans will have to buy health insurance from the federal government because "<u>Thirty-four states</u> have elected to *not* set up their own exchanges; therefore, the Centers for Medicare & Medicaid Services (CMS) will operate the exchanges in those states."[27]

The aforementioned means that although the government may argue that people can buy insurance that does not require a person to pay for abortions and birth control—this is not the case. In many cases American citizens that can't afford the private policies will not have the luxury to abide by the "<u>Conscience Clause</u>."[28] This is why over the current budget debate to defund or delay Obamacare for a year a new "Conscience Clause" has been added to squash the federal overreach that the government was able to place back into the Affordable Care Act under the Centers for Medicare & Medicaid Services.

The above are minor problems concerning the Affordable Care Act because not only will the healthcare policy affect young Americans today, but as time moves forward the cost will grow and get absorbed directly or indirectly by everyone. At the beginning the Congressional Budget Office (CBO) put out a one decade projection of costs for the Affordable Care Act at 940 billion dollars and the new numbers are astonishing.[29]

There is an 830 billion dollar increase in the cost of the Affordable Care Act because the Congressional Budget Office projects the cost of Obamacare for the next decade to total 1.7 trillion dollars.[30]

Somebody has to pick up the tap for the doubling of the cost of the Affordable Care Act and a betting person would probably bet that the cost will even go much higher. The people that will pay are the young and healthy and this will create a schism between the young and the old. The old may think that they are making out, but in short order I am sure that the children of those that voted for President Obama will vote to crank up the death panels to save themselves some money.

The dreaded death panels for a secular society make a lot of sense after all there isn't any heaven or hell. What does it matter to end the lives of individuals that are not up to the standard of living that the state deems insurance worthy? People are living longer and the longer people live the more money that the society needs to pay for the elderly that can no longer work. The American society is not a society that has a great respect for its elderly or as discussed above a respect for the family and extended family in general.

The rich do not have to worry about the Obama death panels, but those that are on Medicare will have to worry about their futures. This is because the federal government is going to take away 716 billion dollars from the Medicare program in the next ten years. There are a few things that people need to understand about Medicare

A and that is that it is compulsory for people to have Medicare A if they hope to receive their Social Security checks.

Do not think that you can avoid the death panels by paying cash for doctor services because this is illegal: "'. . . A 1997 law (Balanced Budget Act, section 4507) forbids private contracts between patients and doctors." This means that "Medicare recipients cannot pay cash for a Medicare-covered service that Medicare denies until the doctor has opted out of Medicare. " [31] It seems that the college students who voted for President Obama also unknowingly signed on for much higher taxes and a healthcare program that will literally kill them.

Presidential Tragedy and Obamacare

The President's approval rating is at an all-time low. Obamacare is in danger of collapsing and it is up to the Republicans to save the people.

The progressives argue that only about <u>fourteen million people</u> will not be able to keep their own health insurance this is disheartening news.[32] The reason why progressives can make such a nonchalant comment about millions of people is the idea that many more people will be helped by the Affordable Care Act. Hence, in a socialist mind the reasoning is always based on the greater good and not the individual. It is like what <u>Marx stated</u>: "From each according to his abilities to each according to his needs." [33]The progressives will have to accept Karl Marx's statement about "his" because the people did not have political correctness when he was writing.

America is or was a country based on <u>rugged individualism</u>. However, individualism is not taught in schools any longer and children are growing up as team players. And as team players children are not even taught the importance of winning, but participation is what gets rewarded. This mindset is what the progressives in the Obama administration are hoping for. It is the "Young Invincibles" that the President is counting on to support his Affordable Care Act. The President is relying on the "Young Invincibles" to buy health insurance from the Affordable Care Act exchanges in order to cover the bills of the old and sick.

Why should the young and healthy pay outrageous prices for health insurance that they do not even need? It is because they are team players. The "Young Invincibles" have been conditioned and taught in school that it is not a matter of how much that they have— because they must share. The liberal progressive teachers if they have done their teaching jobs correctly have brought up a generation of Americans that are like no other generation in history. It is the first generation of willing socialists and the negation of individualism.

The President argues that if a person loses their insurance than they should just "shop around" in the new government markets for health insurance.[34] Yes, perhaps some people would take the President's advice, but the problem is that the site in order to "shop around" is not working at the moment.

The President tricked the American people into voting for him in the 2012 election. Paraphrasing the President this is how he tricked the American people: "If you have insurance and you like your doctor then you can keep your insurance and your doctor—period." The Washington Post fact checker gave the President four Pinocchio's regarding the last statement.[35] It is only now as the Affordable Care Act is rolling out that people are finding out that everything the President stated was not true.

The President in regards to the Affordable Care Act is finding out as Malcolm X stated in a 1963 speech it is "merely a case of "chickens are coming home to roost.'"[36] That is why the President's approval ratings have hit an "all-time low" for his presidency.[37] The Democrats that voted for the Affordable Care Act are now seeing that the results of their votes may cost them in the 2014 mid-term elections. This is why the Democrats in swing districts are starting to distance themselves from the President and the Affordable Care Act. Things are not looking good at all for President Obama.

The next question is what happens next if the entire progressive big government healthcare program falls flat on its face? President Obama and the Democratic Party may be the ones looking for a new constituency. Some can argue that the Democratic Party and its big government vote may dry up because the promises of the President and the Democratic Party did not come to fruition.

The failure of Obamacare could bring about a new direction for America. A whole new way of thinking may come over the American people. Perhaps, the American people will say that it is up to them and not the government in order to better their lives. The first thing that the American people will begin to look at is the economy. The economy because it takes a job and preferably a good job in order to take care of oneself.

Once the American people begin to look at the economy what they will realize is that the President has done nothing to improve it. The American people will begin to understand that the economy has been stuck in low gear for a while. The American people will then look to the President for answers and what they will find is that the President has lied to them—some more.

President Obama likes to take credit for things that go right even though he impeded the growth as much as he could. A perfect example is the fossil fuel industry and the boom that some states are seeing and the jobs that are being created. The President has done everything he can to hinder the development of fossil fuels in America.

President Obama is the big regulation President who has created more regulatory law than any President that came before him. In fact, <u>President Obama in 2012</u> alone has created more regulatory law than President's Bush and Clinton created in their first terms. This means that businesses are being fined. The American people because of their new state of mind will understand that the fines are being passed on to them. The President and his progressive lot do not think that the American people can put two and two together, but this will change as they mistrust the President and the Democratic Party more.

The Republican Party cannot be the party that simply states that we told you so! It is up to the Republican Party to help the American people in this time of tragedy. The Republicans need to help the Democrats who want to help the American people. This is still a great country. It is up to compassionate Americans on both sides of the political aisle to come together and bale the American people out of the mess that the President and his progressive mobsters have put the country in.

Chapter Five

Environmentalism and the
Presidents Green Energy Plans

America Cannot Afford "Green Energy" We Must Drill, Drill, Drill

The one thing to get the American economy moving is to create jobs by tapping into the countries natural resources. This will bring down the cost of energy for Americans and that means the American people will have money to spend on other things.

The <u>Great Green Fleet</u> is the most ludicrous and dangerous thing that our Commander and Chief, King Obama has foisted on the Defense Department, the Navy, and American people.[1] It takes <u>one bushel of corn</u> to make 2.8 gallons of ethanol.[2] At this time the Navy will pay twenty six dollars a gallon for a 50/50 gas, ethanol mix in order to fuel a fleet of ships. The fleet of ships could be filled for the price of three dollars and sixty cents using the regular fuel the Navy has used since the beginning of gas powered shipping. America is in an energy boom for oil and gas why should the country waste the money?

President Obama has cut, cut, and cut defense and now he wants to waste Defense Department money on a product that costs over seven times the price of what the Navy needs to pay. In both the World Wars the United States needed to send food to the American allies so that the civilian populations would not starve. In World War I food was used as an effective weapon. Should America be wasting good corn land and product on ethanol for engines? Of course not the land should be used to feed the people and livestock of America and the world.

America needs to drill, drill and have more drilling, because that would create hundreds of thousands of American jobs at home. Drilling would also keep the American dollar out of the hands of foreign nations. The housing market will not revive and America will not be building new homes anytime soon. There are millions of Americans out of work in the electrical, pipe fitting, and all other types of construction labor jobs that drilling will create. Fossil fuels could be America's way out of the President's "New Normal."

More jobs would be created in the actual drilling of oil, and work in the companies that make the products and materials that are needed. Drilling will take America off the leash of the Middle East, and make the dollar more stable. With Americans back to work and paying taxes the United States Treasury would bring in more money. America could start making some inroads into paying down the federal debt.

The course the President is now on begs the question of why the President doesn't socialize the entire green energy program in America. The Bush administration may have started with the ethanol subsidies, but President Obama has turned green energy into a crusade. The job stimulus package created huge subsidizes and guaranteed government loans for green energy. All the costs went onto the backs of the American taxpayer. The American taxpayer has paid for plenty of the President's green energy boondoggles: solar, wind, electric cars and ethanol. Why don't the environmentalists care about top soil? The federal government and ethanol production continues to ruin good top soil. The federal government keeps turning corn into ethanol rather than utilizing and developing the nation's fossil fuel capacities.

Many scientific tests have proven that America has hundreds of years of oil, natural gas, and coal deposits that can be tapped for production. However, the federal agencies that the Obama administration controls are trying to kill the fossil fuel industries in America. The various governmental agencies that should be helping American business are instead hindering and actually hurting the fossil fuel industry, especially coal.

America needs to stop using thousands of acres of corn to make ethanol: <u>Last year</u>, (2011) for the first time ever, more corn in this country was used to make ethanol than to feed livestock.[3] This means that food prices go up on all livestock products. Increased food costs are due directly to ethanol production. It is this writer's opinion that higher food prices are a tax on the lower middle, middle, and upper middle class families that are paying higher prices for food. The American people are also paying too much for gasoline because of the price of ethanol. President Obama and his Energy Czar will not allow American companies to drill on government land. Someone should remind the President that government land is owned by the American people as a whole, and not just his little <u>green friends</u> who support the President's campaign coffers.[4]

The federal debt in America is over seventeen trillion dollars. If President Obama is reelected it is projected that the President will run trillion dollar deficits for the next four years. America cannot bail itself out of that much debt. America in the near future will be a junk bond nation. The EPA headed by Lisa Jackson and the Secretary of Energy Steven Chu are developing regulations that are causing the loss of thousands of American coal jobs.

Luckily the United States Senate was able to stem the EPA's attempt to kill the coal industry. "Republicans said, the <u>regulations are the most expensive</u> rules ever created by the EPA, and will cost consumers $10 billion a year in addition to killing 50,000 jobs."[5] Many argue that the President wants to double down on green energy. The President thinks that he understands economics. Is not nine billion dollars in <u>stimulus money for solar and wind</u> that only creates nine hundred and ten jobs a bad investment?[6] The cost is equal to ten million dollars per job is that good economics? This is a crime. Much more can be said about the Presidents failures to stimulate the American economy, but let's stick to green energy.

Large corporations are utilizing a green energy loophole to pay no corporate income tax. It is called the federal **Green Energy Tax Credit**. For example, General Electric did not pay any corporate income tax in 2010, because of all the <u>green energy tax credits</u> the company bought from other companies. "For instance, one of the reasons that GE did not pay any taxes in 2010 was their mass accumulation of tax credits from things like wind turbines. It seems General Electric was not really the company that was responsible for building the wind turbines, they were just the organization that gets credit for it."[7] One interesting study about the wind turbine industry demonstrates that since the early 2000's the tax subsidies for wind turbines have had no effect on the price of energy. In fact, the price of energy for the wind turbines continues to go up. One of the main reasons for this phenomenon is due to the third-party development of the industry by corporations like General Electric who are using the energy tax credits and doing absolutely nothing in order to further the wind turbine industry.

When one looks deep enough the only reason why green energy is important is because it is making certain groups of people rich. Green energy ends up costing the average American while the people who are for green energy make money off of the green energy scams. That is why it costs ten million dollars to create one green energy job. Look at all the money that the American people lost by the failure of green energy companies like Solyndra and a bunch of other companies.[8] President Obama is catering to a few at the expense of the average American when it comes to his ideas about the environment. It is time for the American people to speak up.

President Obama's Green Warriors Verse the American People

President Obama's nominee for the EPA Gina McCarthy is discussed in relation to the new regulations that will bring higher costs for the American people.

The one bright spot in the American economy today comes from the energy sector and how that sector will develop and expand in the future. This upsets President Obama and other far left environmentalists in the United States who hope for nothing more than higher fossil fuel prices for all Americans. It is the position of the far left environmentalists to do everything in their power to crush the life blood of American ingenuity and a once vibrant American economy to death.

President Obama's "New Normal" of environmental cronyism and federally funded environmental project failures are weighing the American economy down. The elected officials in Congress who represent the people have no control over what the President is doing with the various agencies that deal with the energy sector in the United States.

Each agency created by the Congress is created by general law and it is the agency that turns that general law into regulative law. The President's ultimate environmental misfit the Environmental Protection Agency (EPA) does exactly what the President tells it to do even though it's funding is authorized by the United States Congress. The EPA is a runaway outfit under the guidance of President Obama.

In <u>President Obama's budget</u> for the Environmental Protection Agency for 2014 the President actually cuts the department by nine percent leaving the agency with a mere total spending amount of eight billion dollars.[9] However, this does not mean that the agency will stop its push towards higher energy prices for all Americans. This is due to the EPA's over regulation since the beginning of the Obama Administration. In fact many of the new regulations by the EPA were not set to go into effect until after the President's re-election in 2012.

<u>Larry Bell wrote</u> a piece for Forbes Magazine titled *EPA's Insanely Ambitious Agenda If Obama Is Reelected* that argues the extent of the Obama Administrations attack on oil, gas and specifically the coal industry.[10] Bell argues that under the auspices of the Clean Air Act (CAA) the EPA is going to develop restrictions industry by industry that will amount to an increase of 300 to 400 billion dollars in costs a year for the energy industry. Bell continues with a discussion of the "Cow Tax" that amounts to charging farmers who own cattle for greenhouse gas admissions and that will mean that small farmers will need permits at an average cost of 23,000 dollars a year.

The thing that is most disheartening about the President and his green warriors is that they do not care about the American people. Environmentalism has nothing to do with future generations of Americans for the green warriors or they would want a robust economy in order to pay down debt and save Social Security and Medicare. Instead Obama's green warriors want a stagnant economy because that means less pollution. The idea of having both a clean environment and a healthy economy never crosses the mind of the green warriors. It is unimaginable for the green warriors that America can have both a clean environment and a healthy energy economy that leads the way for heavy industry and better paying jobs as more companies decide to set up shop in the United States because of cheap energy.

The United States has more coal than any country on the planet. The Obama administration is doing everything in its power to keep that coal in the ground. The Obama policies are and will cause hundreds of thousands of jobs to be lost throughout the entire coal arena including the employees of coal fired power plants. China and India have absolutely no plans on changing the way that they pollute the environment and that makes everything that the United States does miniscule in regards to a healthier environment.

If the green warriors could wrap their minds around the scientific concept of diminishing returns then the green warriors would understand that unrealistic regulations are bad for the economy. The green warriors would realize instead of paying more for energy Americans will have more for consumer spending and that will help the economy grow.

A growing economy will create a larger tax base and more money in federal taxes taken in. With the extra tax money after the federal debt is paid off the United States would have more money for the domestic programs of health, education, and welfare. The aforementioned is why the green warriors continue to try and find new ways to hurt the United States economically through green regulations. The green warriors equate a bad economy with a need for more government handouts and hence, more power in the hands of the federal government.

For instance, "Senators Barbara Boxer (D-CA) and Bernie Sanders (I-VT) recently proposed the Climate Security Act of 2013." This new tax will be a tax on carbon alone or a tax on fossil fuel energy sources alone. The Heritage Foundation argues that the tax will cost a family of four one thousand dollars the first year it is enacted. The tax will mean higher costs for consumers of 20 cents on gas and 20 percent on electric energy.[11] The tax will have a devastating effect on the coal industry and coal production will drop by sixty percent. The Boxer-Sanders bill would cause a loss of forty percent of all coal jobs.

President Obama is also trying to put a new EPA Secretary into position by the name of Gina McCarthy and some think that this means more doom and gloom for the energy sector. McCarthy believes in a zero-tolerance approach towards regulations which means that she does not care about a cost-benefit analysis.[12] McCarthy in this writer's opinion believes in the environment first and animals second. McCarthy is a green warrior who thinks that the American people need to go to the back of the bus. Gina McCarthy believes that environment trumps business, and animals trump people. McCarthy cares little about business except for how much money the EPA can acquire through regulatory fines and how much more money each company must pay to live up to the new EPA regulations.

The Heritage Foundation article *Ten Questions for EPA Nominee Gina McCarthy* lays out the same questions that need to be asked by the Senate in her confirmation hearing.[13] The EPA has grown well beyond what the Clean Water Act (CWA) and the Clean Air Act (CAA) were created to accomplish. In the last thirty years the United States has developed much cleaner air and water than all of the emerging industrial powers for example, both China and India. The idea that America should unilaterally work towards climate change legislation means American businesses cannot compete with foreign companies that do not have the same costly regulations. This means a further erosion of the American manufacturing base and higher costs for all Americans.

The EPA should be replaced by an entirely new environmental agency and one that is responsible to the American people as a whole. This is rather than by business interests or by environmental protectionist green warrior groups. The entire process of stewardship needs to be controlled by the people. The people have the greatest interest in the wellbeing of America and that is why the general public should have more input about national environmental concerns. There should be a mechanism in place that allows the American people to weigh the environmental benefits verse the personal costs of any environmental protection. The idea would be that the American people and the environment could act as one symbiotic unit.

The President's War on Fossil Fuels is a War on the Middle Class

The President would like to tax oil and gas for another two billion dollars so that he can spend the money on green energy projects. The cost of Obama's war on fossil fuels is billions of dollars in fines and higher energy costs for consumers.

In 2009 President Obama took 90 billion dollars from the stimulus package and put it into renewable energy projects. Now in 2013 the President is complaining about the sequester cuts of 84 billion having an impact on his favorite green energy projects. What the President has decided to do is get an initiative on track to take two billion dollars from royalty payments to the federal government for oil and gas offshore drilling and putting that money into green energy projects over the next ten years.[14] In a speech at Argonne National Laboratory outside Chicago President Obama explained how China, Germany and Japan are investing in renewable energy while America is standing around not doing a thing as far as future investments in green energy.

The President thinks that batteries for automobiles need further investment so that America can begin to use less fossil fuel. This country would be in worse shape today if it was not for the fossil fuel explosion in America. The oil and gas jobs created and increased supplies of oil and gas because of drilling in America is keeping the economy afloat today—that is no thanks to the Obama administration.

The stimulus package that gave 90 billion dollars for green energy projects was the largest investment in the history of the United States.[15] The money went to solar projects, wind projects, water projects, high speed rail train projects, 13 million "smart" electrical meters, weatherizing for one million low income families homes, and many other green energy projects. Where did all that money end up? Remember the Solyndra ordeal that cost the American people 535 million dollars because of Solyndra's bankruptcy on federally guaranteed loans.

The excuse by Solyndra was that China was dumping cheap solar panels into the United States so that Solyndra could not compete.[16] One should ask why the President did not put tariffs on the Chinese solar panels so that Solyndra could compete with the Chinese. Solyndra was only one of many boondoggles that cost the American people billions of dollars for little to show for it all. The Obama administration had promised jobs out of the stimulus money for the green energy projects, but the jobs never materialized.

President Obama is waging a war against the American fossil fuel energy sector in oil, gas, and coal that is costing the American people jobs and a bill for higher energy costs. Before exploring the Presidents abuse of the fossil fuel industry there is one glaring energy problem that the President should have dealt with years ago and that is the Keystone XL Pipeline. This problem is glaring because it affects the North American continent and one of America's biggest trading partners our neighbor Canada. It makes no sense for Canada to sell oil to China that could be brought cheaply into the United States, refined and put into the American gas system to lower America's domestic fuel rates and dependence on Middle Eastern oil.

The State Department on March 1, 2013 put out a report that the Keystone XL Pipeline would not have an effect on global warming because the oil would still be developed by Canada either way. President Obama while speaking to law makers yesterday stated that he would make a decision by the end of this year. Derek Wallbank in a Benefitspro article argues that a house bill would route the Keystone Pipeline around Obama. The House of Representatives is working on a bill that would not need the President's signature.[17]

In May (2014) the House will vote on a bill to get the Keystone XL Pipeline back on track. The House of Representatives does not even want to deal with the President any longer.

The American people must understand that this back and forth between the President and Congress has been going on for a while. For instance, the President tried to get a Cap and Trade bill through Congress that failed.[18] The President decided that by using the Environmental Protection Agency (EPA) he could create regulations for greenhouse gases that would have the same results on the coal industry as cap and trade would have. The President will not let up on the coal industry because he wants to destroy it. The American people are going to be forced to pay more for electricity. No one is freed from the President's greenhouse gas emission plans. What the President failed to do through the proper channels of government he accomplished through the long arm of the governmental bureaucracy found in the administrative apparatus.

The President does not care about added fuel costs for the American people. The President fails to do the proper cost benefit analysis about energy before making decisions that will affect the lives of the American people. The cost of gas and electricity are hurting the people of the United States for no good reason. Forty five percent of the electricity in America comes from coal-burning power plants. The added costs that President Obama is forcing on the coal industry and the electric companies are costs that the American people have to deal with.

The higher energy costs amount to taxing the people twice for the same coal. First, by the regulations on the coal and the electric power industry that amounts to paying fines to the federal government. Secondly, by the hidden extra costs that the consumer is forced to pay. Estimates have the EPA's regulations costing the American people 129 billion dollars.[19] This will force the utility plants to take about a fifth of their coal—burning power plants off line and that will cost not only money, but many jobs as well. Is this what one would consider a President for the people?

President Obama wants billions more for his green energy plans that are years away from profitability. This is true because if the technology was worth developing private companies would do the research and development themselves. The Chinese are willing to invest money in the United States by building hundreds of <u>natural gas fueling stations</u> across America in order to get in on the natural gas boom going on in the United States.[20] The new fueling stations will save close to two dollars a gallon in the switch from diesel to natural gas for trucks. This just shows that business knows how to invest for making profit whereas all the federal government can do is take the money from business through regulations and waste it on government programs.

The Chinese are now <u>importing more oil</u> than the United States and that amount will increase as China continues to develop.[21] Naturally the Chinese are interested in buying American fossil fuel in the future or at least helping America to tap its own resources so that the price on the world exchange will stay low. What does it matter if the United States pollutes the least while countries like China use nothing but fossil fuels? What matters is the American people will continue to pay more for gas, electricity, food and everything else that moves by truck. Hence, the living standards of the Chinese will continue to grow while the United States standard of living will continue to decrease. This is all thanks to the environmentalists and President Obama.

The American Working Class
Can't Afford "Green Energy"

Green energy is costing the American people. The people should not have to pay the higher costs for energy because they cannot afford it. President Obama is forcing people out of jobs and destroying the entire coal industry, an industry that this country counts on.

President Obama is on his way to killing the coal industry in the United States.[22] Before Barack Obama became President he was quoted, as saying that he would, "bankrupt the coal industry."[23] The United Mining Association states that 50% of the energy in the United States comes from coal. To put that into perspective according to UMA each person in the United States consumes 3.4 tons of coal in a year. The U.S. Energy Administration states that the demand for coal in 2010 was 1.05 billion tons, and ninety percent of that coal was used in the United States.[25] The United States has the most coal reserves in the world with Russia second, and China third. Coal is the cheapest source of electricity in the United States. UMA argues that for every employee in the coal industry that Obama puts out of work, another 3.5 individuals will lose their jobs somewhere else in the American economy.

President Obama and his "double-down" philosophy for "Green Energy" is costing the American coal industry billions and those billions mean that the American people are paying more for electricity.[26] The Mining Association argues that coal workers are skilled labor and that once the coal workers move it is difficult to find quality workers. Of course the President's hope is that the coal industry just dies. This President is the coal industries worst nightmare. It is also a nightmare for the American people because of the higher costs of electricity due to the Obama policies.

If President Obama wins the 2012 election, then in four years a new presidential administration will not be able to set America on the right energy track again. The new President will have a hard time putting humpty dumpty (<u>American Energy Policy</u>) back together again.[27] America after another four years of President Obama will have to revamp the energy sector and that will cost the American taxpayer billions of dollars. Green energy is thirty years away for the American free enterprise system in terms cost effectiveness. The Obama administration from a public policy perspective should have performed a cost-benefit analysis concerning the green energy market. Secretary Steve Chu and the President knew that their policies in the <u>The Chu Plan </u>were pushing green energy faster than the free market could accept.[28]

The American people are not ready to lose thousands of jobs and pay billions more for energy just so the President can tell the United Nations that he is doing everything in his power to meet expectations for carbon emissions. The President first should worry about the coal workers and the national debt of seventeen trillion dollars before he worries about the United Nations and the international community. Does it really matter if the President must tell the United Nations that he can't meet the seventeen percent drop in carbon emissions that was promised? Mr. Chu believes that in creating artificially higher costs for fossil fuels that people will use less. This is true, but Mr. Chu should be worried about the welfare of the American people more than the welfare of the international community.

The Secretary of Energy Mr. Chu is willing to have thousands of Americans lose their jobs in the worst recession since the Great Depression. Secretary Chu argues in the <u>"The Chu Plan"</u> that it does not matter, nor does he care about American jobs or the cost of living for Americans.[29] Tripling the costs of fossil fuels for the rest of Americans is a good domestic policy according to Secretary Chu.

How can any person with common sense not think that Mr. Chu is doing the job that the Obama administration wants him to do? This Presidential election is about the road that America will go down. We will be either a socialist nation under the Obama administration or a Romney freedom and liberty America.

In this writer's opinion the most tragic thing about President Obama is that he doesn't care about losing billions on bad green energy investments. People in the coal industry and other fossil fuels are losing their jobs, while the American energy sector wastes good money for green energy losses. It seems that the green energy losses do not matter to President Obama. This is probably because the losses will be offset by charging the coal industry more to do business. The new cost of doing business is putting business out of business. President Obama has broken the back of the coal business. President Obama is creating too many regulations on businesses and he is making the cost of doing business too high. It seems that the global citizen (Obama) has spent too much money and now the world is sick. Yes, the old adage lives on "If America sneezes the world catches a cold."

The diagnosis does not look good. America can't help the world, because we are sick ourselves in debt. The National Debt Clock as this paper is written marches closer to eighteen trillion dollars. That amounts to over fifty thousand dollars for every man, woman and child that lives in America. President Obama is no longer about "Hope and Change" his campaign is about "Hype and Blame."[30] It is incredible how intelligent and masterful the United States Constitution is written, because it understands and makes allowances to control the inherent difficulties of human emotions and greed. The 2010 elections meant losses for the Democrats and President Obama and what happened is that the Democrats have changed.

In 2010 the Republican Party became the majority party in the House of Representatives. This allowed for changes in the House committees that control the various cabinet departments and agencies. The new House Committee for the Environmental Protection Agency and the Department of Energy where told that they were being put on a tight leash. Broder did some research and discovered: "A House subcommittee voted on Thursday to strip the Environmental Protection Agency of its power to regulate greenhouse gases,"[31]President Obama vowed that he would veto any legislation that was placed on his desk that would restrict his cabinets from regulating coal and other fossil fuel industries. It is a good thing that President Obama was put in check like he was by the new Republican House of Representatives.

Here are a few facts about the differences between fossil fuels and green energy. It will take 1.3 billion GE Wind Turbines to take the place of the forty eight percent of electricity that coal power plants produce in the United States. GE Wind Turbines are not cheap they run one million dollars per mega-watt. This means that a 1.5 mega-watt GE Wind Turbine costs 1.5 million dollars and two million if it is installed. Green energy will never have the capacity to take care of even twenty five percent of America's power needs.

The title of the article is "Obama Regulations kill Ohio Coal Mine Hundreds of Jobs Wiped Out." [32] How cold of a man is the President? It seems the President can careless about the people who have worked their whole lives to just make ends meet. At Harvard University the President learned about global warming and now no matter who gets hurt the President feels he will do something to stop global warming. The problem is just how far the President is willing to go.

"There will be additional layoffs, not only at Murray Energy, but also throughout the United States coal industry due to Mr. Obama's 'War on Coal' and the destruction that it has caused to so many jobs and families in the Ohio Valley area and elsewhere," said Mr. Murray. "Both Mr. Obama and Vice President Joe Biden stated that there would be 'no coal in America' prior to their elections," said Mr. Piasecki. "They are making good on their intentions while they destroy so many lives and family livelihoods in this area for no benefit whatsoever," he concluded."[33]

The American people must begin to worry about the future of our country. In a Washington Post article Gattuso points out that President Obama and his administrative agencies have created 106 regulations that add up to 46 billion dollars in costs to business.

Former President Bush had 28 regulations with a total regulatory cost to business at 8.1 billion in the same three year time period.[34] Americans are losing high paying jobs for no reason other than the warped ideology of our President.

Prices on fuel, food and many other items that move by truck are going up and costing Americans more money. The extra money spent on necessities means that Americans do not have much discretionary income. This greed and corruption is only the beginning of President Obama's green energy cronyism and what is being called green corruption.[35] America does not have the luxury to worry about clean energy at this juncture in American economic history. This is not the Great Depression; in fact this recession economically will have a greater toll on America for decades to come.

During the Great Depression the American dollar was still backed by gold. The way that President Obama is running up trillion dollar deficits each year a person has to feel bad for the youth of America. This country cannot stand on paper. The floating world exchanges and national abstract numbers will only float for so long. The housing bubble in the United States is nothing compared to a federal government bubble. When the government is no longer valid to the rest of the world, then America will end up like Greece. And when that bubble bursts one can only hope that they live in a good neighborhood with good friends, and a large arsenal. The riots will begin quickly. The people will want their 'Free-stuff" and when they can't get their free stuff from the government. It will be revolution time in America.

Green Energy Regulations make 85 Billion look Cheap

Drilling for oil and gas are two ways out of the economic problem facing America today. The President needs to put Green Energy aside.

The United States has more coal than any other country in the world. Our country has plenty of oil and gas that needs to be tapped. Pipelines like the Keystone pipe line from Canada to the Gulf of Mexico needs to be completed. If President Obama would put his love of green energy and his fallacious belief in climate change aside and move forward with a realistic energy plan this country would have more money to pay down our federal debt.

A realistic legacy for President Obama should be the idea of putting the United States well on its way to fulfilling America's independent energy goal. Another legacy could be the incredible turn around in the American economy and the nation's ability to pay down the federal debt due to the Presidents energy policy. President Obama with a fossil fuel energy plan could become the liberal Twenty First century Ronald Reagan.

The sequester will save 85 billion dollars about two percent of the governments federal budget.[36] President Obama's Environmental Protection Agency (EPA) headed by Lisa Jackson has pressed forward creating a path of regulations that has cost America billions of dollars. For instance, just the mercury policy that Lisa Jackson implemented will cost the American people 100 billion dollars a year according to the Electric Reliability Coordinating Council.[37] This is why President Obama's campaign about sequestration makes little sense. President Obama needs to just call his EPA pit bulls off of the coal industry and other fossil fuel industries and he would have much more than 85 billion.

An article by William Jasper lays out a great case of science and what scientists really think about the idea of CO2 and climate change.[38] President Obama stated in his "State of the Union" address that he would do something to stop the forward motion of climate change for our children. Jasper argues using many sources and references that because of the research of many scientists the idea of global warming is inconclusive to be kind. Mr. President, What climate change?

The United Nations and the statistics that they have developed and put out regarding climate change are considered erroneous by many scientists. This is due to the fact that many scientists who have created data pointing to a climate change are all supported by governmental sources for financing or by NGO's. It is just plain wrong for the President not to take the advice of many of the renowned scientists who do not believe in global warming. The whole idea and the costs to American businesses and citizens are much higher than the benefits that the President is suggesting.

President Obama has stated that he will go around Congress and pass Executive Orders and use his various governmental agencies like the EPA to make his global warming agenda prevalent. The Secretary of Interior has already started the policy of not opening federal government land permits for drilling. This crushes the access that companies need in order to drill on federal land. There are many ways that the Obama administration can hinder national economic growth. America's energy policy should be as free and loose as President Obama was with the American citizens' money for companies like Solyndra. However, unlike Solyndra a loose energy policy at the moment will help grow the American economy and make America energy independent.

The EPA is willing to kill American jobs in order to shutdown coal burning power plants around the country. Close to fifty percent of America's electricity comes from coal. The new technologies for harnessing natural gas mean that the United States can begin to use more natural gas. This is due to the new stringent guidelines on coal due to the new EPA policies. Yes, it will actually be cheaper to just shut down a coal burning power plant than to build and implement a gas fired power plant. The problem is coal makes up forty two percent of America's electric needs.

The only way that the United States Coal Industry can survive is by shipping more coal overseas to the largest coal burning country in the world and that is China. China at one time was putting a coal powered plant on line each week and this was when AL Gore, the United Nations, and other nation-states were all talking about reducing man's carbon footprint and the dangers of global warming. China does not want to have anything to do with the countries bend on ruining their manufacturing base due to unrealistic carbon and mercury emission restrictions.

Let's look at it another way—if the United States is not burning coal than who will pay for the switch from coal to gas? The consumers will pay for it through higher fuel costs for the next ten years because that is the time it will take to switch from coal to gas. In the end the consumer once again will pay for President Obama's green energy policy. Clean air is worthwhile but if America is playing by its stringent environmental rules and countries like China are allowed to be careless about air pollution that will affect the price of American products for export. President Obama is so green minded that it appears that he is not rational about what is best for the United States.

Moving on to oil the same groundwork is being applied as in the case of coal. Federal land leases for drilling that used to take one month are now taking three months to get passed by the federal government. One thing that needs to be answered is who benefits from high gas prices in America? The President insists on keeping the price of gasoline as high as the administration has the capacity to influence such matters. Everyone agrees that America needs to be energy independent. Why is the President not allowing drilling in Alaska and offshore or building pipelines like the Keystone pipe line?

Once again the President seems not to care about the cost of gasoline for the average American. Many Americans are probably traveling further for less money because of taking a job that they are over qualified for due to the length of the latest recession. Hence, gas prices are making the lives of many Americans very difficult while putting them in a situation where they have no extra income to spend. The American economy is a consumer based economy and therefore, people must have extra income to spend. Without spending the American economic environment runs into the stagnation that the United States is seeing with regards to President Obama's "New Normal."

One must argue that President Obama's strategies about many domestic policies are counterproductive. The President thinks that more government is the answer instead of less government and that bureaucracies are better than an American business. The President thinks that green energy is the key to America's future while others say let us worry about the economy today. The United States has some of the cleanest air and water in the world for an industrialized nation and that should be good enough at the moment. The federal debt and entitlement programs are what America needs to concentrate on.

A growing United States economy is what America needs not this lethargic crawl in the American economy today. If increases in fossil fuels outputs and cheap gas prices are the answer to the American economic problem then let's drill. It is quite evident that the drilling on private lands has brought booming economies to areas of the country that have never seen the prosperity that they are now seeing because of oil and gas. The 85 billion in the sequester cuts is a joke. America could make much more than that in taxes each year if the country would just utilize its talents in citizens and technology in regards to fossil fuel drilling.

The Goal of the Progressive Environmentalist is Hurting People

America has environmental issues that must be dealt with, but those issues need to be dealt with in an intelligent manner. The environmentalists are over the top in that their ideas will hurt basic Americans.

What happened to the "Land of the Free?" It is gone! Freedom in America is on a continuous slide and it seems to have been that way since the first progressives. It appears that those who consider themselves progressives believe that they understand what is best for the rest of us. That is why they are progressive and this is a joke. Environmentalism and especially today's progressive environmentalist is a small part of a greater picture concerning the loss of freedom in America today. It is the hi-jacking of America by a small percentage of self-deluded environmentalists that Americans' must look out for.

The progressives are today very illogical and contradictory in how they hope to save the environment as is seen below. American stewardship of the land is dissipating due to the new environmentalism being practiced in America. It is true today that the "We the People" no longer control how the material benefits of the country is disbursed for the betterment of all. It is a small percentage of Americans who force all of us to pay a growing price for the actions of overzealous progressive environmentalists.

Progressive environmentalists in reality seem to care more about animals than they care about human beings. President Obama a progressive and his cronies at the Environmental Protection Agency (EPA) and the Department of Interior are taking away valuable American land from the American people. It is analogous to mouth balling certain areas of the country in order to save the land from the very people that it belongs to. The thing that is most offensive is the manner and how these two agencies do their dirty deeds. It is equal to a kid on drugs who steals money from the family to support their habit. The progressive environmentalist will not stop its addiction from taking away the American peoples natural resources.

One example is the Department of the Interior and the Interior Secretary Ken Salazar wanting to take half of Alaska and half of America's petroleum reserves off limits to drilling. Secretary Salazar states that Alaska is "an iconic place on earth."[39] His statement is what is troublesome because it is a globalist statement. The statement is not one expected from a presidential appointed American leader who is trying to take away trillions of dollars in oil reserves not to mention other resources that belong to the American people.

Secretary Salazar is not happy with only wanting half of Alaska he is also concerned about saving one million acres around the Grand Canyon from the big bad mining companies on this specific federal land. At least Secretary Salazar considers the Grand Canyon "priceless American landscape."[40] It appears the heart of the American West is not up for negotiations with the new globalist regime in Washington.

It is in the small things that are said or done by President Obama and those appointed by him that are frightening as an American. This American does not vote for American leaders who have the world's interest above the United States interest. It appears that President Obama and the people that are working for him care more about the international interests of the world and not the United States interests. It would be nice if the President cared about the thousands of people who work in the coal industry and the people that support them.

The United States has twenty seven percent of the world's coal supply that is more coal than China or Russia.[41] Coal produces forty two percent of America's electricity. We have enough clean coal to last over two hundred years. The new technology for coal burning takes away ninety five percent of the sulfur dioxide in the production of electricity.[42] A gravitation towards clean coal burning by government incentives and leaving the industry alone could put a large dent in the federal deficit over the next ten years. This along with the savings for consumers on electricity will mean that the consumer has more money to spend.

Instead of wanting to tax the oil companies more without giving them anything in return the two sides should cut a deal. President Obama's method only means that the American people pay the tax, not the oil company. Instead help them to make more oil for Americans by giving them the permits needed in a timely fashion. Let the oil companies make more profits and tax them at the same rate—the federal government, the oil company, and the American people will make out.

America needs to open the seas to offshore oil drilling and we need to drill more at home so that other sections of America can achieve the North Dakota Affect.[43] North Dakota is a state that with private oil production has brought jobs and higher pay to most of the people in North Dakota. The Keystone Pipeline is another project that is being held back by the environmentalists. The Keystone Pipeline amounts to thousands of jobs for Americans.

The Obama method to create energy efficiency for America is a joke. Green energy is a dead end at this stage of world technological development! Since there is a want for energy efficiency why not let the private sector create the products that truly are efficient for Americans. If President Obama developed a new energy policy one for all Americans rather than a very small percentage of sick fringe element environmentalists then America would be on the road to energy independence.

Some may question the use in language above, but when you have clean energy like hydroelectric, why dismantle it? The cost is in the billions of dollars all over America to remove the plants due to environmentalists. The dams are being removed because they are in the way of salmon migration or some other little bug or creature.[44] What justifies calling progressive environmentalist a sick fringe is that as stated earlier they care more about living creatures than the wellbeing of the American people.

The reason for this article is partially due to the ultimate argument of insane environmentalism. Yes, insane because the environmentalists are arranging the <u>killing the barred owl</u> in order to save the spotted owl.[45] It is this writer's opinion that environmentalists could care less about the spotted owl. The progressives care more about all the pristine two hundred year old trees that they are saving. If it was a question of ten acres of two hundred year old trees or a few thousand spotted owls the environmentalist in weighing the options would probably save the trees. If there was a bug that was eating the two hundred year old trees that was headed for extinction the environmentalists would save the bug. Instead of logging the trees, and saving the owls—weighing the options the progressive would put the loggers out of work, and kill the spotted owls to save the tree eating bug.

There is not any logic in a progressive environmentalists mind. The progressives are secularists that think it is up to them to play god. The progressives are very sick people. Yes, the progressive environmentalists are nihilists out to hurt the average person with their policy objectives. The only hope for the progressive is something that they do not believe in. It is too bad because we are all God's creatures.

Chapter Six

Big Government and the President

President Obama and Presidential Power

The article makes a comparison between President Obama and Richard Neustadt's book Presidential Power and the Modern President

President Obama is dealing with many problems at the moment and they seem to run one right after another. It is time for the President to take a break and try to figure out how to move forward in his job as the American President. President Nixon's staff was told to read *Presidential Power and the Modern President* by <u>Richard Neustadt</u> which is a very good book on the presidency and presidential power in modern times.[1] There are three things that a president should be aware of and nurture while in the Whitehouse and they are: the power to persuade, the presidents professional reputation, and public prestige. In this article the problems that President Obama faces are highlighted in relation to the three bedrock principles discussed above.

The number one problem that this President faces is his inability to get anything accomplished concerning the development and passage of bills through the Congress. The President's agenda is important and the President must work his agenda through the Congress. However, this President is having a hard time getting anything done in Congress.

The reason why the President is having difficulties with Congress is that the President is not a natural in politics and his knowledge of the political process is weak. <u>Richard Neustadt argues</u> that "The presidency is not a place for amateurs. The sort of expertise can hardly be acquired without deep experience in political office. The presidency is a place for men of politics, but by no means is it a place for every politician (Neustadt 152)."[2] This article suggests that President Obama did not have enough experience in political office before becoming the President of the United States.

The President did not want to have any negotiations with members of Congress when it came to the debt ceiling debate. This is not the place to argue whether the Republicans were right or wrong, but if the President had tried something different or used his "power to persuade" the country would have not shutdown. The only time that President Obama was able to get any legislation passed in Congress was when the Congress was held by a majority of the Democrats from 2008 to 2010.

The President won the battle over the debt ceiling issue, but will he win his war against Congress? Is the President going to get his agenda accomplished in the remainder of his Presidency? It is this writer's opinion that the President has alienated the Republican Party to the point that they will not deal with the President at all. The Republican Party in the House of Representatives took an awful defeat in the polls and in the eyes of the public over the government shutdown fiasco. The President and the Democratic Party came out of the debt ceiling fight in very good shape compared to the Tea Party wing of the Republican Party.

Politics are very volatile. The failure of the Affordable Care Act roll out and the breakdown of the healthcare website are placing the President in a tough position. The President is losing in two ways. First, the President's "professional reputation" is in deep trouble at the moment. The press is arguing that the President was untruthful in his comments that people would be able to keep their own health insurance and their private doctors.

The problem develops because of the accusations that people are not able to keep their current healthcare plan and some argue that they cannot keep their doctors. The press continues to slam the President with tape reruns of him making claims about how individuals will have the ability to keep their healthcare plan. The press shows about ten different instances in many different contexts and this is making the President look terrible. This is doing a lot of damage to the Presidents "professional reputation" at home.

There are two issues at the moment that are testing President Obama's 'Professional reputation" abroad. The first is the NSA leaks that the United States is spying and listening in on the conversations of <u>European leaders</u>.[3] The second is President Obama's Middle Eastern policy towards Iran and Syria. It seems that the President is upsetting are allies in the Middle East like Saudi Arabia and Israel over the confusion concerning America's intent in our dealings with <u>Iran and Syria</u>.[4] The President must be trusted in order to have creditability in the world. It is important that the President clears up the difficulties that he is having with foreign leaders concerning American foreign policy.

President Obama's "public prestige" is in shambles at the moment because of the problems discussed throughout this article. The question is what should the President do to change his fellow Americans and world leaders' opinions of him? The one thing the President should not do is go out on a <u>nationwide tour</u> to raise money for fellow Democrats and talk badly about the Republicans in Congress.[5] This will do nothing to help the Presidents "public Prestige" with the American people. The only thing that the aforementioned would do is further polarize the nation for and against the President.

<u>President Obama served</u> three terms in the Illinois Senate from 1997 to 2004 and was in the United States Senate from 2005 to 2008 before becoming the President of the United States. Many can argue that the problems that President Obama is having concerning Congress is due to his lack of "professional reputation" in Washington.[6] However, it is this writer's contention that if President Obama can improve his overall rating among the American people this would help him with his presidential agenda in Congress.

The "power to persuade" comes when a President has the "public reputation" that allows him to summon action on the part of members of Congress. The idea of a presidential mandate is something that President Obama did not receive by the American people in his last election. The Presidents inability to reach across the aisle when the

Democrats ran the Congress set the President up for defeat once the Republicans won the House of Representatives in 2010. It is time for President Obama to engage with the Republicans and develop his "public reputation."

Because of the problems with the Affordable Care Act and the Presidents lies it is going to be very difficult for the American people to gain trust in the President again. President Obama's lack of "public prestige" is going to ruin his presidency in the years to come. The only hope for progress is if President Obama can remake himself using the three principles discussed throughout this article.

King Obama Exerts his
Power on the Senate

The Democratic Senates use of the "Nuclear Option" has undermined the less populated states influence and power in the Senate.

There is one bright star in the Democratic Senate's decision to change the rules for the nomination of court appointees. The "Nuclear Option" and Senator Reid's use of it will make it much easier for the Republicans to appeal Obamacare. If in 2016 a Republican president is elected and there are simple majorities of Republicans in the House and the Senate than Obamacare can be appealed very easily. It will be much easier to appeal Obamacare in the Senate if instead of sixty votes to appeal Obamacare only fifty one are needed.

There is no reason for the Republicans to stop with the rules put in place now. Why not just take the change in the Senate rules one step further and make it a simple majority vote to put another judge on the Supreme Court or perhaps two. Two strict conservative constructionists added to the Supreme Court would throw the Roe v. Wade liberal baby out with the bathwater. The Supreme Court will have a conservative slant for decades into the future.

It will be a splendid day to watch the liberal progressive Democrats grovel about how they are being treated by the Republicans. Life and circumstances change but progressives only live one moment at a time. Conservatives always hope to conserve and the Senate rules are one thing that the Democrats will wish they were not so progressive about.

The main concern with the change in the Senate filibuster rule and the sixty votes necessary for a presidential nominee to be confirmed is that the President, because of a simple majority has done away with the power of the minority parties Senators. American's will not realize the insipid nature of the changes that are being developed by the many regulatory agencies that make up the administrative branch of the federal government. The Senate changes are more monumental than meets the eye.

One needs to look at today's move by the Democrats in the Senate as another example of how President Obama has run rough shot over the States and state power. The Senate was created to protect the rights of the minorities in the United States. Now what we see is the Democrats taking power away from the less populated states and given more power in the Senate to the large states. This is not a good day for America nor the freedom and rights of the citizens of the less populated states.

The U.S. Court of Appeals for the District of Columbia Circuit (D.C. Circuit) is one of the most powerful courts in the United States. President Obama is upset because the Senate Republicans did not want to nominate three judges to the D.C. Circuit Court that President Obama had put up for judgeship.

Paraphrasing Carol D. Leonnig the Republicans did not think that the court needed anymore judges because the court has eight judges already. The judges are evenly divided between Democrats and Republicans.[7] The added appointees that President Obama hopes to place on the court are said to be pro-government, pro-regulation and bad for business interests.

This move by the President is in essence the same "Court Packing" plan that President Franklin D. Roosevelt tried with the Supreme Court. President Roosevelt lost his bid to change the Supreme Court in the Senate and that is why the Supreme Court is the same today.[8] Today's United States Senate is not as lucky nor is the formation of the D.C. Circuit Court thanks to President Obama. President Obama will go down in history as the President who changed the power of the presidency in many ways.

The judiciary is one way that the President is changing the judicial landscape of the country. The healthcare system and Obamacare is another big change for the federal government, the states, and individual freedom. A change that goes undetected by most Americans is in the underneath or the belly of the federal government. The entire administrative branch of the United States is incrementally getting changed to benefit the federal government over the free market system, individual freedom, and the <u>Republic's 'State Power'</u>. [9] President Obama is making and placing exceedingly more law under the jurisdiction of the federal government that was once under the strict control of each state. Individual liberties and freedoms are also getting trampled upon by the Obama administration.

President Obama defends his actions and the actions of the Democratic Party by blaming obstructionism on the so-called do nothing Republicans. There is nothing wrong with America at a standstill. The country was designed by our Founding Fathers against the radicalism of the progressives. All of the problems that this country faces today are due to the progressives. The progressives have changed the Senate once before.

In the original United States Constitution the United States Senate members were supposed to be appointed by the state legislatures and not by the American people directly. If the United States Constitution was not changed by the Seventeenth Amendment the country would not have had Obamacare or the rest of the trash that this President and the Democrats have rammed down the throats of the American people. This is due to the fact that there are over twenty six states with Republican legislatures. Hence, there would be a majority of Republican Senators in the Senate. This constant changing of the United States Constitution and how America governs is ripping this country apart.

American progressives are going to progress America into a nation that the generation not yet born will not want to live in. And that is if the land we call the United States of America is still a country. Mob rule and a mob without its treats will revolt. American progressives free money pot at the end of the federal rainbow will have imploded on its own massive pile of federal debt. This multiculturalism that progressives celebrate will be a curse that pits race against race—the same way—that we see President Obama manipulating group against group today.

The move by President Obama and the Democratic Senate today will have repercussions for all Americans. The benefits that one group may receive today another group may take away in the future. When the majority of the people in America want free stuff—they will vote for free stuff. This means more taxes for the people that work in order to pay for the free stuff for others. More taxes means less money to spend which means a slowing economy and less work. Less work means more people needing more government assistance. Is the aforementioned the right path for America? President Obama's hi-jacking of the Senate, the administrative branch of the federal government, healthcare, and other actions through Executive Orders makes him the closest thing America has ever had to a king.

President Obama and the Administrative Law Agenda

What laws the President cannot get passed through Congress are laws that he is taking care of through regulations created by the various governmental agencies.

Progressives love big government. This is way progressives cannot stand anything that gets in the way of making government larger. President Obama is using the presidency in ways that it has never been used before. President Obama is developing new precedence for the office that will have lasting effects for future Presidents. It is important that the people have an understanding of the changes and how detrimental they are to the freedom and liberty of the American people.

The federal government is unbelievably large it has <u>456 federal agencies</u> with a lot of overlapping "Bureaucracies inside of bureaucracies." The interaction between federal departments and agencies is massive.[10] The interactions amount to one thing for the American people and businesses and that is more regulations. More regulations amount to more law that the people and businesses have to adhere to.

There are so many different ways for the Executive Branch to direct funds from one agency to another—since the President needs to confer only with his department heads. The Congress votes for a budget for each department and then it is up to the departments to

176

spread that money out among the agencies under the control of the various departments.

The above movement of funds from each <u>department to the various agencies</u> within a department gives the Executive Branch a lot of authority. The President has the authority to tell the departments how the money should be spend among the various agencies. This means that the priorities of the President and his Department heads are what the government accomplishes.[11] The President is making it so that Congress has very little control over the actions of the Administrative Branch of government.

The departments of the Executive Branch are developed by Congress under general law. This is the same way that the agencies are developed and that is through general law. It is up to the President, departments, and agencies to decipher the general law and create that into specific law. This is done by developing regulations that the agency enforces through regulatory fines. It is the hands off by the Congress that allows departments and agencies to actually create more regulations (law) than Congress creates in its regular sessions. It is in the Administrative Branch of government where the President can exert his policies more efficiently.

It is easy to argue that the Executive Branch has much more power than the United States Constitution gave the President. What happened is that the federal government grew and more and more of the governmental hierarchy came under the control of the President for nominations and the Senate to confirm people to the various positions. This is the same way that the United States Federal Court System works. The President nominates a person to the bench and the Senate confirms that nomination. The above system creates a check and balance system between the Executive, Legislative and Judicial branches of government.

The Administrative Branch is the largest branch of the federal government by far and that is why for purposes here it will be referred to as the <u>fourth branch of government</u>.[12] The fourth branch of government is all of the departments and agencies that make up the federal government. The thing that sets the fourth branch of government aside is its ability to create administrative law through regulations and enforcement through fines and shutdowns.

The courts give the laws created by agency regulation validity and it is important that the Senate plays a role in what judges sit on the various courts that make the decisions regarding administrative law. President Obama is very active in dismantling the equilibrium between the three branches of government when it comes to this colossal fourth branch of government.

The President has made recess appointments using the *Recess Appointment Clause.* The Senate was actually in Pro-forma sessions of three days while technically on recess for twenty days. The Senate Republicans argue that the Senate has the right to make the rules of how the Senate operates and what rules are to be followed.[13] In other words the Senate was not in recess and the President should not have made the three appointments to the National Labor Relations Board (NLRB).

There has not been a President that tried to exert power in regards to recess appointments in the manner that President Obama did.[14] This is why the Supreme Court is going to hear the case regarding the Presidents recess appointments. The President has received a lot of harsh criticism from conservative groups.

The Democrats in the Senate under the Majority Leader Senator Harry Reid have gone down a road with the Presidents encouragement to invoke what is called the "Nuclear Option." What the "Nuclear Option" does is make it necessary so that only fifty one votes instead of sixty votes are needed for a judge to be confirmed. Since the Democrats are in power in the Senate the "Nuclear Option" takes the power of the minority away from the Senate Republicans.[15] What this has done is allow President Obama to run judges through the Senate that probably would not have received a confirmation if it was not for the change in the voting structure of the Senate.

The first act after the "Nuclear Option" was to place three liberal judges on what many consider the second most important court in the country—the Washington D.C. Circuit Court of Appeals. By putting his own judges in place the President effectively takes away the check that the court should provide. Some argue that the D.C. Circuit

<u>Court</u> will now allow the President to move his agenda forward.[16] The President's agenda would have stalled if it was not for the "Nuclear Option" being invoked.

Keep in mind that this is after the President has already taken the power away from the minority party in the Senate. Hence, the President controls the Administrative Branch, the confirmation process in the Senate and the courts for any regulations (laws) that the departments and agencies develop. In other words what we have is a King and not a President. The President has effectively dismantled the entire checks and balance system for what is discussed here as the four branches of government: Executive, Legislative, Judiciary, and Administrative.

Just think if a Supreme Court judgeship comes up for grabs the "Nuclear Option" will probably get invoked by the direction of the President even though it is not supposed to get used. The legacy of President Obama will not be what he accomplished by compromise in Congress, but what he accomplished by running rough shot over the entire American political system. The one thing that can slow this President down is a large victory by the Republican Party in the 2014 elections. However, that does not mean that the damage already done can be easily reversed, because it cannot.

Social Darwinism and the American Dream

America is not moving forward economically and the country continues to lean towards Socialism. The free market is based on Social Darwinism

Discussions in the United States are beginning to echo a change in America. David Simon argues that what we have are two America's the rich and the poor. Simon argues that the American people have a moral choice to make. Simon's argument is a choice between Laissez-faire economics or socialism and that is the basic premise behind his emotional plea.[17] The arguments are a choice a moral choice—are Americans all in this plight of life together or is each person on their own?

What ever happened to the ideas about Social Darwinism? America is the way that it is today because of Social Darwinism! Socioeconomics in America are in a large part developed at the individual level and not the family or group level of society.[18] Americans need to stop taking the easy way out of blaming race for why they continue to exist at the socioeconomic level that they do. The United States has been under the curse of affirmative action for fifty years now. After fifty years one would expect that it would be the white male that was without a job and in poverty.

Simon argues that in politics it is the rich that control the politics in America. The idea is that the populace does not have complete control over who gets elected. The argument is that Congress and the President are elected by the interests of money and not of the people.

This is a very good argument and there is a lot that can be said for money, politics and who wins a political race. However, studies tell a different story the <u>*Washington Post*</u> ran a column on the subject and came to the conclusion "Money doesn't dominate elections nearly as much as some of the news coverage would suggest—but in the right context, ads can still have very large effects." [19]There are many reasons to think that money would matter, but there are good reasons to think that American's can see through advertising.

It is the contention of this article that money matters, but not in how much the candidates' spend on the election; money matters because most people vote on the premise of how much money the politician promises to redistribute or not. American politics more than ever today is a fight over redistribution and that is why there is so much obstructionism in Washington. The war is on—in America between the have and the have-nots and those in between. The outcome of the battle will mark the direction that America walks in the future. Will America continue to be the land of opportunity or will it become the land of hand outs and stagnation?

The answer to the question above in regards to politics seeps through at the local, state and federal levels and this war is fought district by district and state by state. The battlefield is Washington. The Executive, Congress, and Judicial structure developed by the United States Constitution mark the rules of conduct for the war for America's future. The big question is will Americans get sold on the ideas of morals? There are two different arenas for morals one is secular humanism and the other is religion. The question is what spectrum of American morality should carry more weight—freedom and liberty or chains and punishment?

Let's look at what is meant by chains and punishment. For the context of this article taxation is a punishment and mandates are chains. The Democratic Party is all about taxation and mandates while the Republican Party is about freedom and liberty. Some would argue that the previous sentence is not at all accurate and that the Democrats are about helping the poor and less fortunate. This is while the Republicans are all about not caring and not wanting to help the less fortunate. It is said that the Democrats want to give people benefits while the Republicans want to take benefits away.

The broad sweeping statements and perceptions painted above make the choices of who to vote for easy. A secular humanist is all about morality when it comes to other people's money. Yes, the secular humanist votes for the Democratic Party of tax the rich and give the money to the needy. However, when it comes to taking a dime out of their own pocket or time out of their day—in the mind of a secularist—that job is supposed to be accomplished by the government. The idea is that the system and not the individual should worry about each citizen.

A religious person on the other hand believes that it is their responsibility to give money to charities and time to the soup kitchen to help the less fortunate in the surrounding area. In fact, the United States is the most charitable nation in the world when it comes to helping other nation-states. This is because America is also the most Christian based nation in the world. The bottom line is that a religious Republican will take it upon himself to help the people in need with their own money and time.

The two aforementioned paragraphs demonstrate the two moral perspectives of how and who should help the poor in America. The answer to the question is that Democrats favor government intervention and Republicans favor the individual or church effort. One would think that this should be the end of the argument but it is not. The Democrats have created this monster that they call the free enterprise system. It is the evil behind all of the misfortune in America. From the perspective of the evil free market system the Democrat figures out all the different methods to tax and mandate in order to create leveling.

It is in the above sense that Democrats control the people and take away their freedom and liberty. Let's face it if a person's money is taken through taxation they lose the freedom to spend that money. A person's liberty to acquire whatever they want to buy declines because the person no longer has the money due to taxation to buy what they want to buy. The Presidents socialist healthcare system mandates people to buy something that they may not want to buy or get fined. This is slavery you must buy healthcare or you will get the whip of a fine. However, this is how the socialist left wants to deal with the rich getting richer while the group of the poor is growing.

The Republican Party on the other hand try's to establish less government and less taxation for the people. This is in order to give the people more freedom and liberty the way that our Founding Fathers expected the country to operate. It should be noted that federal taxation was illegal until the <u>Sixteenth Amendment</u> in 1913.[20] Republicans try to create a society that is conducive to a person's ability to start their own business, go to school, and do what they wish in America in order to better oneself.

The crux of the argument is that the Democratic Party hopes to bind people through socialism and the Republican Party wants to free the people through the free enterprise system. Some people will end up at the top and others will end up at the bottom. This is part of human existence. Secular Democrats that believe in Darwin should acknowledge the ideas demonstrated by Social Darwinism and embrace them. Socialism is un-American.

The Differences between the
Political Powers in Washington

The Democrats, establishment Republicans (neo-conservatives) and the Tea Party are discussed. The two main parties are just about the same.

In this article the writer tries to distinguish between the general philosophies of the different political groups in American politics. It is easy to see why many Americans do not bother voting because of their thinking that all politicians are the same. In many ways all politicians are the same. However, as discussed below the Democrats and neo-conservative Republicans have a lot more in common with each other than they do the Tea Party.

In researching the <u>Rockefeller Republicans</u> [21]in a comparison with the <u>Neoconservatives</u> the only real difference between the two is foreign policy.[22] First, let's put the Rockefeller Republicans to rest, because they are an endangered breed, except for the Governor of New Jersey, Chris Christie and some rare sightings in the smaller Northeastern states. The neo-conservatives took over the Republican Party when George W. Bush Jr. became President. The neo-cons used the 9/11 tragedy to seize America and begin a new unipolar "benevolent hegemony" approach to foreign policy. A benevolent hegemony—because America will use are overwhelming military and economic power with good intentions.

The neo-conservative foreign policy is an interventionist philosophy that brought about the "<u>Bush Doctrine of Preemption</u>." In theory the doctrine gives the United States the right to take preemptive action against any rogue state that is deemed a threat to America.[23] The neo-conservatives believe in American exceptionalism; the idea that the United States is a virtuous nation that is above all others. This idea justifies America's aggressive behavior towards other nation-states.

The foreign policy of the neo-conservatives argues that because of the collapse of the Soviet Union, the United States, and liberal democracy must become the default governmental system for the nation-states of the world. Hence, in the War on Terror the United States at times must use force in order to purge terrorists from nation-states that plan to harm America. The Iraq War was the result of the neo-conservative liberal democratic nation-building ideology.

The above are the reasons why the Republican neo-conservatives who represent the establishment Republicans can get along with the Democrats and President Obama on foreign policy when the Tea Party conservatives cannot. The Tea Party conservatives are foreign policy American isolationists. Many on the left of the Democratic Party are against war, but President Obama and his entire <u>foreign policy team are liberal interventionists</u>.[24] To save time neo-conservatives and liberal interventionists both believe in universal human rights and using the United States military to promote liberal democracies around the world.

Some argue that the President's foreign policy team varies from the neo-conservatives in one way and that is their belief in international institutions. Neo-conservatives think that the United States alone can make the difference in the world. The liberal interventionists believe in developing international relations with other nation-states that will help develop liberal democracies through nation-building. President Obama's use of force in Libya is an example of the liberal interventionist philosophy.

It is the above arguments that are an example of why both the Democrats and the Republicans would like to do away with the Tea Party conservatives. The Tea Party is considered "wacko's" and members of the extreme right or far right by both the Democrats and the establishment Republicans. One can argue that the entire government shutdown was a set-up by President Obama and the Republican establishment against the Tea Party in order to change American politics in the direction of the neo-conservatives and liberal interventionists who are both supported by big business and big money donors.

In time the government shutdown ended and the debt ceiling debate was kicked down the road. President Obama made a statement about immigration and how <u>immigration reform</u> should be the next thing to get addressed by Congress.[25] Once again it is the Tea Party in the House of Representatives and the few in the Senate who would like to create strict immigration law and border security without amnesty. This annoys the President and the neo-conservative Republican establishment.

The President, Democrats, and Republican establishment together would like to pass amnesty and open border immigration reform that will devastate the poor working class who will be forced to compete in the workforce with the new immigrants. The President's Affordable Care Act will get inundated on the Medicaid side by the new immigrants who have just received their amnesty from the Democrats and the Republican establishment. This because of the Obamacare system will create higher taxes for the middle class in the government healthcare exchanges.

The only reason why immigration reform will not get passed is due to the Tea Party conservatives. This is another reason why the Democrats and Republican establishment are working together to get rid of the Tea Party coalition.

The neo-conservatives are not really that interested in small government they believe in big government and big spending on domestic programs. This is one reason why America saw the run up in debt by the Bush II administration. Government spending is another place where people get confused between the neo-conservatives and the Democrats because they are both big spenders and for big government. The Tea Party argument for small government goes against both the Democrats and the neo-conservative Republican establishment.

The one thing that the Democrats, Republican establishment, and the Tea Party can agree on is free-trade and open markets. However, free-trade takes jobs away from the American people in manufacturing, textiles, and other areas because of regulations and higher pay for workers in the United States. This makes it difficult for American businesses to compete so they pack up and move to foreign countries. In order to win elections it takes campaign funds from business and business owners who give a lot of money to candidates of all stripes. This is why the aforementioned groups all support free-trade instead of protectionism.

The Tea Party is being attacked by the Democrats and the neo-conservative Republicans. The Tea Party is not far right. The Tea Party is a conservative group that is about the same in conservatism as the Democrat John F Kennedy was in 1960. The neo-conservatives (establishment Republicans) are to the left on the political scale and the progressives (Democrats) are further to the left, but the Tea Party is about as right as the conservative Democrats of 1960.

It is not the Tea Party that is wrong. It is the thinking and policies of the majority in both parties that is causing the problems Americans face today. The whole purpose of the Tea Party is to restore America and the American people to a standard of living and morals that are better for the next generation instead of worse. The Tea Party is the best hope for America.

1964 Goldwater Conservatism will fail the Tea Party Conservatives

The article assumes the shutdown of the federal government and what the implications of that will mean for the Tea Party and the Republicans

The Tea Party conservatives will lead the moderate Republicans to heavy losses in future elections. One can only hope that the government shutdown does not last long and the debt ceiling fight can end quickly without the Tea Party conservatives tearing down what is left of the Republican Party. Senator Ted Cruz is turning out to be the Barry Goldwater of the new Republican Party. The moderates or Nelson Rockefeller Republicans of the 1964 convention were booed off the stage and Barry Goldwater took the reins of the Republican Party.[26] What the Republican Party ended up with was a landslide loss to the Democrats and President Lyndon B. Johnson.

The favorite Nelson Rockefeller lost in the California primary of the Republican Party. At that point the Republican Party moderates tried an eleventh hour party takeover by supporting Governor of Pennsylvania Bill Scranton.[27] The "Draft Scranton" movement of moderate and liberal Republicans by a Harris poll found that sixty two percent of the Republican Party would support Scranton over ultraconservative Barry Goldwater.[28] The victory of Barry Goldwater at the 1964 Republican Convention was the beginning of the end of the Republican Party for the 1964 presidential election.

Senator Ted Cruz and the Tea Party conservatives in the House of Representatives are going to take a perfect political moment and turn it into a possible disaster for the 2014 election. The Democrats will blame the Republicans for everything bad that happens due to a government shutdown. It is not hard for Tea Party conservatives to take over red districts in various states around the country. However, those districts are safe from the Democrats no matter who the Republicans decide to run.

In the Senate, Senator Ted Cruz comes from a very red state and that is why he can be as outspoken as he is without fear of the electorate. This does not help Republicans that are in difficult elective territory or in the states and districts that can go either for a Democrat or a Republican. The Tea Party is not going to help the Republican Party as a whole in the future unless the Democratic Party and its policies fail the American people.

The failure of the Affordable Care Act is a necessary outcome if the Republican Party is going to have any traction for the 2014 campaign and especially for the 2016 presidential election. However, even if Obamacare is a complete failure the possibility for Senator Ted Cruz, Senator Marco Rubio or Senator Rand Paul winning a general election for the presidency is slim. President Ronald Reagan was not a crazy conservative like the three amigos just mentioned above.

President Ronald Reagan dealt with a different political climate than the one in the United States today. For instance, the United States was still fighting a cold war so arguing for more defense spending was very easy. President Ronald Reagan argued for "Peace through Strength" [29] and this allowed for deficit spending and support for an aggressive American foreign policy unlike the foreign policy that a Rand Paul, Ted Cruz or Marco Rubio can argue in today's political environment of isolationism.

President Reagan passed tax deduction but also ran up public debt. In 1980 the United States public debt was 711.9 billion dollars [31] and when President Reagan left office the public debt had risen to 2, 1907 trillion dollars. [32] Today the Republican Party wants to cut the public debt, which is completely out of control at over seventeen trillion dollars. The debt is something that will cost the country economic growth in the process of debt reduction. Debt reduction although popular with the American people will be very difficult to achieve regardless of who wins the presidency in 2016 because at that point the public debt will be greater.

How can the Republicans begin the damage control that will be necessary after the dust settles and the Senate Democrats live up to their threat to shut down the federal government? The first thing that will be required is a sobering of the Republican Party and a complete reconfiguring of how the moderates of the Republican Party can reinstitute control over the party. If the moderates are unable to re-establish control over the Tea Party conservatives in the House and Senate the Republican Party will end up on life support.

Everything depends on the Affordable Care Acts failure and what happens to the American economy if the government is shut down for any length of time. The failure of the American economy will be blamed on the Republican Party even though it is becoming obvious that the Obama recovery is losing steam. If the Affordable Care Act holds its own until the 2014 elections then the Republican Party will be in deep trouble.

The future of the Republican Party is hanging on the balance of many economic and political factors that are well out of the control of humans at this time. The Affordable Care Act depends on the young and whether they sign up for Obamacare. If only the lame, old and poor sign up for the Affordable Care Act the entire healthcare system will be on its way downhill. The price of health insurance will go through the roof and the American people and businesses will not want to buy it. This will raise prices even further and so it goes.

The Republicans will need the help of the young and it is a good thing that they are self-centered and naïve. Young voters overwhelmingly voted for President Obama and they may be the group that takes the President down. If the youth reject Obamacare then the youth will bring the President and the Democrats down— that will be ironic. Ironic because the young adults today were supposed to have been trained to be good little socialists by the liberal unionized teachers and apparently they will have not.

If the moderate distracts of states reject the Tea Party who win the Republican primaries the Republicans are in trouble. In trouble because that will mean that Democrats win and if the Democrats win then they will retake the House of Representatives. If that happens the country is in real trouble. This may well be the demise of the Tea Party. In the years after the 2014 election if the United States has a good economic environment and a warming of the American people towards Obamacare the Tea Party will fall away from the American political landscape. The 2016 Republican primary race may end up being a re-run of the1964 Republican Party Convention and hopefully the Tea Party loses because the Republican Party and America in general cannot take another four years of a Democratic president.

The Republicans can strangle the Leviathan

The power of the administrative branch is discussed. It shows that the Republicans "power of the purse" is stronger than the President's executive power.

The Republican House must slow down the regulations that are going to be implemented in the next four years. The Obama Administration will administrate under the strict guidance of the President—the imperial President. Administration more specifically the government's administration through federal agencies is where the real battle will be fought for the underpinnings of American economics and free enterprise from all four corners of the United States. The most important item for the Republican House and the Republican Senators is to figure out how to starve the leviathan monster that is the administrative branch of the federal government.

Today there are about two thousand <u>agencies, commissions and departments</u> that in many cases answer in procedure to the President and Congress; however in reality for the most part the agencies run themselves with the President's and not Congresses best interest at heart. This is because Congress in the development of an agency creates each agency using general law.[33] One example of what general law means is that if the Congress wants clean air and water it tells the Environmental Protection Agency (EPA) to make sure the nation's air and water are clean. Congress has all the best interests of the people at heart because everyone would agree that clean air and water are important.

The problem is the devil in the details because what is needed to have clean air takes on two different meanings. It seems that the Congress has one interpretation of what the agency is supposed to do. The second is how each agency perceives their duties on the issue and how to implement the general law of Congress. The agency creates the rules and regulations that businesses must follow. Hence, the agencies have a lot of power to interpret and make new law through regulations.

The agencies regulations in some cases eat away at the profits of corporations. The corporations then pass the losses on to the American people. In other words what Congress expected and what occurs is sometimes two different things. In many cases an overzealous agency can end up making regulations so stringent that the American people end up paying an indirect tax.

The problem is that the President, the cabinet secretary and the agency try to define clean air differently than Congress intended. Thus, in many cases the American people who like the idea of clean air at the same time do not want to pay high energy costs. The balance between cost and benefits becomes a major issue that does not normally get addressed properly by the governmental process.

Two factors come into play at the point that agencies like the Presidents EPA and the EPA originally created by Congress come into conflict. This is most important in a President's second term because neither the President nor the EPA is accountable to the American people. The bureaucrat's that make up the administrative branch are not elected by the people. The President cannot run for election again and this means that neither is responsible to the people. Congress is accountable to the people that are why it is the responsibility of the Congress to check the EPA. The Congress has two ways to check the EPA one is through the power of the purse and the money budgeted to the EPA. If the previous does not work it is also in the power of the Congress, and Congress alone to do away with the agency in its entirety.

The power of the purse is all that the House Republicans have to stop a Presidents spending in theory. In the negotiations over the "fiscal cliff" the spending cuts are the most important weapon that the House Republicans have against the Senate and the President and they need to use it. If it is necessary they should even allow the country to go over the cliff. In power politics sometimes the individual leader of a country can change without warning. President Obama may change so that he avoids being remembered like the former <u>President Herbert Hoover</u> the "Do Nothing" president?[33] Does anyone think that one veto and the same bill hitting his desk a second time would not get signed?

President Obama thinks he has a good hand of cards against the Republican Party. The Republicans have the money that President Obama needs for Obamacare, Homeland Security, and the Department of Health and Human Services just to name the most important in need of funding. President Hoover took office right after the stock market crash of 1929 and some historians can argue Hoover's problems were worse than what President Obama was left by the former President Bush.

When President Hoover left office the country was in shambles and Hoover was a tired, broken down and beaten man. President Hoover came into the presidency a confident man and left as a worthless no good President, the <u>"Do Nothing" president</u>.[34]President Obama will not allow what happened to Hoover to happen to him. The fiscal cliff will bring America right back into a recession and a long road back to normal with many individuals hurt by President Obama's arrogance if he doesn't do what is right for the country.

The President can say what he wants to say, but the Republicans must be strong and show the President what power they hold over the Executive Branch. The Administrative Branch is a powerful tool in the hands of any President. Congress must show the fortitude to strangle the leviathan and that is the only weapon that Republicans are holding against the President. The House of Representatives controls the money and the President needs to understand that is the case. Republicans must be strong and stand up to President Obama for the good of the country.

President Obama Needs to be Impeached

President Obama has changed the laws of the Affordable Care Act so many times that the bill originally signed by Congress no longer exists. The President has gone way too far with his executive authority and the Congress must put the King in check.

Is this President just drunk on power? The <u>President argues</u> that he has a pen and can sign Executive Orders to get things done without Congress.[35] If President Obama makes one more move that oversteps the office of the Presidency, then the House of Representatives Judiciary Panel needs to proceed with the Articles of Impeachment. The Judiciary Panel should begin impeachment hearings immediately on past actions of the President; and all other actions that the President may undertake that erodes and dissolves the laws of the Constitution of the United States of America. This President can be impeached for many things that have already occurred and are discussed below, but all of the Presidents impeachable offenses fall under <u>Article II, Section 4</u>—High Crimes and Misdemeanors.[36]

The Speaker of the House of Representatives John Boehner is correct—the President may have a pen and telephone, but it is Congress that has the United States Constitution. In 2014 it is very likely that the Republicans will take control of the United States Senate. At that time the Republicans in the Senate will have the majority—a majority to impeach the President. President Obama after being indicted for crimes in the House of Representatives can be put on trial in the Senate. The Senate will be acting on Alexander

Hamilton's enlightened argument on impeachment that is found in Federalist number 65.[37]

There are many crimes that the President can be indicted on in the House of Representatives. Fast and Furious, Benghanzi, the NSA scandal and these are just a few of the many illegal actions authorized by the President. However, it may be difficult to prove that the President authorized any of the aforementioned crimes. The Presidents breaking of the law under the Affordable Care Act must be argued front and center as the grounds for the Presidents impeachment.

The Affordable Care Act is a law. The President in his continued manipulation of the Affordable Care Act by developing exemptions, and the changing of deadlines has broken the law. President Obama was pledged into the office of the Presidency to uphold all of the laws of the United States. The bottom line is the President refuses to uphold the letter of the law developed under the Affordable Care Act. This in itself is enough for a trial of impeachment in the Senate under *High Crimes and Misdemeanors*.

The *American Thinker* argues that the Presidents failures to "faithfully execute the laws" of the United States of America are enough for impeachment. The President's "High Crime" of **abuse of power** is the main reason for the Senate to impeach the President.[38] Remember that the President has a pen and a telephone. The President by his own words and actions can care less about the legislative process of the United States of America. The President must be stopped and impeachment is the method that are Founding Fathers gave Americans. Mr. Obama you are not a king!

The Founding Fathers understood what type of office that the Executive Branch of government could turn out to be. This is why George Washington was called on to be the first United States President. President George Washington understood how important it was that he set precedence for how the President should operate as the Commander and Chief of the United States of America. President George Washington refused to run for a third term, a term that he would have easily won. It is the progressives like President Franklin Delano Roosevelt that relish the idea of abusing the power of the presidency. Progressives want to usurp power under the control of the federal government. President Obama has tried like President Franklin Delano Roosevelt to change the courts and the laws of the United States of America for his own ends. Progressives do not believe in representative democracy they believe in government control and dictatorship.

The American Recovery and Reinvestment Act of 2009 (ARRA) was revised and gave the President <u>831 billion dollars to invest</u> ". . . direct spending in infrastructure, education, health, and energy, federal tax incentives, and expansion of unemployment benefits and other social welfare provisions." [39]What did the President do with the money that he was given to get America out of the Great Recession? Many argue that the President spent the money foolishly in many ways. The Washington Post argues that President Obama spent <u>90 billion dollars</u> on green energy projects that did little to spur economic growth and that the growth that was developed cost the American people to much for each job.[40]

The current unemployment extension of three months that the President is hammering for is at a cost of <u>6.4 billion dollars</u> that the Republicans want to pay for by cutting another program.[41] The Democrats want to just add the money to the existing seventeen trillion dollar federal debt. If the President was so worried about the unemployed perhaps he should have put some of his green energy money aside for more unemployment insurance. The problem with President Obama is that neither he nor his economic advisors really understand how the American economy operates. The entire ARRA was based on Keynesian Macroeconomics rather than <u>Supply-side economics</u> like America had under the Reagan economic recovery.[42]

The President has also gone on a rant about immigration reform. The President has already made comprehensive changes in immigration policy remember that the President by Executive Order instructed <u>Homeland Security to halt deportation</u> of young illegals.[43] Many libertarians and scholars argue that the President's actions where illegal. It was by the inherent power of Homeland Security that the President was able to get away with it.

Senator Rubio argues that the President may take it upon himself to pass a more comprehensive immigration reform on his own. It would be an immigration reform for the eleven million illegals already in the United States.[44] This in many ways is an impeachable offense on its own. This is regardless of any law that Homeland Security perverts in the in favor of any Presidential Executive Order for immigration reform. Immigration reform without legislation would undermine the country. The President needs to be stopped—he is out of control.

Progressives especially their leaders are very dangerous people. In the name of freedom and liberty they break the laws that give the American people their freedom to begin with. Progressives argue that fairness gives them the right to take property (money is property) and give it to others that do not have property. This is not the American way it is the perverse pseudo-reality of many progressives. Nothing comes for free and the American people should not allow themselves to be manipulated by President Obama and the rest of his progressive army of revolutionaries.

Chapter Seven

American foreign Policy

Predictions on the Iranian Nuclear Deal

President Obama is interested in his own interests and not the interests of Israel. Israel must take action against Iran for survival.

It is time for Israel to state the obvious and that is the only nation-state that cares about the survival of Israel is Israel. Netanyahu called the deal made with Iran a "historic mistake."[1] This was before President Obama decided to call the Prime Minister and try to explain the deal made with Iran. Prime Minister Benjamin Netanyahu after speaking with President Obama made this comment to his Cabinet "[Israel] has the right and duty to defend itself by itself."[2] Iran's President Rouhani made it perfectly clear that the deal made with the P5+1 meant that Iran would still be able to enrich Uranium.[3] Exactly what do the above developments mean concerning certain ramifications in the Middle East for Israel and some of the Arab nation-states like Saudi Arabia?

The first thing that must be explored is how likely is it that Iran will live up to the agreements made for the next six months. This writer argues that Iran will continue to enrich uranium and work on its nuclear program for the next six months while it drags its feet with the international community. The seven billion in sanctions that are being lifted have only confirmed to the Iranian leadership that the Western nations are weak. President Obama's missteps in Syria and the "Red Line" comment were heard loud and clear by Iran and in

Iran's view the United States is not going to take any military action against Iran.[4]

In the days leading up to the negotiations in Geneva Supreme Leader Ayatollah Ali Khamenei gave a speech to the paramilitary organization Basij. Supreme Leader Khamenei stood in front of about fifty thousand members and he was firm in his convictions about Israel and Prime Minister Netanyahu who he described as a "Rabid Dog."[5] The Supreme Leader Khamenei also called for the annihilation of Israel. Suzanne Maloney argues that the Khamenei in his speech made it clear: ". . . American immorality, greed and wickedness; [Khamenei]who detests Israel; and who anticipates the ultimate triumph of the Islamic world over what he sees as a declining West and illegitimate Israel."[6] In light of Khamenei's full speech how can Secretary of State Kerry believe that he can make deals with such a regime?

There is something inherently wrong with the idealistic thinking of the liberal left. President Obama and those around him like Secretary of State Kerry believe in soft power as a legitimate way of thinking when it comes to foreign policy and Iran. Perhaps, on a good day America can make concessions using soft power with fellow allies of the West like Germany, France, and England. However, in the current international environment using soft power in the Western arena is pushing the envelope.

The problem with the Iranian deal is that America has crawled under the covers with China and Russia in order to make a deal with Iran and this is just plain dumb. Russia supports Syria and Iran is supporting Syria so those two have mutual interests at the moment in the Middle East. China has deals with Iran for oil so they do not want to upset the Iranians. The aforementioned is why Iran was able to get away with such an unrealistic deal with the United States in Geneva on Sunday.

It is easy to make predictions on how the next six months will play out with the Iranians and their nuclear program. The first thing that America and the West will see is that the inspections are not going as negotiated in Geneva. The Iranians will make excuses on why they cannot go along with certain aspects of the nuclear inspection team. This will raise red flags that the Iranians will once again work to extinguish with the West.

Secretary of State Kerry will meet with Iranian President Rouhani who will appease Secretary of State Kerry and make him think that the nuclear inspection team can do what it is expected to do. Secretary of State Kerry will make an announcement to the world about how once again he has put the negotiations back on track with Iran. This will make things look good while the Iranians continue to build nuclear centrifuges, enrich uranium, and develop nuclear launch capabilities. All this will happen at secret underground facilities that the world will not know about until they are pointed out by Israel.

It is time that Israel walks away from the United States while President Obama remains in power in America. Israel needs to understand that President Obama is not interested in the security of Israel. President Obama is interested in placing obstacles between the thinking of the American people and the Affordable Care Act's failure at this time. Foreign policy, immigration reform, and anything else that the President can do to take the American peoples mind off the Affordable Care Act he will do. It is very important that Prime Minister Netanyahu takes Iranian policy into his own hands and realizes that President Obama will not help him in anyway militarily.

It can be argued that not only will the United States refuse to help Israel with any efforts to attack Iran on its own, but the United States will do everything in its power to stop Israel from acting in its own best interest. This is a bad time for Israel and Iran is going to take full advantage of the opening that has been given to them by the P5+1 in regards to the Iranian nuclear program. It is obvious that before President Obama leaves office Iran will have nuclear weapons at their disposal and aimed at Israel.

Egypt and Israel's Iranian Problem

President Obama's foreign policy threatens Israel. The military in Egypt must be supported for a secular Egypt. Iran is America's problem.

As the Middle East burns in Lebanon, Syria, and Egypt what happens to Israel in the perpetual violence and killing that continues to go on in the region. Just two years ago Turkey was foreseeing the concept of Turkey and Egypt becoming an anchor in the Middle Eastern region.[7] The whole idea of Egypt in any sort of peace in the future seems to put a damper on the whole Egyptian and Turkey anchor business. Especially as we watch the Iraq and Syrian Sunni's begin to attack Lebanon with terrorist measures that killed 22 in Beirut in one of the deadliest attacks since the civil war in Lebanon ended in 1990.[8] Hezbollah's leader has vowed to send even more men to fight for the Bashar al-Assad government against what he calls Sunni extremists.

The worst thing for Israel to come out of current events in the Middle East is that Iran and Hezbollah are beginning to reach out to the Muslim Brotherhood.[9] This creates a new problem for Israel as it moves forward with its ideas on Iran without American help. America may even become part of the problem with Israel as the United States Congress flirts with the idea of cutting aid to Egypt. If aid to Egypt is cut the 1979 Egypt-Israel Peace Treaty goes up in smoke and Israel is once again completely alone in the Middle East.

The Obama Administration is a complete failure when it comes to the Middle East and all other Muslim strongholds around the world. The Obama Administrations failure is terrible for the United States and its foreign policy.

President Obama did not know what his 2009 "New Beginning" speech in Cairo would do to America's image among the Islamic nations. The Presidents' idealism sounded like this: "I have come here to seek a new beginning between the United States and Muslims around the world; one based upon mutual interest and mutual respect; and one based upon the truth that America and Islam are not exclusive, and need not be in competition."[10] President Obama's wish for soft power idealism with the Muslim world has caused problems that America and its allies are only beginning to see and it looks as if problems in the world among Islam and the Western world will only grow.

Some believe that President Obama since the beginning of his presidency has talked about soft power, but that all his actions seem like more of the same Bush Administration lone cowboy approach to foreign policy problems. This is due to his increased use of drones on terrorists. The unilateral action in the takedown of Osama Bin laden in Pakistan; and the President's increase in troops in Afghanistan along with his inability to close Guantanamo. President Obama seems to "talk softly and carry a big stick" like President Theodore Roosevelt. However, this is not the way that soft power should be projected in the 21st century. Especially, when the enemy or terrorists are not harmed by the big stick approach and that is why the "War on Terrorism" is so difficult to win. In fact President Obama refuses to refer to the terrorist problem as a war.

Let's turn to the Presidents handling of events in the Middle East since he has been president. One of the largest problems in the Middle East is the way that the Obama Administration deals with Israel. Since the beginning it seems that President Obama has put Israel into the backseat in his dealings in the Middle East. In fact, the American Enterprise Institute thinks that President Obama dislikes Israel a great deal and that projection is picked up by many in the Muslim communities in the Middle East.[11]

The Russians and Chinese understand the dislike of Israel that President Obama disseminates and that is why problems in Iran and Syria continue with the aid of Russia to Syria and China with Iran. China and Russia have a very unique relationship that provides for balance against the interest of the United States and in favor of their own interests. In regards to Iran Michael Singh thinks: ". . . From Beijing's perspective, Iran serves as an important strategic partner and point of leverage against the United States." China worries about China and it can careless about Israel since Israel has nothing to offer the Chinese in comparison with Iran. Hence, the United States finds itself in regards to the United Nations and Iranian nuclear plans in a precarious position with only the European Union and Japan on its side, but who are all exempt from Iranian sanction control.

The problems in Egypt are good for Iran because it helps to place a wedge between Israel and the United States in relation to Egypt and hence, a further separation between the alliance of Israel and the United States. The Turkey and Egypt anchor would have helped the Middle Eastern region so that Hezbollah and the Muslim Brotherhood did not find themselves in a position to help each other. Iran is a Shia stronghold and the Shia Hezbollah makes up 41 percent of Lebanon and if the Sunni Muslim Brotherhood decides to converge with Hezbollah this will change the dynamics in Iraq and Syria which will further strengthen Islam against Israel. Of course this is a likely projection given all of the various divisions within both the Sunni and Shia groups in the Middle East.

Iran now more than ever is looking forward to becoming a nuclear power in the Middle East and one that can counter the nuclear weapons that Israel possesses. Iran sees itself as the future hegemon in the Middle Eastern region and this is what the United States would like to stop. The problem is that President Obama is not taken seriously by the Muslim world. Iran with the help of China, Russia, Japan and ten other European nations make sanctions against Iran worth the sacrifice for its future victory by becoming a nuclear hegemon in the Middle East.

Israel will have to strike Iran in the future with or without the help of the United States. It seems that President Obama has through his inaction against Syria when the red line was drawn about chemical weapons is evidence to the world that the United States has turned into a paper tiger. The Middle East is in a more volatile position today than it has been in since the Yom Kipper War in 1973.

The only hope for the region is for the military in Egypt to win over the people and create a secular governmental apparatus like the one that exists in Turkey. Turkey is only a secular country today because of its military and if that is the way it needs to be in Egypt than that is what other nations that have interests in the Middle East need to have happen.

Israel's survival rests on peace in the Middle East and at this time the Middle East is a complete disaster. The United States should help Israel stay strong while the rest of the Middle East kills itself in religious clashes. The largest problem in the Middle East today is not the war in Syria or the problems in Egypt. The main problem in the Middle East is Iran and the threat of a nuclear Iran to rival Israel. The United States needs to support the military in Egypt so that Iran with the help of the Muslim Brotherhood does not take over Egypt and create another enemy for Israel. A strong Israel is the bedrock of good American foreign policy in the Middle East.

Pray for the Syrian People

President Putin and President Obama are both going to win on the Syrian issue. Putin will keep Syria under its wing and Obama will save face

It is obvious that President Vladimir V. Putin has a different ideological way of looking at the history of the world. Everyone has their own way of looking at the world and it develops from their experiences throughout life. President Putin has lead a very different life than that of President Obama and that could be one of the reasons why the two leaders have so much difficulty finding any common ground when it comes to world events. However, they must put those differences aside when it comes to Syria. President Putin is holding all the cards when it comes to the Syria problem.

In the first place President Putin and Bashar al Assad are good friends and allies so it is the United States and Secretary of State Kerry that are at the immediate disadvantage when it comes to negotiations about chemical weapons. President Putin is the man in charge. President Obama must listen to President Putin as the negotiations move forward about the turning of chemical weapons over to the United Nations.

President Obama's weak position makes him the floundering fish in the Middle East. In regards to the Syrian Crises the President lost the Congress and the American people on the entire issue of attacking Syria. The President's "Red Line" argument was the beginning of his problems, but that issue is mute as the Syrian situation moves forward.

Because of President Obama's garbling and stumbling on the Syrian problem the Syrian people will suffer and many more lives will be lost in the continuing Civil War. This is due to the concessions that will be required for any concrete movement forward on the chemical weapons issue and the help of President Putin.

Of course Bashar al Assad will need things in return for his allowance of the United Nations into his country for the verifying of the chemical weapons removal. President Putin will offer Bashar al Assad weapons, planes, missiles and whatever else that Assad asks for in return for his accommodation in the relinquishing of his chemical weapons program.

President Putin will have a green light to arm Bashar al Assad with what he needs to defeat the rebels in his country. It does not matter how many more of the Syrian people will die as long as three inevitable things happen. One is President Putin wins by keeping Syria under the control of the Russians. Secondly, Bashar al Assad wins because he has the conventional weapons in order to defeat the rebels and continue on in power. Thirdly, President Obama and the international community can claim the victory for removing some of the largest stockpiles of chemical weapons in the world.

Secretary of State Kerry will give the credit to the President for his persistence and vigor for moving forward during tough negotiations. In fact, the President and the international community will be giving the aforementioned concessions (conventional weapons) via Russia to Bashar al Assad. The only real losers are the Syrian people and the countries that border Syria who will need to take care of all of the refugees from continued warfare and carnage in Syria.

To understand <u>Vladimir V. Putin's article</u> in the *New York Times* a few details need to be interjected in order for history to be properly discussed.[12] First of all let us look at World War II and the allied powers, specifically the United States. The Soviet Union received equipment through the United States <u>Lend-Lease</u> Act that helped the Soviet Union force the Nazi's to retreat from the Soviet Union.[13] Before the United States began to arm the Soviet Union the Red

Army did not even have enough guns for its soldiers on the frontlines. The guns where in retrospect nothing compared to the amount of tanks, tactical vehicles, and planes that the United States and the Allies provided the Soviet Union.

President Putin should understand the reason for the failure of the League of Nations was the fact that the United States was not a part of it. The United States Senate never ratified the treaty. Now on to the United Nations that term was created by Franklin D. Roosevelt in his description of the Allied troops and later became the name used in the creation of the Atlantic Treaty.[14] In 1945 the UN Conference of International Organization was held in San Francisco and it involved about fifty different countries and some non-governmental organizations.

Today the Headquarters of the United Nations is in New York City. The Security Council ratified the charter and signed it into legal standing in France, and the first meeting of the United Nations was in London. Beyond the two variations most of what the United Nations stands for was developed by the United States except for the ICESCR.[15]

President Putin's comments about American exceptionalism may have some truth to it. It is strange that President Putin ends his op-ed with God, because that is what America is lacking today. If America is no longer exceptional it is due to the progressives.

The original progressives in the United States had a strong belief in God and this was one of its strengths in the fight for equality and rights for all Americans. However, today the progressives have absolutely no inclination towards God. Secularism is what is tearing away at the fabric of America and this nation is not the dream of John Winthrop's "City upon the Hill."[16] America has replaced morality with the Rule of Law. It was not long ago that morals and right and wrong in America did not have to be written into law. Morality came from the teachings of the Bible.

If we are to learn from the ruins of the Soviet Union it is that the state is not a god. That is what was wrong with the Soviet Union. In Russia today the church is multiplying and growing. There is little separation from church and state the head of the Russian church Patriarch Kirill supports Vladimir Putin and works out of the Kremlin.[17] It may not be a good idea for the church and state to be so close but after years of secularism in the Soviet Union it is good to see the church is playing an active role in governmental policies that affect the church.

President Putin will have the day when it comes to the Syria problem. President Obama and his type of progressivism is what have given President Putin the driver's seat on the Syrian issue. American foreign policy in the Middle East is at its lowest level since the 1979 Hostage Crises in Iran. America needs to avoid entanglements in the Middle East and change its foreign policy as it relates to the region. It will take another President before the United States has a sound foreign policy and one that is understood by the world.

Syria is not Worth American Blood and Treasure

Russia, China, Iran and Iraq have enough influence to stop Bashar al—Assad from using chemical weapons. The US should not act unilaterally.

Syria is not worth American blood and treasure. President Obama's foreign policy in the Middle East is not consistent and it changes depending on the circumstances or problems that arise in the Middle East. President Obama has not lived up to one of his promises in the Middle East so why should he start now just because some women and children have been killed by chemical weapons.

Syria is a Russian problem and it should be up to Russia and its sidekick China to put Al Assad in his place for using chemical weapons. After all Russia and China sit on the United Nations Security Council and instead of vetoing the other members regarding Syria, perhaps they could do something productive. From an international perspective it becomes obvious that it should be up to Russia and China to do some heavy lifting for a change.

Russia has been arming Bashar al-Assad since the beginning of the civil war in Syria.[18] Zachary Laub writing for the Council of Foreign relations points out that Russia and China has vetoed three United Nations Security Council resolutions.[19] Laub goes on to discuss the heavy military and economic ties that both China and Russia have with Syria.

Why should the United States continue to think that are military can do what the Russians could not do for example in Afghanistan? Remember Vietnam where the Chinese armed the North Vietnamese well in this instance it is the money that China is pouring into Iran and Iraq that is being funneled indirectly to Bashar Al-Assad for arms and the propping up of the Syrian faltering economy.

Let us look at Iraq briefly and who is benefiting the most from the last Iraq War—and that is China. *The New York Times* points out that since 2003 when the United States invaded Iraq the main beneficiary has been China.[20] In 2014 Iraqi oil is predicted to increase beyond the 1.5 million barrels a day that it is producing now. The Iraqi's point out that billions of dollars will come from the investment of the Chinese so that more oil can be produced and therefore more can be sold to China.

Iraq is important because it is speculated that many of the al Qaeda fighters that are fighting against Mr. Assad are the same Al Qaeda that he created a "rat line" for in order to move Al Qaeda fighters into Iraq to kill Americans from 2003-2011.[21] It seems that al-Assad flew al Qaeda from North Africa to Damascus and then moved the groups of fighters into Iraq to kill Americans. It is ironic that now it is these same fighters that are against al-Assad. If the al Qaeda fighters do not have their eye on al-Assad they would definitely turn to killing American's once Basher al-Assad was toppled and any United States military were still in Syria.

It is estimated that some 6000 jihadists or al Qaeda who are linked to al-Nursa Front are fighting al-Assad in Syria at the moment.[22] It is argued that the al-Nursa Front make very good fighters who hate America as much as Mr. Assad. Why would President Obama contemplate one boot on the ground in order to stop the killing in Syria? It is this writer's opinion that one United States solder is worth more than all the dead in Syria to date. Some argue that the al Qaeda in Iraq do not see eye to eye with the al-Nursa but the al-Nursa can be ruthless in getting what it wants: food, oil, weapons and all the other items needed for war.

Turning from Iraq to Iran it was a much simpler time when the United States could arm whoever was losing in the Iraq and Iranian

War in order to make sure that neither side won the war. Iran is another one of al-Assad's allies in the war against the insurgents in Syria. The Iranians are willing to do a lot in order to keep Bashar al-Assad in power including supplying him with <u>supplies from Bagdad straight to Damascus.</u>[23] Right now it is the air routes from Iran to Syria that are supplying the al-Assad army with needed supplies.

Some argue that a no-fly zone would stop the Iranians from moving supplies to al-Assad by air. Is it really the United States job to create a no-fly zone in order to keep Iranian supplies bought with Chinese funds indirectly from reaching al-Assad? It is not as if a no-fly zone would be an easy task since the Russians have supplied the <u>Syrians with antiship cruise missiles.</u>[24] The missile defense system would make it difficult to create a block-aid around Syria or to establish a no-fly zone. It is clear that the Russians, Chinese, Iraqis, Iranians, Hezbollah are all on the side of Bashar al-Assad.

The innocent women and children who are being killed by al-Assad's chemical weapons are being killed because the opposition forces are using them as human shields. One must remember that President Obama and his security team cannot determine if the Syrian opposition forces are al Qaeda.

Al Qaeda and jihadists that are hoping to drag American forces into the Syrian conflict in order to kill American forces or take American pilots hostage after one of our planes go down. The Russians and Chinese would consider it a victory without firing a shot if the United States decides to take down al-Assad with ground troops or waste billions of dollars developing a no-fly zone.

America's foreign policy and especially that in the Middle East is not worth much to the player's in the region. It should not matter if President Obama was dumb enough to put American credibility on the line by creating chemical weapons redline. A redline that the al-Assad regime was told not to cross or there would be consequences. The Consequences are higher for America to do something in Syria unilaterally. Hence, the President is correct in asking for international approval and resources. What President Obama will see is more of the same by the Russians and the Chinese in regards to the United Nations.

There will be more chemical attacks in Syria because disregarding the military objective al-Assad is getting the support from all the aforementioned players who are helping al-Assad. What President Obama should do is listen to the generals "Outlining options for the use of U.S. military force, Chairman of the Joint Chiefs of Staff General Martin E. Dempsey reported to Congress in July 2013 that even limited interventions, such as the establishment of no-fly zones or buffer zones, or limited strikes on Syrian military assets, could cost billions, would not ensure civilian safety, and could quickly lead to unintended escalation. "Deeper involvement is hard to avoid," he warned.""[25]

The world understands that the Democratic Party of the United States does not have a proper perspective on realpolitik. It will be easy for the world to understand the missteps of President Obama. President Obama should just get back to domestic politics and let the Middle East play itself out until a Republican President can re-establish a Middle Eastern foreign policy.

Iran Needs a Wake-up Call

President Obama needs to try a new foreign policy approach with Iran. The United States should listen to Israel and others concerning Iran.

If the Iranians are smart they have learned from the North Koreans about what it takes to manipulate the United Nations Security Council and more importantly the United States. It seems that Iran is doing a very good job of moving forward with its nuclear program. It should be obvious that Iran will not stop until they are the nuclear and conventional hegemon in the Middle East. This is obvious to many of America's allies like Saudi Arabia and Israel. There are many familiarities between the road that North Korea and Iran have gone down in their dealings with the West and their nuclear ambitions.

The Secretary of State John Kerry should listen to our allies and not try to lead on the Iranian nuclear front. In fact, it would probably be best if the United States did not even try to negotiate with Iran. The only thing that the United States needs to make clear is that— Iran is looking down the barrel of the United States militaries might and that the United States is not very happy.

Below are some of the outcomes of the hundreds of meetings that went on over the decades between the United States and North Korea—before and after—North Korea became a nuclear power. Iran is on the same track unless new tactics are taken quickly. It is important that the United States realizes that sanctions do not work on totalitarian states. The United States military and a credible belief

215

by a nation-state that the United States is ready to attack is the only thing that will work with a totalitarian regime.

In 1994 President Bill Clinton was hawkish towards the North Korean threat to build nuclear grade uranium.[26] President Clinton sent fifty thousand troops to South Korea and stationed an array of 50 ships and over 400 combat planes to convince Kim-Il Sung that the United States was willing to go to war to stop him from producing nuclear weapons.

President Bill Clinton gave permission to former President Jimmy Carter to enter negotiations in order to convince Kim-Il Sung to stop with his plans to develop nuclear grade uranium. Former President Jimmy Carter brokered a deal and told President Bill Clinton only hours before the deal was signed. Ann Coulter argued that the Clinton administration: "Under the terms of the "agreed framework," we gave North Korea all sorts of bribes—more than $5 billion worth of oil, two nuclear reactors and lots of high technology. In return, they took the bribes and kept building nukes."[27]

The United States Senate never ratified the treaty and the two light-water nuclear reactors were never sent to North Korea. If the United States under President George Bush had delivered the two light-water nuclear reactors the fuel rods that where under lock and key would have been removed from North Korea, but that never happened.

President George W. Bush took over after President Clinton and he decided not to negotiate with North Korea at all. At the same time President Bush was trying to get the Iraqi War underway in the Gulf. The changing of the guards in Washington meant that the ball on North Korea was dropped. The death of Kim-Il and the empowerment of Kim Jong-Il created a situation of crises. In the end North Korea's Kim Jong-Il was sitting on nuclear enriched uranium, fuel rods, and weapons grade plutonium.[28] The Bush administration and the CIA did not know enough about North Korea's high technology missile-systems or the extent of North Korea's nuclear development.

During the Obama administration we have seen no change in the way that North Korea acts. There seems to be nothing that the United States can do to stop North Korea from flexing its nuclear muscle in the Pacific.[29] The history of the negotiations between the United States and North Korea demonstrates nothing but failure. It must be obvious that using the same methods with Iran that the United States used with North Korea and expecting different results is ludicrous.

The Iranians have found ways around the sanctions for years now. China has imported over <u>500 million in fuel oil</u>, which is easily converted into crude oil in 2013 alone.[30] China is not the only country that has found ways around United Nations sanctions. In fact, many nations have found ways to trade with Iran through the years.

Some argue that the United States and the Obama administration have begun to loosen sanctions against Iran in secret deals. The <u>Washington Post writes</u> that the United States had lifted financial sanctions on Iran prior to the negotiations on nuclear weapons. Other sources mentioned in the same article argue that President Hassan Rouhani and the United States actually began easing sanctions right after Iran's new President took office.[31]

The French decided that they would not accept the deal that the United States had tried to put on the table with the Iranians in Geneva. <u>Al Jazeera</u> was able to get the Iranian side of the story: "Iranian President Hassan Rouhani has said his country will not give up the right to enriching uranium . . . We have said to the negotiating sides that we will not answer to any threat, sanction, humiliation or discrimination."[32] How is anyone to argue with someone like the President of Iran when his position is as entrenched as President Obama's was in his dealings with the Republicans? The President could look in the mirror and see that his team will get nowhere with the Iranian regime.

<u>Many argue</u> that it is Israel and its threat of airstrikes that brought the meeting together in Geneva although Israel has no seat in the negotiations. Israeli Prime Minister Benjamin Netanyahu has the most to gain and lose through the talks concerning Iran.[33] Most scholars who have studied the Iranian nuclear issue and have dealt with it over the years are aware that Iran is not going to stop moving forward on its nuclear program.

The only thing that will stop the Iranian nuclear program is for the United States and Israel to bomb the Iranian nuclear program back into the Stone Age. It is not until the United States comes to its senses that America will once again have some clout in the world. The Obama administration has weakened the United States in foreign policy around the world. At this time there isn't a country not even are allies that take the United States seriously. The United States is the greatest military power to ever exist. It is time that the United States makes that perfectly clear to the rest of the world.

Terrorism a Weapon against America's Soft Power

Terrorists are the most dangerous commodity that a weak nation-state or group can use against its perceived enemies. The problem is that it places fear in the hearts of civilians and this alone is a problem for any nation-state that is fighting against terrorists.

Soft power is important in the twenty-first century and it will continue to be the most important element of American foreign policy in the future. President Obama has squandered America's soft power and has left are allies in many peculiar predicaments around the world. In the Middle East the United States has lost the respect of both Israel and Saudi Arabia. In Europe the United States has left the NATO alliance on shaky grounds. In the Pacific the United States is letting Japan and South Korea fly alone in the heavy winds of an assertive China and North Korea. President Putin seems to walk all over the United States when it comes to the Security Council of the United Nations. The bottom line is that America's foreign policy has left the world a much more dangerous place.

Joseph S. Nye Jr seems to think that soft power embellishes more than just the action of the nation-state. Nye argues that individuals, the private sector, and civil society play a role in the operation and the use of soft power. Nye argues that the previous must be coupled with a nation-states culture, political values, and the perceived moral authority of the nation-state in question. Hence, soft power is both material and psychological; and soft power derives its strength from many different perspectives and facades of a nation-state.[34] The world looks at the culmination of the aforementioned and draws perspective about the credibility of a specific nation-state. In the international arena perception and credibility is everything. President Obama has damaged America's credibility greatly.

In this article the issue of soft power is looked at from the realist perspective—classical and neo-realism are both represented in the overall outline of the discussion about soft power and terrorism. At the moment the United States is weak when it comes to credibility. For the most part America's weakness comes from not living up to its friends and allies expectations. America is losing the "War on Terror."[35]

One aspect of soft power is of course hard-power. Hard power has three elements one is the population of a nation-state. This was a much more prevalent element before defense technology made the size of an army irrelevant. The second element is the economy of a country because it takes money to build and pay to keep a solid military apparatus. The last thing that is important is the size of a nation-states military; its ability to project that military power around the world, and the sophistication of the weapons systems that the military has at its disposal.

In 2012 the United States spent more money on defense than the next ten countries with the highest defense spending combined.[36] The United States by far has the greatest military to ever exist on earth. The United States Navy can project America's military might anywhere in the world. The United States has the largest economy in the world and a population more than adequate to fight wars on two different fronts. The world marvels at the ability of the United States military and what that military is capable of achieving. The United States hard power is not the issue when it comes to America's capabilities—it is the nation's resolve.

America's War on Terror reflects on the nation's ability to use soft power. Terrorism affects the civil society of all the nation-states that are affected by terrorism. Terrorism is the weapon of the weak that wreaks havoc on a civil society. By affecting the nation-states civil society terrorists are actually breaking down that nation's soft power.

The reason why terrorism is important to America's enemies is it affects America at the individual, and group level. Terrorism also erodes America's civil society. It is the fear that terrorism creates that makes terrorism such an effective weapon against the United States. Terrorism is the only weapon in many cases for America's enemies. Terrorism takes away the American peoples' resolve to fight wars.

President Obama has attempted to be the nice guy around the world to many Islamic nations and the terrorists of those nations. Some can argue that the President's drone capabilities and actions have played into the hands of some terrorists by getting rid of other terrorists groups that are in conflict with each other.

Not all terrorists groups have the same objectives or are out to achieve the same goals. Many terrorists are more than happy to manipulate the United States intelligence network into a situation where their dirty work is done for them. This is accomplished very easily by one Islamic group arguing that another Islamic group represents terrorists and that they are working to attack American interests even though in reality they are not.

The above actions have led the United States to use drone attacks that have collateral damage that destroys America's reputation among the different nation-states around the world. In other words, in many nations the CIA is a terrorist organization. What is established by the term terrorist is nothing more than semantics concerning what side a nation-state is on.

The United States is losing the patience and resolve of the American people to fight terrorism by going to war in other nation-states like Iraq and Afghanistan. The United States by using drones to fight its War on Terror is actually telling the world that America is impotent. The world understands that American's are no longer willing to go to war to protect the homeland against terrorism. The American people expect that Homeland Security will protect them. If a terrorist act takes place on American soil then America will just have to cope with its leaderships failures when it comes to the War on Terror.

The ability of the terrorists to inflict fear in the American people and the ability of the Islamic world to stop American hard power has left America's soft power in jeopardy. The terrorists have created fear in the individual which has seeped through into the entire American civil society. Terrorists have achieved their objective of turning America into a paper tiger. President Obama's inability to deal with nation-states like Iran and Syria has left the United States even weaker when it comes to the nation's soft power. It seems that the United States cannot do anything to stop terrorism and that the terrorists are winning under the Obama administration.

"MAD" a Good Middle East Policy for America

An argument can be made that a nuclear stand-off in the Middle East between Israel and Iran could bring about a greater incentive for peace. A perfect example was the cold war neither the Soviets or the United State would dare use nuclear weapons because it would mean the destruction of the world.

President Obama's idea for peace in the Middle East must be Mutual Assured Destruction (MAD) between Iran and Israel.[37] The President and Secretary of State Kerry are not stupid men they must understand that Iran will never stop at a peaceful end to its nuclear development. Iran will not stop until it is a nuclear power in the Middle East. In the mind of Iran's Supreme Leader Sayyid Al Khamenei it is necessary for Iran to have nuclear parody with Israel in the Middle East. Nuclear weapons make perfect sense—why is it acceptable for Israel to have nuclear weapons[38] and not Iran in the international scheme of things?

Every nation in the P5+1 have nuclear weapons except for Germany who does live up to the Non-Proliferation Treaty. Germany does possess the technology and capacity to create nuclear weapons.[39] However, Germany belongs to the NATO Alliance and because of that bond they do not need nuclear weapons. In the minds of the Iranians there is nothing that can stop Israel from using nuclear weapons. If Israel used nuclear weapons there maybe world condemnation but

223

that would not do a nuked Iran any good. What is done is done when it comes to nuclear weapons—ask the Japanese.

Israel is in a tough position when it comes to the P5+1 nuclear talk's with Iran. There really isn't a country that supports the views of Israel. Not even the United States supports Israel in the eyes of the Israeli's. The Obama administration disregards Israeli input concerning the Iranian nuclear talks. Israel believes that the United States should take a much stronger stance on Iran than the one demonstrated recently in the current nuclear talks. Israel and a majority of the United States Senate believe that the Obama administration is not handling the Iranian nuclear situation well.

President Obama's little poodle in the Senate Harry Reid has blocked a vote for a new round of United States sanctions on Iran. Senator Reid's block on sanctions is on sanctions that are contingent on an Iranian failure to live up to its present obligations. The *Weekly Standard* argues that President Obama is being tough on the pro-Israeli lobby in the United States Senate. Some argue that the President is using Majority Leader Harry Reid to do his dirty work.[40] President Obama ever since becoming President has not shown any real respect for America's ally Israel.

Majority Leader Harry Reid and other Democrats loyal to the President have gone as far as calling the Senators that support sanctions on Iran warmongers. There are some Democrats that support United States sanctions in the Senate, but the President is being tough on members of his own party for supporting Israel. This is threatening the US-Israel alliance in the eyes of many who follow the relationship between the two countries. It can be argued that the Presidents dealings with Iran are counterintuitive towards the people of Israel and the Israeli government.

President Obama has also shown utter contempt for the Israeli Prime Minister Binyamin Netanyahu by refusing to take his phone calls and pushing him off to Secretary of State John Kerry.[41] Secretary of State John Kerry seems like a lap dog in the United States negotiations with Iran. How else would anyone consider the results in the negotiation process with Iran from a foreign policy perspective?

The United States is supposed to stop Iran from moving forward with nuclear weapons capability. Senator John Kerry signed a treaty that allows Iran to continue to <u>enrich uranium and build centrifuges</u>.[42] Senator John Kerry will lift a majority of the sanctions on Iran over the next six months so that Iran can continue on its nuclear merry way. This writer may not be a foreign policy expert, but commonsensically a person does not sell a car by giving the car away and call it good business.

Secretary of State John Kerry is no friend of Israel to begin with especially after his visit to Israel in <u>December of 2013</u>. In December Secretary Kerry talked with both Palestinian Authority President Mahmoud Abbas and Prime Minister Benjamin Netanyahu on two separate occasions concerning the Israeli-Palestinian problem.[43] How many decades and American diplomats does it take to figure out that neither Israel nor the Palestinians will ever make an agreement with each other?

The reason why the Israeli-Palestinian issue is brought up here is just to show how in all negotiations the Obama administration places Israel on the losing end. In fact, <u>Tova Dvorin</u> of *Aurtz Sheva* called the Secretary of State John Kerry's visit to Israel an utter disaster: ". . . after he reportedly threatened a third intifada and then pledged over $75 million in financial support to the Palestinian Arabs."[44] And if the aforementioned was not bad enough Secretary Kerry on Monday <u>postponed his latest trip</u> to Israel.[45] This happened because it was apparent that neither Israel nor the Palestinians' could come to a conclusion over the security issues in the Jordon Valley.

At this place in time it would probably be best if Secretary of State John Kerry dealt with the Iranian problem and put the Israeli-Palestinian issue to the side. The Supreme Leader of Iran Al Khamenei gave a <u>speech to the Basij</u> commanders. In the speech the leader demonstrated nothing but contempt for the United States. Paraphrasing Al Khamenei the United States thinks that they own the Middle East region. How can the United States to tell another people what they can and cannot do in their own sovereign land? Al Khamenei went on to say that when it comes to Iran's nuclear

ambition—Iran is not obligated to listen to the "arrogant powers"—
that act in one way and tell another nation that they cannot.[46]

President Obama believes that people are rational. The problem
that President Obama has is that ideologically he thinks in terms of
Western values and the Leader of Iran thinks in terms of the Quran.
Iran is at war with the entire Western philosophy and how people
should be treated—especially women. The United States will never
get Iran to accept the existence of Israel. The United States foreign
policy towards the Middle East should be a big stick, but no boots
on the ground. Violence is the only thing that a terrorist nation will
understand. America cannot negotiate with Iran and expect positive
results in the long run.

Secretary of State John Kerry
and a Less Stable World

Secretary of State John Kerry does not understand the complexity behind international relations. For instance, the Secretary does not seem to have an understanding of America's involvement in Central America over the last hundred years. In his view all the Americans that died for the Monroe Doctrine do not really matter.

It is just unbelievable that the United States President would appoint an idiot to the job of Secretary of State. Secretary of State John Kerry has absolutely no understanding of the world of power politics. The whole idea of other nation-states not wanting to compete with the United States for the worlds resources through the use of the military, economics, and politics within the international arena is just nonsensical. China would like to be the regional hegemon of Asia and Iran would like to become the hegemon in the Middle East, but Secretary of State John Kerry hopes to relinquish the United States hegemony over the entire Western Hemisphere. On November 18, 2013 in Washington D.C. in front of the Organization of the American States Secretary of State John Kerry said, "The era of the Monroe Doctrine is over."[47]

Forgive this writer for not hearing about the above ludicrous comments until just recently it is important that someone discusses exactly what Secretary of State John Kerry is actually telling the world. Regarding Russia, Japan, and India the three main players in

Asia the Secretary of State is actually arguing that the United States no longer wants to live up to its role in the world. In a manner of speaking the Secretary of State Kerry is suggesting that the United States is willing to give up on the entire idea of hegemony as a worthless international political theory for nation-states to live by. In other words, Secretary of State Kerry is telling the world that the United States gives up its role as the hegemon of the Western Hemisphere.

The whole idea of throwing away close to two hundred years of precedence is nuts. The Secretary of States remarks are like throwing away years of blood and treasure that America has fought to achieve in Central America alone. The <u>Monroe Doctrine</u> created by President James Monroe and John Quincy Adams[48] took more strength of character than President Obama or Secretary of State John Kerry will ever come close to.

The only thing that America's allies and friends can expect from America today is apologies to our perceived enemies in the hopes that they will like us. This is why Secretary of State John Kerry is giving away the Middle East to Iran. In less than ten years Iran will be the hegemon of the Middle East—because of the foreign policy of today's Commander and Chief—President Obama.

President Theodore Roosevelt knew how important the south of the border was when he created the <u>Corollary to the Monroe Doctrine</u>: "The corollary states that the United States will intervene in conflicts between European countries and Latin America countries to enforce legitimate claims of the European powers, rather than having the Europeans press their claims directly."[49] Secretary of State John Kerry is basically telling the other nations in the Western Hemisphere that the United States will no longer protect their interests.

The United States is suggesting to nations like Venezuela and other countries that it is fine to sell oil and other raw materials directly to the Chinese and other rogue nation-states. The Secretary of State is expressing to China and the world that America is no longer interested in the Western Hemisphere as a hegemonic necessity. Secretary of State John Kerry is suggesting that it is fine for all and every nation to play in the United States backyard. The Senate needs to put the brakes on any and all foreign policy treaties that this Secretary of State attempts to place America in. It is proper that the Senate moves forward with stricter sanctions on Iran regardless of what the President thinks.

It is up to the Senate to vote down all trade treaties that the Obama Administration tries to place America under. The members of the Senate must let the United Nations and the world understand that President Obama and his Secretary of State do not speak for the United States as a whole. America is entering into some troubling times due to the lack of knowledge that the Obama Administration has about international theories of nation-state behavior. It is obvious that the President and Secretary of State are poisoned by the idealism of their Ivy League educations.

John Mearsheimer argues that American's are just too liberal to think in terms of realist theory. Realism suggests that there is no "911" for a nation-state to call if they are in trouble because of attack by another nation-state.[50] In other words the United Nations is as useless as it seems to be in reality. NATO is the same way unless the United States takes the helm. In realist theory what the previous suggests is that nations like China, Iran, Russia, India and just about all other nations have to find some way to protect their own interests.

Realists believe that nation-states will balance with other nation-states in order to protect their own interests. This is why Mearsheimer believes that India and Russia will move closer to the United States if China begins to flex its muscle in Asia. There are many different scenarios that various nation-states will adhere to in order to balance the international system. However, one must remember that never in the history of the League of Nations or the United Nations has a war been avoided. It is up to the individual powers to create alliances in order to protect each other's personal interests.

President Obama and Secretary of State Kerry are creating a much less stable world by relinquishing American power around the world. The one thing that will happen as time moves forward is the world will begin to balance itself without the United States guidance. In the aforementioned manner the United States will have weakened its position in the world.

The more moving parts (nation-states) in the world the less stable the world becomes. The former makes it much easier for war to break out. All of the peace and cooperation that the current administration is working towards will in actuality make the world less peaceful and unstable. This will lead to less trust among the various nation-states in the world and less cooperation. Hence, everything that the administration is trying to accomplish will boomerang on itself. President Obama's peace initiative will make America the major player in the next great historical war.

China's Day is on the Horizon

The world economic problems among the Great Powers are likely to turn to war in order to control domestic politics and nationalism.

The world is in turmoil and international organizations like the United Nations will be of no use in the future outlook of world politics. The breakdown of the great economies and war machines will cause unrest, anger and the end result will be world war. For example, the two authoritarian states China and Russia have domestic problems that are increasing as their economies are beginning to show strain and weakness. The United States will soon face the same problems that are seen in the European Union of high unemployment, increased taxation and member states on the verge of bankruptcy (American states and cities). The aforementioned are the world powers and the world is not balanced at the moment. Russia and China are working in tandem to attempt to balance against America and the European Union, and this creates a perfect recipe for war.

Some writers argue that the weight of the communist regime in China and a slowing economy means that the millions of Chinese that were lifted out of poverty will find themselves once more in poverty. China needs resources in order to keep its economy running. This is why China is attempting to deal with anyone who can provide China with the energy products that they need in order to compete on the world stage.

Russia who's GDP is based on oil and gas income will not have the money that the Putin government has promised the people of Russia. The Russian people will not have the money required to build their economy because the Putin government will not have the money to put into the economy. This is due to increased production in Canada and America that is keeping the price of oil down. Low oil and gas prices means less money for Russia and hence, the Russian economy. This will cause problems in Russia among the average citizenry and that will cause riots in the streets like those that have already been seen in Russia.

The European Union is a powder keg ready to exploit and the explosion may cause the actual breakup of the European Union and a move back towards their original nation-state boundaries and individual sovereignty. This is evident in the fact that the state of Germany is not at all interested in the continued bail out of the other component states that make up the European Union. A continued weak world economy is dangerous for the European Union which is tied down in heavy debt and a recession at the moment.

The United States is not immune to the problems that face the other great nations of the world and in many cases the United States is in a worse position than that of the other great nations. The living standards of Americans are decreasing from year to year and this has become evident to many Americans.

The elders of the last economic generation want the money that they think is deserved in regards to Social Security and Medicare. This is because they have paid for their parents, but the problem is that because of longer life expectancies both generations are asking the current generation to pay for them. The programs of Social Security and Medicare are placing a heavy burden on the American people as the payment out to recipients continues to outpace the money that is being brought into the system.

The children of the last generation are now expected to pay for their parents and grandparents and this is a tremendous burden on the current economic generation from the ages of thirty to retirement. This generation is losing ground economically because the middle class is shrinking and people are working harder for less.

The above is an outline for a world that will need war in order to control the domestic environment of each given nation-state written about above. War draws the people off of the streets and away from protesting. The nation-state is free to develop a new mentality wrapped up in nationalism. The country with the most to gain from a war is China and the new leadership of China is beginning to see that. In a recent <u>trip to Moscow</u> the Chinese bought four submarines and 24 Sukhoi Su-35 fighter planes this is a sign of what the new President of China Xi Jinping is looking to increase its military capabilities.[51] The sale of weaponry demonstrates the alliance of China and Russia who have through the years had a rocky relationship with one another especially on the border that the two countries share.

Most recently China has been flexing its muscle in the South China Sea. A <u>Chinese navy flotilla</u> was seen 1,250 miles from China and this aggressiveness is something that has not been seen by the Chinese in the past.[52] Some countries have appealed to the United States for action over the aggressiveness of China who hopes to take control of 1million square miles of fishing and energy waters. What is also vital about the Chinese movement is that without the shipping lanes of the South China Sea half of the world's shipping would conceivably be under the control of the Chinese government.

Some military experts believe that this movement by the Chinese is only the beginning of a problem for America in Asia. Some think that President Xi Jinping believes that he can move wherever he wants to because President Obama and his administration are timid. The South Asian Sea is shared by Vietnam, the Philippines and Taiwan and besides the fishing and energy resources of the sea; the Chinese wish to lay claim to a larger prize Taiwan. President Obama needs to move a fleet back to Asia for his "Asia Pivot" before Xi Jinping takes the United States inaction as a green light to do whatever he pleases in the East Asia region.

<u>Patrick Buchanan</u> thinks that China is not a threat to America's vital interest. Buchanan argues that even if the Chinese where to annex Taiwan that would not be a reason for the United States to go to war with China.[53] The <u>Bush administration</u> went from one extreme to the other in regards to America's commitment to Taiwan. In the

first months of the Bush administration President Bush went as far as stating that if Taiwan was attacked then America would defend Taiwan.[54] However, from 2003 forward the United States changed its commitment with Taiwan in order to receive help from China on the nuclear problem with North Korea.

The Obama Administration has decided on discussions between the United States, China and Taiwan in regards to respect for one another with China respecting Taiwan's sovereignty. However, that policy was before the latest movements from China in the South Asian Sea. President Obama has put forward his new Asian policy and it was to coordinate with America's allies in the region and tread lightly with China.[55] However, the latest actions by China demonstrate that the new President in China wants to push the United States and see what the reaction will be.

It is this writer's opinion that China believes that it can take back Taiwan without any reprisal from the United States and still maintain good relations with Russia. If China's economy begins to falter and there is unrest in China among the people then Xi Jinping will take the opportunity to develop nationalism at home while at the same time reuniting Taiwan with China. The United Nations will have nothing to say about the matter and in no time the Chinese will be back in international favor.

The Chinese will be the economic and military power of the world and stronger than any other nation-state in less than fifteen years. The United States will have massive military and economic difficulty, the European Union may not exist anymore and Russia will have its own internal domestic problems to deal with. China's day is on the horizon.

Notes

One. The Elites and the Progressives

1. Lowell Video: "Joe Biden Says Ken Cuccinelli is the "absolute . . . antithesis . . . of change and progress," *Blue Virginia,* November 4, 2013, available at http://www.bluevirginia.us/diary/10561/video-joe-biden-says-ken-cuccinelli-is-the-antithesis-of-change.
2. Joe Blackman, "Obamacare's Three Broken Promises," *The Daily Caller,* November 5, 2013, Available at http://dailycaller.com/2013/11/05/obamacares-three-broken-promises/.
3. United Nations. It's Your World. The Universal Declaration of Human Rights Available at http://www.un.org/en/documents/udhr/.
4. Russell Kirk, The Conservative Mind From Burke to Eliot. 7th ed Regnery Publishing, Inc. 1999.
5. United Nations Human Rights. International Covenant on Economic, Social and Cultural Rights available at http://www.ohchr.org/EN/ProfessionalInterest/Pages/CESCR.aspx.
6. Patrick J. Buchanan, "We Need More Economic Nationalists," *WND,* June 18, 2012, available at, http://www.wnd.com/2012/06/we-need-more-economic-nationalists/
7. Ibid. 1.
8. Charles Scaliger, "Obama the Deficit Hawk?" *The New American,* February 21, 2013, available at, http://www.thenewamerican.com/economy/commentary/item/14581-obama-the-deficit-hawk.

9. Wikipedia The Free Encyclopedia, "2009 United States Federal Budget," January 24, 2013, available at, http://en.wikipedia.org/wiki/2009_United_States_federal_budget.

10. Katherine Q. Seelye, "Health Care's Share of U.S. Economy Rose at Record Rate," *The New York Time,* February 4, 2010 available at, http://prescriptions.blogs.nytimes.com/2010/02/04/us-health-care-spending-rose-at-record-rate-in-2009/?_php=true&_type=blogs&_r=1&.

11. Chris Jacobs, "Defunding Obamacare: The Next Best Option," The Heritage Foundation, July 30, 2013, available at, http://www.heritage.org/issues/health-care/obamacare.

12. ED.GOV, 'The Federal Role in Education," February 13, 2012, available at, http://www2.ed.gov/about/overview/fed/role.html.

13. Wikipedia The Free Encyclopedia, "Darwinism," February 12, 2014, available at, https://en.wikipedia.org/wiki/Darwinism.

14. Wikipedia The Free Encyclopedia, "White Guilt," December 15, 2013, available at, http://en.wikipedia.org/wiki/White_guilt.

15. Jeff Sessions, U.S. Senate Committee on The Budget Republicans, "CRS Report: Welfare Spending The Largest Item In The Federal budget," October 18, 2012, available at, http://www.budget.senate.gov/republican/public/index.cfm/budget-background?ID=3c687e99-a5c5-46f2-9f9d-0ea5a62c3183.

16 Ibid. 1.

17 Ibid. 1.

18. Wikipedia The Free Encyclopedia, "Group Think," February 12, 2014, available at, http://en.wikipedia.org/wiki/Groupthink.

19. Joshua Kennon, 'The New Elite: A Look In the 1% of Wealth in the United States," October 9, 2011, available at, http://www.joshuakennon.com/the-new-elite-a-look-in-the-top-1-percent-of-wealth-in-the-united-states/.

20. Wikipedia The Free Encyclopedia, "White Anglo-Saxon Protestant," February 11, 2014, available at, http://en.wikipedia.org/wiki/White_Anglo-Saxon_Protestant.

21. Patrick Poole, "Homeland Security: You're All 'Militia Extremists Now," Common American Journal, February 5, 2012, available at, http://commonamericanjournal.

com/homeland-security-you%E2%80%99re-all-%E2%80%98militia-extremists%E2%80%99-now/.

22. Prof. Charles D. Kay, "Justice as Fairness," Department of Philosophy, (1997) available at, http://sites.wofford.edu/kaycd/rawls/.

23. Charles Krauthammer, "Obama's Ultimate Agenda is Social and Economic Leveling," Pittsburgh Post-Gazette, April 4, 2009, available at, http://www.post-gazette.com/opinion/Op-Ed/2009/04/04/Charles-Krauthammer-Obama-s-ultimate-agenda-is-social-and-economic-leveling/stories/200904040133.

24. Fox News Politics, "Obama Call for 'International Order' Raises Questions About U.S. Sovereignty," May 24, 2010, available at, http://www.foxnews.com/politics/2010/05/24/obama-international-order-raises-questions-sovereignty/.

25. David Brooks, "Why Our Elites stink," New York Times, Opinion pages, July 12, 2012, available at, http://www.nytimes.com/2012/07/13/opinion/brooks-why-our-elites-stink.html?_r=0.

26. Charles Murray, "The tea party warns of New Elite. They're right.," Washington Post, October 24, 2010, available at, http://www.washingtonpost.com/wp-dyn/content/article/2010/10/22/AR2010102202873.html.

27. Martin E. Marty, "The Establishment That Was," Christian Century, November 15, 1989 p. 1045, available at, http://www.religion-online.org/showarticle.asp?title=906.

28. Alan Wolfe, "The Power Elite Now," The American Prospect, November 16, 2001, available at, http://prospect.org/article/power-elite-now.

29. RationalWiki, "Secular Religion," February 13, 2014, available at, http://rationalwiki.org/wiki/Secular_religions.

30. Mark L. Movsesian, "Walter Russell Mead on Christianity and American Elites," Center For Law and Religion Forum, July 9, 2012, available at, http://clrforum.org/2012/07/09/walter-russell-mead-on-christianity-and-americas-elites/.

31. Shamus Khan, "The New Elitists," New York Times, July 7, 2012, available at, http://www.nytimes.com/2012/07/08/opinion/sunday/the-new-elitists.html?pagewanted=all&_r=0.

32. Mark L. Movsesian, "Walter Russell Mead on Christianity and American Elites," Center For Law and Religion Forum, July 9, 2012, available at, http://clrforum.org/2012/07/09/walter-russell-mead-on-christianity-and-americas-elites/.

33. Wikipedia The Free Encyclopedia, 'Meritocracy," February 9, 2014, available at, http://en.wikipedia.org/wiki/Meritocracy.

34. Christopher Hayes, "Why Elites Fail," *The Nation,* June 6,2012, available at, http://www.thenation.com/article/168265/why-elites-fail.

35. Ibid., 1.

36. Ibid., 1.

37. Wikipedia The Free Encyclopedia, "The Sixteenth Amendment of the United States Constitution," February 12, 2014, available at, http://en.wikipedia.org/wiki/Sixteenth_Amendment_to_the_United_States_Constitution.

38. Dan Bigman, "John Stossel: Tax The Rich? The Rich Don't Have Enough. Really.," *Forbes,* April 3, 2012, available at, http://www.forbes.com/sites/danbigman/2012/04/03/john-stossel-tax-the-rich-the-rich-dont-have-enough-really/.

39. John Hayward, "Here Comes The Obamacare Tax Avalanche," *Human Events,* December 27, 2013, available at, http://www.humanevents.com/2013/12/27/here-comes-the-obamacare-tax-avalanche/.

40. Ibid. 1.

41. Laura Meckler, "Obama Signs Stimulus Into Law," *The Wall Street Journal,* February 18, 2009, available at, http://online.wsj.com/news/articles/SB123487951033799545.

42. Arthur C. Brooks, "Why the Stimulus Failed," National Review Online, September 25, 2012, available at, http://www.nationalreview.com/articles/328432/why-stimulus-failed-arthur-c-brooks.

43. Nick Schulz, "How effective was the 2009 stimulus program?" American Enterprise Institute, July 5, 2011, available at.

http://www.aei.org/article/economics/fiscal-policy/how-effective-was-the-2009-stimulus-program/.

Two. Immigration and Affirmative Action

1. Frosty Woolridge, "Illegal Aliens Education Impart—US Losing its Mind," Rense, April 14, 2008, available at, http://www.rense.com/general81/illega.htm.
2. Caroline May, "Senate Dems block amendment to restore benefits by closing illegal immigrant welfare loophole," *The Daily Caller* December 18, 2013 available at, http://dailycaller.com/2013/12/18/senate-dems-block-amendment-to-restore-veteran-benefits-by-closing-illegal-immigrant-welfare-loophole/.
3. John Dillin, "How Eisenhower solved illegal border crossings from Mexico," *The Christian Science Monitor,* July 6, 2006, available at, http://www.csmonitor.com/2006/0706/p09s01-coop.html.
4. Ibid., 2.
5. David Emery, "Theodore Roosevelt on Immigrants" About.com, Urban legends, October 29, 2005, available at, http://urbanlegends.about.com/library/bl_roosevelt_on_immigrants.htm.
6. U.S. Immigration Support, "Your Online Guide to U.S. visas, Green Cards and Citizenship," February 1, 2014, available at, http://www.usimmigrationsupport.org/no-route.html.
7. History, "Coolidge signs stringent immigration law," This Day in History, May 26, 1924, available at, http://www.history.com/this-day-in-history/coolidge-signs-stringent-immigration-law.
8. Vicki D. Westling, "Immigration and the U.S. Constitution," *Observer Today,* August 18, 2010, available at, http://www.observertoday.com/page/content.detail/id/544129.html?nav=5046.
9. Doug Whallon, "A Code of Ethics for the Christian Evangelist," *Student Leadership Journal, (1989),* available at, http://cms.intervarsity.org/slj/fa00/fa00_code_of_ethics.html.

10. CIS "Three Decades of Mass Immigration: The Legacy of the 1965 Immigration Act," Center for Immigration Studies, September 1, 1995, available at, http://www.cis.org/articles/1995/back395. html.

11. "56e, Lyndon Johnson's "Great Society," U.S. History, February 1, 2014, available at, http://www.ushistory.org/us/56e.asp.

12. CIS "Three Decades of Mass Immigration: The Legacy of the 1965 Immigration Act," Center for Immigration Studies, September 1, 1995, available at, http://www.cis.org/articles/1995/back395. html.

13. Michele Waslin "Remembering the Benefits of IRCA, 25 Years Later," American Immigration Council, Immigration Impact, November 8, 2011, available at, http://immigrationimpact.com/2011/11/07/ remembering-the-benefits-of-irca-25-years-later/.

14. NumbersUSA, "The Seven Amnesties Passed by Congress," February 1, 2014, available at, https://www.numbersusa.com/ content/learn/illegal-immigration/seven-amnesties-passed-congress.html.

15. Alex Pappas, "Marco Rubio doesn't mention Tea Party in victory speech," *The Daily Caller,* August 25, 2010, available at, http://dailycaller.com/2010/08/25/ marco-rubio-doesnt-mention-tea-party-in-victory-speech/.

16. Tim Brown, "Rubio Thinks Rove's Anti-Tea Party Pac IS A "Good Idea,'" Freedom Outpost February 20, 2013, available at, http://freedomoutpost.com/2013/02/ rubio-thinks-roves-anti-tea-party-pac-is-a-good-idea/.

17. James Kitfield, "Accepting the Neocon Torch: Marco Rubio," *National Journal,* April 25, 2012, available at, http:// www.nationaljournal.com/2012-presidential-campaign/ accepting-the-neocon-torch-marco-rubio-20120425.

18. Patrick Krey, "Is Conservatism Dead?" *The New American,* January 5, 2009, Available at, http://www.thenewamerican.com/ usnews/politics/item/2488-is-conservatism-dead.

19. Taylor Rose, "Senator To "Gang of 8" Secure Border First," WND February 15, 2014, available at, http://www.wnd.com/2013/04/senator-to-gang-of-8-secure-border-first/.

20. Wikipedia The Free Encyclopedia, "Universal Declaration of Human Rights," February 7, 2014, available at, http://en.wikipedia.org/wiki/Universal_Declaration_of_Human_Rights

21. Eric Holder, "Holder Calls Amnesty a 'Civil Right,'" Fox Nation, Holder Speech on C-SPAN, April 24, 2013, available at, http://nation.foxnews.com/amnesty/2013/04/26/holder-calls-amnesty-civil-right.

22. Wikipedia The Free Encyclopedia, "International Court of Justice," February 5, 2014, available at, http://en.wikipedia.org/wiki/International_Court_of_Justice.

23. Wikipedia The Free Encyclopedia, "United Nations Human Rights Council," February 7, 2014, available at, http://en.wikipedia.org/wiki/United_Nations_Human_Rights_Council.

24. Wikipedia The Free Encyclopedia, "International Covenant on Economic, Social and Cultural Rights," February 3, 2014, http://en.wikipedia.org/wiki/International_Covenant_on_Economic,_Social_and_Cultural_Rights.

25. Wikipedia The Free Encyclopedia, "United Nations Charter," February 9, 2014, available at, https://en.wikipedia.org/wiki/United_Nations_Charter.

26. Terry Greene Sterling, "Obama's Dreamer Immigration Move Boosts His Standing With Arizona Latino's," *The Daily Beast*, June 20, 2012, available at, http://www.thedailybeast.com/articles/2012/06/20/obama-s-dreamer-immigration-move-boosts-his-standing-with-arizona-latinos.html.

27. Josh Blackman "Ice Agents Sue President For Failing To Enforce Immigration Law," Josh Blackman's Blog, August 27, 2012, available at, http://joshblackman.com/blog/2012/08/27/ice-agents-sue-president-for-failing-to-enforce-immigration-laws/

28. Caroline May, "House Homeland Security Committee Chair demands answers from ICE on illegal immigration release," *The Daily Caller*, February 27,

2013, available at, http://dailycaller.com/2013/02/27/rep-mccaul-questions-ice-on-illegal-immigrant-release/

29. George Stith, "Operation Wetback," Digital History (2013), available at, http://www.digitalhistory.uh.edu/disp_textbook.cfm?smtID=3&psid=593

30. NPR Staff, "A Reagan Legacy: Amnesty For Illegal Immigrants," NPR, July 4, 2010 available at, http://www.npr.org/templates/story/story.php?storyId=128303672

31. CBS News, "10 ICE agents sue over Obama immigration policy," (CBS/AP) Dallas, August 24, 2012, available at, http://www.cbsnews.com/news/10-ice-agents-sue-over-obama-immigration-policy/

32. Julia Preston and John H. Cushman Jr., "Obama to Permit Young Migrants to Remain in U.S.," *New York Times,* June 15, 2012, available at, http://www.nytimes.com/2012/06/16/us/us-to-stop-deporting-some-illegal-immigrants.html?pagewanted=all&_r=1&

33. Fox News, "Protesters Defend Carrying Mexican Flags," Associated Press, Phoenix, April 6, 2006 available at, http://www.foxnews.com/story/2006/04/06/protesters-defend-carrying-mexican-flags/

34. Jenny Portney, "Chris Christie trumpets signing of Dream Act in Union City," *The Star-Ledger,* January 7, 2014, available at, http://www.nj.com/politics/index.ssf/2014/01/chris_christie_trumpets_signing_of_dream_act_in_union_city.html

35. "New Jersey Unemployment," Department of Numbers, January (2014), available at, http://www.deptofnumbers.com/unemployment/new-jersey/

36. Charlie Spiering, "Video montage of MSNBC's Chris Christie lovefest on 'Morning Joe,'" *Washington Examiner,* November 6, 2013 available at, http://washingtonexaminer.com/video-montage-of-msnbcs-chris-christie-lovefest-on-morning-joe/article/2538614

37. Steve Salvi "The Original list of Sanctuary Cities USA," Ohio Jobs & Justice PAC, November 9, 2013, available at, http://www.ojjpac.org/sanctuary.asp

38. Michael Bargo Jr., "Sanctuary cities and states will bear the lion's share of amnesty cost," *American Thinker,* May 12, 2013, available at, http://www.americanthinker.com/2013/05/sanctuary_cities_and_states_will_bear_the_lions_share_of_amnesty_cost.html.

39. Ibid., 1.

40. Wikipedia The Free Encyclopedia, "Silent Majority," February 8, 2014, available at, http://en.wikipedia.org/wiki/Silent_majority.

41. Stephen Dinan, "Nearly 20 million illegal immigrants in U.S., former Border Patrol say," *The Washington Times,* September 8, 2013, available at, http://www.washingtontimes.com/news/2013/sep/9/nearly-20m-illegal-immigrants-us-ex-border-patrol/.

42. Patrick J. Buchanan, "Buchanan: Has the Bell Begun to Toll for China," *Human Events,* March 1, 2013, available at, http://www.humanevents.com/2013/03/01/has-the-bell-begun-to-toll-for-china/.

43. Theodore Roosevelt, "Idea's on Immigration and being American in 1907," Snopes.com April 12, 2006, available at, http://www.snopes.com/politics/quotes/troosevelt.asp.

44. Matthew Larotonda, "Biden Defends Voting Rights Act Provision in Selma, Alabama," ABC News Blog, March 3, 2013, available at, http://abcnews.go.com/blogs/politics/2013/03/biden-defends-voting-rights-act-provision-in-selma-alabama/.

45. Jessie Kindig, "Bloody Sunday, Selma, Alabama, (March 7, 1965)," BlackPost.org, December 30, 2011, available at, http://www.blackpast.org/aah/bloody-sunday-selma-alabama-march-7-1965.

46. Nina Totenberg, "Supreme Court Weighs Future of Voting Rights Act," NPR February 27, 2013, available at, http://www.npr.org/2013/02/27/173012038/supreme-court-weighs-future-of-voting-rights-act.

47. George E. Curry, "Supreme Court Justice Equates Black Voting Rights with 'Racial Entitlements.'" *The Sacramento Observer,* March 4, 2013, available at, http://sacobserver.com/2013/03/supreme-court-justice-scalia-equates-black-voting-rights-with-racial-entitlements/.

48. University of California, Irvine, "A brief history of Affirmative Action," Equal Opportunity and Diversity, May 3, 2010, available at, http://www.oeod.uci.edu/aa.html.

49. Ibid., 1.

50. Julie Peterson, "U.S. Supreme Court rules on University of Michigan Cases," Michigan News University of Michigan, July 23, 2003, available at, http://ns.umich.edu/new/releases/20237.

51. Bill Frezza, "To Finally Abolish Affirmative Action, All Americans Should Check The Minority Box," *Forbes Magazine,* October 17, 2012, available at, http://www.forbes.com/sites/billfrezza/2012/10/17/to-finally-abolish-affirmative-action-all-americans-should-check-the-minority-box/.

52. Bloomberg Law, "Fisher v. University of Texas at Austin," Scotus Blog, June 24, 2012, available at, http://www.scotusblog.com/case-files/cases/fisher-v-university-of-texas-at-austin/

53. Noel Sheppard, "Obama twice uses MSNBC slogan 'Lean Forward' while addressing disaster relief," Fox.News.com, October 31, 2012, available at, http://www.foxnews.com/opinion/2012/10/31/obama-twice-uses-msnbc-slogan-lean-forward-while-addressing-disaster-relief/

Chapter Three. Economics and the Obama Way

1. Jonathan1352 of VA, "Homeland Security Sub Committee Presses DHS Officials on Policy of Administrative Amnesty," NumbersUSA, October 6, 2011, available at, https://www.numbersusa.com/content/nusablog/jonosborne/october-6-2011/homeland-security-subcommittee-presses-dhs-officials-policy-admin.

2. Lachlan Markay, "An Administrative Amnesty," TexasInsider.com, February 28, 2013, available at, http://www.texasinsider.org/an-administrative-amnesty/.

3. Mark Mazzetti and William K. Rashbaum, "Bin Laden Relative with Qaeda Past to Have New York Trial," *New York Times,* March 7, 2013, available at, http://www.nytimes.com/2013/03/08/world/middleeast/

bin-laden-son-in-law-is-being-held-in-a-new-york-jail. html?_r=1&.

4.   Wikipedia The Free Encyclopedia, "All the Presidents Men (film)," February 8, 2014, http://en.wikipedia.org/wiki/ All_the_President%27s_Men_%28film%29.

5.   Bob Adelmann, "Agencies Set to Unleash Tsunami of Regulations after the Election," *The New American,* November 1, 2012, available at, http://www.thenewamerican.com/economy/ markets/item/13475-agencies-set-to-unleash-tsunami-of-regulations-after-the-election.

6.   Ibid., 1.

7.   Steve Goreham, "Lisa Jackson leaving EPA and path of economic destruction," *The Washington Times,* January 2, 2013, available at, http://communities.washingtontimes.com/ neighborhood/climatism-watching-climate-science/2013/jan/2/ lisa-jackson-leaving-epa-and-path-economic-destruc/.

8.   Steve McCann, "Obama's Second Term Transformation Plans," American Thinker, January 28, 2014, available at, http:// www.americanthinker.com/2012/05/obamas_second_term_ transformation_plans.html.

9.   Russell Kirk, "The Essence of Conservatism," The Russell Kirk Center for Cultural Renewal, February 8, 2014, available at, http://www.kirkcenter.org/index.php/detail/essence-1957/.

10. "Woodrow Wilson," New World Encyclopedia, June 11, 2006, available at, http://www.newworldencyclopedia.org/entry/ Woodrow_Wilson.

11. "Franklin Delano Roosevelt's "Court Packing" Plan." United States Senate Committee on the Judiciary, February 6, 2014, available at, http://www.judiciary.senate.gov/about/history/ CourtPacking.cfm.

12. "The Years of Lyndon Johnson: Master of the Senate," February 2, 2014, available at, http://www.robertacaro.com/senate.htm.

13. Mary Anastasia O'Grady "Brady's Sound Dollar Act," *The Wall Street Journal* April 24, 2012, available at, http://online.wsj. com/news/articles/ . . .

14. Evan Schnidman, PhD, "The Sound Dollar Act: A worthwhile debate in Congress," The Hill Blogs, April 6, 2012, available at, http://thehill.com/blogs/congress-blog/economy-a-budget/220363-the-sound-dollar-act-a-worthwhile-debate-in-congress.

15. Matthew Campione, "Quantitative Easing: Only in America," *Forbes*, April 20, 2012, available at, http://www.forbes.com/sites/matthewcampione/2012/04/20/quantitative-easing-only-in-america/.

16. Matt Egan "Treasury Secretary Tim Geithner Will Not Serve a second Term," Fox Business January 25, 2012, available at, http://www.foxbusiness.com/politics/2012/01/25/treasury-secretary-tim-geithner-will-not-serve-second-term-report/.

17. Maureen Farrell, "Bond Twist after Operation Twist," CNNmoney, September 21, 2011, Available at, http://money.cnn.com/2011/09/21/markets/bondcenter/bonds_fed/.

18. "Sequestration Update Report 2013," Congressional Budget Office, August 1, 2013 available at, http://www.cbo.gov/latest/Budget/Sequestration-Reports.

19. Daniel Halper, "Obama's Budget to Add 4.4 Trillion to Debt in Next Four Years," *The Weekly Journal Blog,* August 23, 2012, available at, http://www.weeklystandard.com/blogs/obamas-budget-add-44-trillion-debt-next-four-years_650614.html.

20. Lucy Madison, "In Farewell remarks, Panetta rails against Congress, sequestration," CBSNEWs, February 6, 2013, available at, http://www.cbsnews.com/news/in-farewell-remarks-panetta-rails-against-congress-sequestration/.

21. Louis Woodhill, "Under Obama Economic Stagnation Is the New Normal," Real Clear Markets, December 10, 2012, available at, http://www.realclearmarkets.com/articles/2012/12/10/jobs_under_obama_economic_stagnation_is_the_new_normal_100035.html.

22. Grover Norquist, "Reagan vs. Obama: The Record," *Human Events,* February 6, 2013, available at, http://www.humanevents.com/2013/02/06/norquist-reagan-vs-obama-the-record/.

23. Ed Morrissey, "Guess which President has raked in the most Wall Street bucks in a generation?" Hot AIR, October 10, 2011, available at, http://hotair.com/archives/2011/10/10/guess-which-president-has-raked-in-the-most-wall-street-bucks-in-a-generation/.

24. Michael O'Connell, "Sequestration will not happen, Obama says in final debate," Federal News Radio, October 23, 2012, available at, http://www.federalnewsradio.com/394/3089313/Sequestration-will-not-happen-Obama-says-in-final-debate.

25. Kim Peterson, "Unemployment benefits at stake in fiscal cliff deal," MSN Money, December 19, 2012, available at, http://money.msn.com/now/post.aspx?post=e7e43083-5fc3-4cae-99bb-def05a3de58d.

26. Lori Montgomery, "Obama says he fears economy could enter 'New Normal' of low job growth," *The Washington Post*, November 7, 2010, available at, http://www.washingtonpost.com/wp-dyn/content/article/2010/11/07/AR2010110705223.html.

27. Joel B. Pollak, "1.6 Trillion? Obama Doesn't Want A Deal," *Breitbart News*, November 13, 2012, available at, http://www.breitbart.com/Big-Government/2012/11/13/1-6-Trillion-Obama-Doesnt-Want-a- . . .

28. Parag Khanna, "How's that New World Order Working Out?" New America Foundation, December 1, 2010, available at, http://www.newamerica.net/node/40674.

29. David E. Sanger, Deficits May Alter U.S. Politics and Global Power, *New York Times*, February 1, 2010, available at, http://www.nytimes.com/2010/02/02/us/politics/02deficit.html?_r=2&.

30. Dennis Gallagher, "Overcoming Obama's New Normal," Conservative Daily News December 27, 2012, available at, http://www.conservativedailynews.com/2012/12/overcoming-obamas-new-normal/?utm_source=rss&utm_medium=rss&utm_campaign=overcoming-obamas-new-normal.

31. "The Dignity of the Human Person," Catechism of the Catholic Church, February 3, 2013, available at, http://www.vatican.va/archive/ccc_css/archive/catechism/p3s1c1a6.htm.

32. Charles Krauthammer, "It's Nothing But a Power Play," National Review Online, December 6, 2012, available at, http://www.nationalreview.com/articles/335009/it-s-nothing-power-play-charles-krauthammer.

33. Jackie Calmes, Demystifying the Fiscal Impasse That is Vexing Washington, *The New York Times,* November 15, 2012, available at, http://www.nytimes.com/2012/11/16/us/politics/the-fiscal-cliff-explained.html?pagewanted=all&_r=1&.

34. "What's the Fiscal Cliff," DNEWS, December 13, 2012, available at, http://news.discovery.com/human/life/fiscal-cliff-obama-121107.htm.

35. Ibid., 1.

36. Thomas Reddlem, Establishment Screams: Avoid Fiscal Cliff and Borrow, Borrow, Borrow, *The New American,* November 25, 2012 available at, http://www.thenewamerican.com/economy/item/13726-establishment-screams-avoid-fiscal-cliff-and-borrow-borrow-borrow.

37. Mark Peters, Douglas Belkin, and Josh Mitchell, "States Brace for Possibility That 'Fiscal Cliff' Isn't Averted, *The Wall Street Journal,* November 16, 2012, available at, http://online.wsj.com/news/articles/SB10001424127887324595904578121454207085678?mg=reno64-wsj&url . . .

38. Jon Hilsenrath and Kristina Peterson, "Fed Acts to Fix Jobs Market," *The Wall Street Journal,* September 14, 2012, available at, http://online.wsj.com/news/articles/SB10000872396390444023704577649602607207034?mg=reno64-wsj&url . . .

39. Erik Wemple, "Palin's freedom v. 'free stuff' line: Viable?" *The Washington Post*, September 12, 2012, available at, http://www.washingtonpost.com/blogs/erik-wemple/post/palins-freedom-v-free-stuff-line-viable/2012/09/12/b19a4af0-fcf7-11e1-8adc-499661afe377_blog.html.

40. Otto von Bismarck, "Otto von Bismarck-Quotes-Quotable Quote," Good Reads, December 7,

2013, available at. http://www.goodreads.com/quotes/424187-politics-is-the-art-of-the-possible-the-attainable.

41. Paul Roderick Gregory, "President Obama's Legacy: $20 Trillion in Debt for 2016 Victor," *Forbes Magazine,* December 25, 2012, available at, http://www.forbes.com/sites/paulroderickgregory/2012/12/25/president-obamas-legacy-20-trillion-in-deficits-for-2016-victor/.

42. Bob Adelmann, Rep. Paul Ryan's New Budget to Repeal Obamacare, Replace Medicare, *The New American,* March 11, 2013, available at. http://www.thenewamerican.com/usnews/congress/item/14741-rep-paul-ryan-s-new-budget-to-repeal-obamacare-replace-medicare.

43. Ken Wandrel, "How Did World War II Help U.S. Recover From the Great Depression," Demand Media, April 10, 2013, available at, http://classroom.synonym.com/did-world-war-ii-us-recover-great-depression-18222.html.

44. Jeremy W. Peters and Jonathan Weisman, "2 Parties' Budgets Show Big Rift as G.O.P. Renews 2012 Proposals, *New York Times,* March 12, 2013, available at, http://classroom.synonym.com/did-world-war-ii-us-recover-great-depression-18222.html.

45. Wikipedia The Free Encyclopedia, "List of Recessions in America," February 8, 2014, available at, http://en.wikipedia.org/wiki/List_of_recessions_in_the_United_States.

46. Wikipedia The Free Encyclopedia, "American Recovery and Reinvestment Act of 2009," February 6, 2014, available at, http://en.wikipedia.org/wiki/American_Recovery_and_Reinvestment_Act_of_2009.

47. Mary Bruce, "Obama Heads to Capitol Hill in Search of Deficit Deal," ABCNEWs, March 12, 2013 available at, http://abcnews.go.com/blogs/politics/2013/03/obama-heads-to-capitol-hill-in-search-of-deficit-deal/.

48. Erik Wasson, "Senate Democrats' budget includes nearly $1 trillion in new taxes," The Hill Blog, March 12, 2013, available at, http://thehill.com/blogs/on-the-money/budget/287625-senate-dem-budget-includes-nearly-1-trillion-in-new-taxes.

49. Wikipedia The Free Encyclopedia, "Race to the Bottom," February 8, 2014, available at, http://en.wikipedia.org/wiki/Race_to_the_bottom.

50. Paul Krugman, "A Permanent Slump?" *The New York Times Opinion Pages,* November 17, 2013, available at, http://www.nytimes.com/2013/11/18/opinion/krugman-a-permanent-slump.html?_r=0.

51. Kevin C. Caffrey, "The Power Elite and American Politics," The Nolan Chart, February 13, 2013, available at, http://www.nolanchart.com/article10119-the-power-elite-and-american-politics.html.

52. Seth Mclaughlin, "Sen. Rand Paul pushes' 'economic freedom zones' for Detroit," *The Washington Times,* December 6, 2013, available at, http://www.washingtontimes.com/news/2013/dec/6/rand-paul-pushes-economic-freedom-zones-detroit/.

53. Wikipedia The Free Encyclopedia, "Urban Enterprise Zones," February 6, 2014, available at, http://en.wikipedia.org/wiki/Urban_Enterprise_Zone.

54. Kevin Cirilli, Rand Paul to make economic pitch to Detroit," PoliticoPro, December 5, 2013, available at, http://www.politico.com/story/2013/12/rand-paul-economic-pitch-detroit-100711.html.

55. Greg Richter, "Rand Paul: 'Enterprise Zones on Steroids' Can Save Detroit," Newsmax, December 5, 2012, available at, http://www.newsmax.com/US/detroit-rand-paul-enterprise/2013/12/05/id/540101

56. Stephen Billings, 'Do Enterprise Zones Work? An Analysis at the Borders," Center for Economic Analysis, November 5, 2007, available at, http://www.colorado.edu/econ/papers/Wps-07/wp07-09/wp07-09.pdf.

57. Matthew Boyle, "Exclusive-Rand Paul: 'Economic Freedom Zones' For Detroit, Other Cities," Breitbart Big Government, December 5, 2013, available at, http://www.breitbart.com/Big-Government/2013/12/05/Exclusive-Rand-Paul-to-Detroit-for-conservative-anti-bailout-minority-outreach-mission-of-inner-city-Economic-Freedom-Zones

58. Wikipedia The Free Encyclopedia, "United States federal government shut-down of 1995 and 1995-1996," Available at, http://en.wikipedia.org/wiki/United_States_federal_government_shutdown_of_1995_and_1996.

59. No Author, "United States Unemployment Rate," Trading Economics, January 1, 2014, available at, http://www.tradingeconomics.com/united-states/unemployment-rate.

60. Alex Pappas, "Republicans Show Rare display of Unity after Obamacare Vote," The Daily Caller, September 20, 2013, available at, http://dailycaller.com/2013/09/20/republicans-show-rare-display-of-unity-after-obamacare-vote/.

61. Lori Montgomery and Philip Rucker, "House passes GOP spending plan that defunds Obamacare," The Washington Post, September 20, 2013, available at, http://www.washingtonpost.com/politics/house-passes-gop-spending-plan-that-defunds-obamacare/2013/09/20/4019117c-21fe-11e3-b73c-aab60bf735d0_story.html.

62. Stephanie Condon, "Cruz says he'll filibuster spending bill if it doesn't defund Obamacare," CBSNEWS, September, 19, 2013 available at, http://www.cbsnews.com/news/cruz-says-hell-filibuster-spending-bill-if-it-doesnt-defund-obamacare/

63. No Author, "NTSB analyzing data recorders to determine cause of deadly NYC train derailment," Fox News, December 2, 2013, available at, http://www.foxnews.com/us/2013/12/02/federal-authorities-probe-cause-of-new-york-city-train-derailment/.

64. Susan Jones, "Lahood Says $48B Stimulus for DOT Wasn't Enough; 'Should Have Been $480B,'" CNSNEWS, December 2, 2013, available at, http://cnsnews.com/news/article/susan-jones/lahood-says-48b-stimulus-dot-wasnt-enough-should-have-been-480b.

65. Emily Goff, "Government Shutdown and the Future of Transportation Funding," The Heritage Foundation, October, 3, 2013, available at, http://www.heritage.org/research/reports/2013/10/government-shutdown-and-the-future-of-transportation-funding

66. Brian M. Riedl, Why Government Spending Does Not Stimulate Economic Growth: Answering the Critics," The Heritage Foundation, January 5, 2010, available at, http://www.heritage.org/research/reports/2010/01/why-government-spending-does-not-stimulate-economic-growth-answering-the-critics.

67. No Author, "State Gasoline Tax Rates 2009-2013," Tax Foundation, available at, http://taxfoundation.org/article/state-gasoline-tax-rates-2009-2013.

Chapter Four. The Affordable Care Act and its Problems

1. Wikipedia The Free Encyclopedia, "Patient Protection and Affordable Care Act," February 3, 2014, available at, http://en.wikipedia.org/wiki/Patient_Protection_and_Affordable_Care_Act

2. Jacqueline Klingebiel, "Obama: Mandate is Not a Tax," ABCNEWs, September 20, 2009, available at, http://abcnews.go.com/blogs/politics/2009/09/obama-mandate-is-not-a-tax/.

3. Lizette Alvarez and Robert Pear, 'Florida Among States Undercutting Health Care Enrollment," *New York Times*, September, 17, 2013, available at, http://www.nytimes.com/2013/09/18/us/florida-among-states-undercutting-health-care-enrollment.html?pagewanted=all&_r=0.

4. Joe Wolverton, II, J.D., "Family-run Businesses Successfully Defend Faith Against ObamaCare Mandate," *The New American*, April 24, 2013, available at, http://www.thenewamerican.com/usnews/health-care/item/15189-family-run-businesses-successfully-defend-faith-against-obamacare-mandate.

5. Merrill Matthews, "I'm Shocked! ObamaCare Costs More Than Promised," *Forbes*, March 15, 2012, available at, http://www.forbes.com/sites/merrillmatthews/2012/03/15/im-shocked-obamacare-costs-more-than-promised/.

6. John Bresnahan and Jake Sherman, "Lawmakers, aids may get Obamacare exemption," PoliticoPro, April 24, 2013, available at, http://www.politico.com/story/2013/04/obamacare-exemption-lawmakers-aides-90610.html.

7. Wikipedia The Free Encyclopedia, "Impeachment of Bill Clinton," February 16, 2014 available at, http://en.wikipedia. org/wiki/Impeachment_of_Bill_Clinton.

8. Reuters, "Obama Will Push Immigration after Fiscal Crises is Resolved," *Huffington Post,* October 15, 2013, available at, http://www.huffingtonpost.com/2013/10/15/obama-immigration_n_4103898.html.

9. Jessica Zuckerman, "Obama Grants Amnesty to Illegal Immigrants Without Congress," The Heritage Network, The Foundry, August 30, 2013 available at, http://blog.heritage. org/2013/08/30/obama-grants-amnesty-to-illegal-immigrants-without-congress/.

10. Janet Novack, "The Hidden Tax Lesson In Chief Justice Roberts' Obamacare Ruling," *Forbes Magazine,* July 27, 2012, available at, http://blog.heritage.org/2013/08/30/obama-grants-amnesty-to-illegal-immigrants-without-congress/.

11. Sam Cappellanti, "Premium Increases for "Young Invincibles" Under the APA and the Impending Premium Spiral," The American Action Forum, October 3, 2013, available at, http:// americanactionforum.org/research/premium-increases-for-young-invincibles-under-the-aca-and-the-impending.

12. Ibid., 1.

13. Brenton Smith, "Facts on Obamacare Prove Potus Will Break These 4 Promises," Policy Mic, October 15, 2013, available at, http://www.policymic.com/articles/67167/facts-on-obamacare-prove-potus-will-break-these-4-promises.

14. Ibid., 1.

15. Lisa Barron, "Obamacare Website cost $634 Million, Faces Months of Glitches," Newsmax, October, 10, 2013, available at, http://www.newsmax.com/Newsfront/obamacare-website-millions-glitches/2013/10/10/id/530382.

16. Ashley Parker and Robert Pear, "Obama Moves to Avert Cancellation of Insurance," *The New York Times,* November 14, 2013, available at, http://www.nytimes.com/2013/11/15/us/politics/obama-to-offer-health-care-fix-to-keep-plans-democrat-says.html?ref=healthcarereform&_r=1&.

17. Jeffrey Young, "Obamacare Enrollment Numbers Fall Far Short of Target (VIDEO)," *The Huffington Post,* November 13, 2013, available at, http://www.huffingtonpost.com/2013/11/13/obamacare-enrollment_n_4266865.html.

18. Ibid., 1.

19. Jeffrey Young, "17 Million Americans Could Get Obamacare Subsidies: Report," *The Huffington Post,* November 5, 2013, available at, http://www.huffingtonpost.com/2013/11/05/obamacare-subsidies_n_4214605.html.

20. David Hogberg, "Why The "Young Invincibles" Won't Participate In The ObamaCare Exchanges and Why It Matters," National Policy Analysis, August 2013, available at, http://www.nationalcenter.org/NPA652.html.

21. Paul Roderick Gregory, "President Obama's Legacy: $20 Trillion in Debt for 2016 Victor," *Forbes Magazine,* December 25, 2012, available at, http://www.forbes.com/sites/paulroderickgregory/2012/12/25/president-obamas-legacy-20-trillion-in-deficits-for-2016-victor/.

22. Bret Baier, "George Will: Trivial" Ryan-Murray Budget Deal A "Rounding Error On The Debt," Real Clear Politics Video, December 10, 2013, available at, http://www.realclearpolitics.com/video/2013/12/10/george_will_trivial_ryan-murray_budget_deal_is_a_rounding_error_on_the_debt.html.

23. Augustino Fontevecchia, "QE4 Is Here: Bernanke Delivers $85B-A-Month Until Unemployment Falls Below 6.5%," *Forbes Magazine,* December 12, 2012, available at, http://www.forbes.com/sites/afontevecchia/2012/12/12/qe4-is-here-bernanke-delivers-85b-a-month-until-unemployment-falls-below-6-5/.

24. Avik Roy, "Obamacare Bends the Cost Curve-Upward," National Review Online, available at, http://www.nationalreview.com/corner/359352/obamacare-bends-cost-curve-upward-avik-roy.

25. Claire Chretien, "Problematic Obamacare unfair to young people, married couples," *The Crimson White,* October 8, 2013, available at, http://cw.ua.edu/2013/10/08/problematic-obamacare-unfair-to-young-people-married-couples/.

26. Robert Rector, "The New Federal Wedding Tax: How Obamacare would Dramatically Penalize Marriage, The Heritage Foundation, January 20, 2010, available at, http://www.heritage.org/research/reports/2010/01/the-new-federal-wedding-tax-how-obamacare-would-dramatically-penalize-marriage?utm=&utm_source=heritagefoundation&utm . . .

27. William Saunders and Mary Harned, "30 States Have No Opt-Out Laws Stopping Abortion Funding for Obamacare," LifeNews.com, July 5, 2013, available at, http://www.lifenews.com/2013/07/05/30-states-have-no-opt-out-laws-stopping-abortion-funding-under-obamacare/.

28. Dahlia Lithwick, "Conscience Creep: What's so wrong with Conscience Clauses?" Slate, October 3, 2013 available at, http://www.slate.com/articles/news_and_politics/jurisprudence/2013/10/is_there_a_principled_way_to_respond_to_the_proliferation_of_conscience.html.

29. Brian Koenig, "CBO: Obamacare Price Tag Shifts from $940 billion to $1.76 Trillion," Yahoo News, March 14, 2012, available at, http://news.yahoo.com/cbo-obamacare-price-tag-shifts-940-billion-1-163500655.html.

30. Ibid., 1.

31. Doug Book, "Obamacare Death Panels will begin their work with Medicare recipients," The Western Center For Journalism, October 9, 2013, available at, http://www.westernjournalism.com/obamacare-death-panels-will-begin-work-medicare-recipients/.

32. Megyn Kelly, "White House knew millions would lose doctors despite Obama's promise," The Kelly file, October 28, 2013, available at, http://www.foxnews.com/on-air/the-kelly-file/transcript/2013/10/29/white-house-knew-millions-would-lose-doctors-despite-obamas-promise.

33. Karl Marx, "From each according to his abilities, to each according to his needs," Brainy Quote, February 1, 2014, available at, http://www.brainyquote.com/quotes/quotes/k/karlmarx136396.html

34. Associated Press, "Obama: 'shop around' if you lose your health insurance plans," Fox News Politics, October 31, 2013,

available at, http://www.foxnews.com/politics/2013/10/31/obama-shop-around-if-lose-your-health-insurance-plans/.

35. Glenn Kessler, "Obama's pledge that 'no one will take away' your health plan," *The Washington Post,* October 30, 2013, available at, http://www.washingtonpost.com/blogs/fact-checker/wp/2013/10/30/obamas-pledge-that-no-one-will-take-away-your-health-plan/.

36. Wikipedia The Free Encyclopedia, "On the Justice of Roosting Chickens," February 11, 2014, available at, http://en.wikipedia.org/wiki/On_the_Justice_of_Roosting_Chickens.

37. Paul Steinhauser, "President ends year at all-time CNN polling low," CNN Poltics, December 20, 2013, available at, http://politicalticker.blogs.cnn.com/2013/12/20/president-ends-year-at-all-time-cnn-polling-low/.

Chapter Five. Environmentalism and the President's Green Energy Plans

1. Fox News, "Republicans critical of Navy's 'Great Green Fleet,' $26 a gallon fuel," Fox News Politics, July 2, 2012, available at, http://www.foxnews.com/politics/2012/07/02/gop-in-congress-critical-navy-great-green-fleet/.

2. Illinois Corn, "How much ethanol will one bushel of corn produce," ilcorn.org, March 10, 2012, available at, http://www.ilcorn.org/ethanol/ethanol-faq.

3. Dustin Dwyer, "After Backlash, Ethanol Industry is Thriving," NPR, April 26, 2012 available at, http://www.npr.org/2012/04/26/151417943/checking-in-on-eurozone-economies.

4. Kate Anderson Brower and Mark Drajem, "Environmental Groups Back Obama as Campaign Donations Trial," Bloomberg.com, April 18, 2012, available at, http://mobile.bloomberg.com/news/2012-04-18/environmental-groups-back-obama-as-campaign-donations-trail?category=.

5. Audrey Hudson, "Senate Kills Effort to Block EPA Regulations on Coal-Powered Plants," *Human Events,* June 20, 2012,

available at, http://www.humanevents.com/2012/06/20/senate-kills-effort-block-epa-regulations-coal-powered-plants/.

6. Michael W. Chapman and Fred Lucas, '$9 Billion in 'Stimulus' for Solar, Wind Projects Made–910 Final Jobs—$9.8 million per job," CNSNEWS.com, June 20, 2012, available at, http://cnsnews.com/news/article/9-billion-stimulus-solar-wind-projects-made-910-final-jobs-98-million-job.

7. Jessica R. Lovering, "Give (Tax) Credit Where Credit is Due," The Breakthrough, June 22, 2011, available at, http://thebreakthrough.org/generation_archive/give_tax_credit_where_credit_i.

8. Joe Stephens and Carol D. Leonnig, 'Solyndra Scandal," *The Washington Post,* December 25, 2011, available at, http://www.washingtonpost.com/politics/specialreports/solyndra-scandal/.

9. No author, "FY 2014 Planning and budget," EPA, December 12, 2013, available at, http://www2.epa.gov/planandbudget/fy2014.

10. Larry Bell, "EPA's Insanely Ambitious Agenda If Obama Is reelected," *Forbes Magazine,* November 4, 2012, available at, http://www.forbes.com/sites/larrybell/2012/11/04/epas-insanely-ambitious-agenda-if-obama-is-reelected/.

11. David W. Kreutzer Ph.D. and Kevin Dayaratna, "Boxer-Sanders Carbon Tax: Economic Impact," The Heritage Foundation, April 11, 2013, available at, http://www.heritage.org/research/reports/2013/04/boxer-sanders-carbon-tax-economic-impact?utm_source=Newsletter&utm_medium=Email&utm_campaign=Heritage%2BHotsheet.

12. Nicolas Loris and Katie Tubb, "EPA Administrator Nominee Gina McCarthy IN Her Own Words," The Heritage Foundation, April 10, 2013, available at, http://www.heritage.org/research/reports/2013/04/epa-administrator-nominee-gina-mccarthy-in-her-own-words?utm_source=Newsletter&utm_medium=Email&utm_campaign=Heritage . . .

13. Nicolas Loris, Diane Katz, and Katie Tubb, "10 Questions for EPA Nominee Gina McCarthy," The Heritage Foundation, April 10, 2013, available at, http://www.heritage.org/research/reports/2013/04/10-questions-for-epa-

nominee-gina-mccarthy?utm_source=Newsletter&utm_medium=Email&utm_campaign=Heritage%2BHotshee

14. AFP, "Obama Defends Green Energy Push After Budget Cuts," Breitbart—Big Government, March 15, 2013, available at: http://www.breitbart.com/system/wire/CNG—8d7f28a5931211dad296db4d6589f747—4e1.

15. John M. Broder, "After federal Jolt, Clean Energy Seeks New Spark," *The New York Times,* October 23, 2012, available at, http://www.nytimes.com/2012/10/24/business/energy-environment/future-of-american-aid-to-clean-energy.html?pagewanted=all&_r=2&.

16. The Week Staff, Solyndra's bankruptcy: 'political catastrophe' for Obama," *The Week* September 1, 2011, available at, http://theweek.com/article/index/218795/solyndras-bankruptcy-political-catastrophe-for-obama.

17. Derek Wallbank, "House Republicans back off debt limit demands," Benefitspro, February 5, 2014, available at, http://www.benefitspro.com/2014/02/05/house-republicans-back-off-debt-limit-demands.

18. Stephen Power, "Senate Halts Effort to Cap CO2 Emissions," *The Wall Street Journal,* July 23, 2010, available at, http://online.wsj.com/news/articles/SB10001424052748703467304575383373600358634.

19. Kerry Picket, Picket: EPA imposes Obama's cap and trade regs-energy prices 'Skyrocket,'" *The Washington Post,* August 20, 2011, available at, http://www.washingtontimes.com/blog/watercooler/2011/aug/20/picket-obama-08-energy-prices-will-skyrocket-under/.

20. Nichola Groom, Reuters, 'Chinese Company Is Quietly Building Natural Gas Fueling Stations Across the US," Business Insider, March 14, 2013, available at, http://www.businessinsider.com/china-pumping-money-into-a-new-us-network-of-natural-gas-fueling-stations-2013-3.

21. No Author, "China Now Importing More Oil Than Any Other Nation: Let The Fighting Begin," Before It's News, March 5, 2013, available at, http://beforeitsnews.com/

opinion-conservative/2013/03/china-now-imports-more-oil-than-any-other-nation-let-the-fighting-begin-2593046.html.

22. Jim Hoft, "Top Obama EPA Official Admits to Plan to Destroy the Coal Industry in America (Video)," Gateway Pundit, June 5, 2012, available at, http://www.thegatewaypundit.com/2012/06/top-obama-epa-official-admits-to-plan-to-destroy-the-coal-industry-in-america-video/.

23. Thomas Pyle, "Obama Pushing a Stealth Cap-and-Trade Policy," U.S. News, October 13, 2011, available at, http://www.usnews.com/opinion/blogs/on-energy/2011/10/13/obama-pushing-a-stealth-cap-and-trade-policy.

24. Hal Quinn, "The Stability of Coal in a changing Market," National Mining Association, March 7, 2012, available at, http://www.nma.org/index.php.

25. No Author, "U.S. Coal Supply and Demand: 2010 Year," U.S. Energy Information Administration, June 1, 2011, available at, http://www.eia.gov/coal/review/

26. No Author, "Obama Doubles Down On More Solyndras," Investors Business Daily, April 18, 2012, available at, http://news.investors.com/ibd-editorials/041812-608263-first-solar-and-fisker-announce-layoffs.htm.

27. Stephen Moore, "An Obama War on Coal," *The Wall Street Journal,* May 14, 2012, available at, http://online.wsj.com/news/articles/SB10001424052702304192704577403913961019378?mg=reno64-wsj&url=http%3A%2F%2Fonline.wsj.com% . . .

28. Ralph R. Reiland, 'The Chu Plan" The American Spectator, May 13, 2012, available at, http://spectator.org/articles/35910/chu-plan.

29. Ibid., 1.

30. David Boyer, *Washington Times,* "RNC Debuts New Obama Slogan: "Hype and Blame,'" Fox Nation, May 3, 2012, available at, http://nation.foxnews.com/rnc/2012/05/03/rnc-debuts-new-obama-slogan-hype-and-blame.

31. John M. Broder, "House Panel Votes to Strip EPA of Power to Regulate Greenhouse Gases," Holsteinworld, February 8, 2012, available at, http://www.holsteinworld.com/story.php?id=3418.

32. John Hayward, "Obama Regulations Kill Ohio Coal Mine, Hundreds of jobs Wiped Out," Human Events, August 1, 2012, available at, http://www.humanevents.com/2012/08/01/obama-regulations-kill-ohio-coal-mine-hundreds-of-jobs-wiped-out/.

33. Ibid., 1.

34. James Gattuso and Diane Katz, "Gattuso and Katz: Regulation and Obama's numbers," *The Washington Times,* March 15, 2012, available at, http://www.washingtontimes.com/news/2012/mar/15/regulation-and-obamas-numbers-game/.

35. David Limbaugh, "Green Energy Losses Not 'Minor Blips,'" New Max, August 7, 2012, available at, http://www.newsmax.com/Limbaugh/Green-Energy-Blips-Solyndra/2012/08/07/id/447824.

36. Dan Weil, "Economists: Sequester Would Put Damper on Economic Growth," Money News, February 22, 2013, available at, http://www.moneynews.com/newswidget/sequester-spending-cuts-economists-GDP/2013/02/22/id/491526?promo_code=F46F-1.

37. Steve Goreham, "Lisa Jackson leaving EPA and path of economic destruction," *The Washington Times,* January 2, 2013, available at, http://communities.washingtontimes.com/neighborhood/climatism-watching-climate-science/2013/jan/2/lisa-jackson-leaving-epa-and-path-economic-destruc/

38. William F. Jasper, "Obama Vows to Bypass Congress on Climate Change," *The New American* February 15, 2013, available at, http://www.thenewamerican.com/usnews/politics/item/14542-obama-vows-to-bypass-congress-on-climate-change

39. Juliet Eilperin, "Salazar plan puts half of Alaska petroleum reserve off-limits to drilling," *The Washington Post,* August 13, 2012, available at, http://www.washingtonpost.com/national/health-science/salazar-plan-puts-half-of-alaska-petroleum-reserve-off-limits-to-drilling/2012/08/13/d542863c-e57f-11e1-8741-940e3f6dbf48_story.html.

40. Adam Fetcher, "Secretary Salazar Announces Decision to Withdraw Public Lands near Grand Canyon from New Mining," U.S. Department of Interior, January 9, 2012, available at, http://www.doi.gov/news/pressreleases/Secretary-Salazar-Announces-Decision-to-Withdraw-Public-Lands-near-Grand-Canyon-from-New-Mining-Claims.cfm.

41. No Author, "Coal" Institute for Energy Research, February 1, 2014, available at, http://www.instituteforenergyresearch.org/energy-overview/coal/.

42. No Author, "Sulfur Dioxide Scrubbers" Duke Energy, January 18, 2014, available at, http://www.duke-energy.com/environment/air-quality/sulfur-dioxide-scrubbers.asp.

43. Amy Harder, "What Does North Dakota's Oil Boom Mean For America?" *National Journal,* August 26, 2013, available at, http://www.nationaljournal.com/policy/insiders/energy/what-does-north-dakota-s-oil-boom-mean-for-america-20130826.

44. Lori Anne Dolqueist, "Let it Flow—The Case for Dam Removal," Environmental Leader, August 15, 2012, available at, http://www.environmentalleader.com/2012/08/15/let-it-flow-the-case-for-dam-removal/.

45. Michelle Malkin "Obama the Job-Killing Owl-killer," Michelle Malkin, November 28, 2012, available at, http://michellemalkin.com/2012/11/28/obama-the-job-killing-owl-killer/.

Chapter Six. Big Government and the President

1. Richard Neustadt, review by Leif Ellington, "Presidential Power and Modern Presidents," Regis Education, January 10, 2014, available at, http://academic.regis.edu/jriley/414%20Power%20to%20Persuade.htm.

2. Ibid., 1(p. 152).

3. Martha T. Moore, "NSA denies Obama knew of spying on German Leader," *USA Today,* October 27, 2013, available at, http://www.usatoday.com/story/news/nation/2013/10/27/rogers-house-intelligence-chief-nsa-europe/3282161/.

4. Graham E. Fuller, "With Syria, Iran, has Obama broken the mold in US foreign policy," *The Christian Science Monitor,* October 3, 2013, available at, http://www.csmonitor.com/Commentary/Global-Viewpoint/2013/1003/With-Syria-Iran-has-Obama-broken-the-mold-in-US-foreign-policy.

5. Matea Gold, President Obama heads into intensive fall fundraising stretch," *The Washington Post,* October, 25, 2013, available at, http://www.washingtonpost.com/blogs/post-politics/wp/2013/10/25/president-obama-heads-into-intensive-fall-fundraising-stretch/.

6. Wikipedia The Free Encyclopedia, "Barak Obama," February 10, 2014, available at, http://en.wikipedia.org/wiki/Barack_Obama.

7. Carol Leonnig, "Senate's filibuster decision could reshape influential D.C. federal appeals court," *The Washington Post,* November 21, 2013, available at, http://www.washingtonpost.com/politics/senates-filibuster-decision-could-reshape-influential-dc-federal-appeals-court/2013/11/21/3b3fd76a-52de-11e3-a7f0-b790929232e1_story.html.

8. No Author, "Franklin Dalano Roosevelt's "Court Packing" Plan," United States Senate Committee on the Judiciary, October 10, 2013, available at, http://www.judiciary.senate.gov/about/history/CourtPacking.cfm.

9. No Author, "Republic of the United States of America," History, February 7, 2014, available at, http://www.republicoftheunitedstates.org/what-is-the-republic/history/.

10. Carol Howell, "Agencies of the Federal Government," Center for Small Government, December 8, 2013, available at, http://www.centerforsmallgovernment.com/small-government-news/agencies-of-the-federal-government/.

11. No Author, "Government Departments and Agencies," USA.gov, February 7, 2014, available at, http://www.usa.gov/Agencies.shtml.

12. Jonathan Turkey, "The rise of the fourth branch of government," *The Washington Post,* May 24, 2013, available at, http://www.washingtonpost.com/opinions/the-rise-of-the-fourth-branch-of-government/2013/05/24/c7faaad0-c2ed-11e2-9fe2-6ee52d0eb7c1_story.html.

13. Michael Kirkland, "Constitutional shoving in the high court," UPI, December 15, 2013, available at, http://www.upi.com/Top_News/US/2013/12/15/Constitutional-shoving-in-the-high-court/UPI-73241387096200/.

14. Ibid., 1.

15. Liberty Counsel, "President Obama Stacks the Court in frightening Power Grab," *Cananda Free Press,* November 21, 2013, available at, http://canadafreepress.com/index.php/article/59408.

16. Alfred S. Regnery, "Obama's Court Packing Plan," Breitbart Big Government, June 12, 2013, available at, http://www.breitbart.com/Big-Government/2013/06/12/Obamas-Court-Packing-Plan.

17. David Simon, "David Simon: "'There are now two Americas. My country in a horror show,'" *The Observer,* December 7, 2013, available at, http://www.theguardian.com/world/2013/dec/08/david-simon-capitalism-marx-two-americas-wire.

18. Robert C. Barnister, P.h.D, "Social Darwinism," Colorado Education, November 10, 2013, available at, http://autocww.colorado.edu/~blackmon/E64ContentFiles/SociologyAndReform/SocialDarwinism.html.

19. Jonathan Bernstein, "When money matters in an election," *The Washington Post,* May 6, 2013, available at, http://www.washingtonpost.com/blogs/post-partisan/wp/2013/05/06/when-money-matters-in-elections/.

20. Wikipedia The Free Encyclopedia, "Sixteenth Amendment to the United States Constitution," February 10, 2014, available at, http://en.wikipedia.org/wiki/Sixteenth_Amendment_to_the_United_States_Constitution.

21. Patrick J. Buchanan, "Rockefeller Republicans," Lew Rockwell, September 18, 2010, available at, http://archive.lewrockwell.com/buchanan/buchanan144.html.

22. Francis Fukayama, "Neo-conservatism," Institute for Policy Studies, February 5, 2014, available at, http://rightweb.irc-online.org/profile/Fukuyama_Francis.

23. Ivo H. Daalder, "Policy Implications of the Bush Doctrine of Preemption," Council on Foreign Relations, November 16, 2002. Available at, http://www.cfr.org/international-law/policy-implications-bush-doctrine-preemption/p5251.

24. David Bosco, "What divides neocons and liberal interventionists," *Foreign Policy Magazine,* April 9, 2002, available at, http://bosco.foreignpolicy.com/posts/2012/04/09/what_divides_neocons_and_liberal_interventionists.

25. Elise Foley, "Barak Obama Immigration Reform," *The Huffington Post,* January 13, 2014, available at, http://www.huffingtonpost.com/tag/barack-obama-immigration-reform.

26. No Author, "The 1964 Republican Campaign," PBS American Experience, February 6, 2014, available at, http://www.pbs.org/wgbh/americanexperience/features/general-article/rockefellers-campaign/.

27. Jules Witcover, "Scranton was GOP moderate," *The Telegraph,* April 3, 2013, available at, http://www.nashuatelegraph.com/opinion/perspectives/1012429-474/scranton-was-gop-moderate.html#.

28. Wikipedia The Free Encyclopedia, "William Scranton," February 3, 2014, available at, http://www.nashuatelegraph.com/opinion/perspectives/1012429-474/scranton-was-gop-moderate.html#.

29. Frank Freidel and Hugh Sidney, "Ronald Reagan," The White House, February 1, 2014, available at, http://www.whitehouse.gov/about/presidents/ronaldreagan.

30. Mike Tirone, "Presidents and Their Debt: From FDR to Obama," Wealth Wire, July 22, 2011, available at, http://www.wealthwire.com/news/finance/1520.

31. Ibid., 1.

32. No Author, "The Organization of the Bureaucracy," USHistory.ORG, February 4, 2014 available at, http://www.ushistory.org/gov/8b.asp.

33. No Author, "How did Hover respond to the Great Depression?" Answers, February 8, 2014, available at, http://wiki.answers.com/Q/How_did_hover_respond_to_the_great_depression.

34. No Author, "The Hoover Administration," UShistory.com, February 8, 2014, available at, http://www.u-s-history.com/pages/h1445.html.

35. Ian Schwartz, "'Obama: "We're Not Going T0 Be Waiting For Legislation . . . I Can Use That Pen To Sign Executive Orders,"' [video], Real Clear Politics, January 14, 2014, available at, http://www.realclearpolitics.com/video/2014/01/14/obama_were_not_going_to_be_waiting_for_legislation_i_can_use_that_pen_to_sign_executive_orders.html.

36. No Author, 'Constitution Article 2, Section 4," Shmoop We Speak Student, February 2, 2014, available at, http://www.shmoop.com/constitution/article-2-section-4.html.

37. Alexander Hamilton, "Federalist No. 65 The Powers of the Senate Continued" Academic Brooklyn, March 7, 1788, available at, http://academic.brooklyn.cuny.edu/history/johnson/fedimpeachment.htm.

38. Richard Winchester, "Why Obama Should be Impeached, but Won't," *American Thinker,* November 24, 2013, available at, http://www.americanthinker.com/2013/11/why_obama_should_be_impeached_but_wont.html.

39. Wikipedia The Free Encyclopedia, "American Recovery and Reinvestment Act of 2009," February 3, 2014, available at, http://en.wikipedia.org/wiki/American_Recovery_and_Reinvestment_Act_of_2009.

40. Brad Plumer, "A closer look at Obama's "90 billion for green jobs,"' *The Washington Post,* October 1, 2012, available at, http://www.washingtonpost.com/blogs/wonkblog/wp/2012/10/04/a-closer-look-at-obamas-90-billion-for-clean-energy/.

41. Brad Plumer, "7 reasons why Congress's failure to extend unemployment insurance matters," *The Washington Post,* January 14, 2014, available at, http://www.washingtonpost.com/blogs/wonkblog/wp/2014/01/14/an-extension-of-unemployment-insurance-just-failed-in-the-senate/.

42. John R. Hendrickson, "What is Supply-Side Economics?" Tax Education Foundation, February 3, 2014, available at, http://www.taxeducationfoundation.org/briefs/2012-01.htm.

43. Olleg Shynkarenko, "Obama's New Immigration Policy Explained: 7 Key Factors," *The Daily Beast,* June 15, 2012, available at, http://www.thedailybeast.com/articles/2012/06/15/obama-s-new-immigration-policy-explained-7-key-facts.html.

44. Brad Plumer, "Can Obama legalize 11 million immigrants on his own?" *The Washington Post,* November 11, 2013, available at, http://www.washingtonpost.com/blogs/wonkblog/wp/2013/11/14/can-obama-legalize-11-million-immigrants-on-his-own/.

Chapter Seven American Foreign Policy

1. David Simpson and Josh Levs, "Israeli PM Netanyahu: Iran nuclear deal 'historic mistake,'" CNN, November 25, 2013, available at, http://www.cnn.com/2013/11/24/world/meast/iran-israel/.

2. No Author, "Obama calls Netanyahu after Israeli leader slams Iran nuke deal," FOXNEWS Politics, November 24, 2013, available at, http://www.foxnews.com/politics/2013/11/24/obama-calls-netanyahu-after-israeli-leader-slams-iran-nuke-deal/.

3. Jeremy Bowen, "Iran agrees to curb nuclear activity at Geneva talks," BBC News, November 24, 2013, available at, http://www.bbc.co.uk/news/world-middle-east-25074729.

4. Glenn Kessler, "President Obama and the 'red line' on Syria's chemical weapons," *The Washington Post,* September, 6, 2013, available at, http://www.washingtonpost.com/blogs/fact-checker/wp/2013/09/06/president-obama-and-the-red-line-on-syrias-chemical-weapons/.

5. Suzanne Maloney, "As Nuclear Talks Inch Forward Iran's Supreme Leader Tacks Right With A Blistering Speech," Brookings Education, November 22, 2013, http://www.brookings.edu/blogs/iran-at-saban/posts/2013/11/21-khamenei-iran-supreme-leader-speech.

6. Ibid., 1.

7. Anthony Shadid, "Turkey Predicts Alliance with Egypt as Regional Anchors," *The New York Times,* September 18, 2011,

available at, http://www.nytimes.com/2011/09/19/world/middleeast/turkey-predicts-partnership-with-egypt-as-regional-anchors.html?pagewanted=all&_r=3&.

8. No Author, "Hezbollah reaffirms support for Syria's Assad," Aljazeera, August 17, 2013, available at, http://www.aljazeera.com/news/middleeast/2013/08/201381619185852996.html.

9. Ariel Ben Solomon, "Report: Iran seeking closer relations with Muslim Brotherhood," *The Jerusalem Post,* August 14, 2013, available at, http://www.jpost.com/Middle-East/Report-Iran-seeking-closer-relations-with-Muslim-Brotherhood-323043.

10. Barak Obama, "Text: Obama's Speech in Cairo," *The New York Times,* June 4, 2009, available at, http://www.nytimes.com/2009/06/04/us/politics/04obama.text.html?pagewanted=all.

11. Danielle Pletka, "Does Obama hate Israel?" American Enterprise Institute, September 25, 2012, available at, http://www.aei.org/article/foreign-and-defense-policy/does-obama-hate-israel/.

12. Vladimir V. Putin, "A Plea for Caution From Russia," *The New York Times* Opinion Pages, September 11, 2013, available at, http://www.nytimes.com/2013/09/12/opinion/putin-plea-for-caution-from-russia-on-syria.html?pagewanted=all&_r=0.

13. No Author, "Lend Lease Tanks and Aircraft for Russia 1941-1945," WW2-weapons.com, February 10, 2014, available at, http://ww2-weapons.com/History/Production/Russia/Lend-Lease.htm.

14. Wikipedia The Free Encyclopedia, "United Nations," February 6, 2014, available at, http://en.wikipedia.org/wiki/United_Nations.

15. No Author, "International Human Rights Law," United For Human Rights, February 8, 2014, Available at, http://www.humanrights.com/what-are-human-rights/international-human-rights-law-continued.html.

16. John Winthrop, "City upon a Hill," mtholyoke.edu, February 5, 2014, available at, https://www.mtholyoke.edu/acad/intrel/winthrop.htm.

17. Jim Newman, "Putin Kisses Staff of Russian Orthodox Church," Skeptic Money, July 27, 2013, available at, http://www.skepticmoney.com/russian-orthodox-church-and-putin/.

18. Judson Berger, "Clinton calls on Russia to stop arming Assad regime," FOXNEWS Politics, available at, http://www.foxnews.com/politics/2012/06/13/state-department-rejects-russia-accusation-arming-syrian-opposition/.

19. Zachary Laub and Jonathan Masters, "Syria's Crisis and the Global Response," Council on Foreign Relations, September 11, 2013, available at, http://www.cfr.org/syria/syrias-crisis-global-response/p28402.

20. Tim Arango and Clifford Krauss, "China Is Reaping Biggest Benefits of Iraq Oil Boom," *The New York Times,* June 2, 2013, available at, http://www.nytimes.com/2013/06/03/world/middleeast/china-reaps-biggest-benefits-of-iraq-oil-boom.html?pagewanted=all&_r=1&.

21. Rowan Scarborough, "Al Qaeda 'rat line' from Syria to Iraq turns back against Assad," *The Washington Times,* August 19, 2013, available at, http://www.washingtontimes.com/news/2013/aug/19/al-qaeda-rat-line-from-syria-to-iraq-turns-back-ag/.

22. Ghaith Abdul-Ahad, "Syria's al-Nusra Front ruthless, organized and taking control," *The Guardian,* July 10, 2013, available at, http://www.theguardian.com/world/2013/jul/10/syria-al-nusra-front-jihadi.

23. Will Fulton, Joseph Holliday, and Sam Wyer, "Iranian Strategy in Syria," Institute for the Study of War, February 1, 2014, available at, http://www.understandingwar.org/report/iranian-strategy-syria.

24. Michael R. Gordon and Eric Schmitt, "Russia Sends More Advanced Missiles to Aid Assad in Syria," *The New York Times,* May 16, 2013, available at, http://www.understandingwar.org/report/iranian-strategy-syria.

25. General Martin E. Dempsey, "General Dempsey's Letter to Senator Levin on the U.S. Military and Syrian Conflict, July 2013," Council on Foreign Relations, July 19, 2013, available at, http://www.cfr.org/syria/general-dempseys-

letter-senator-levin-us-military-syrian-conflict-july-2013/
p31198.

26. Fred Kaplan, "Rolling Blunder," *Washington Monthly Magazine,*
May 2004, available at, http://www.washingtonmonthly.com/
features/2004/0405.kaplan.html.

27. Ann Coulter, "Clinton's 1994 'Peace' with N. Korea," Real
Clear Politics, October 12, 2006, available at, http://www.
realclearpolitics.com/articles/2006/10/clintons_new_glow_job.
html.

28. Barbara O'Brien, "Blame Bush for North Korea's Nukes, Part
I, Mahablog, February 10, 2005, available at, http://www.
mahablog.com/oldsite/id34.html.

29. Daryl Kimball, "Chronology of U.S.-North Korean Nuclear
and Missile Diplomacy," Arms Control Association, February
10, 2014, available at, http://www.armscontrol.org/factsheets/
dprkchron.

30. Natalie Ornell. "China Skirts U.S. Sanctions On
Iranian Oil," China Digital Times, August 21, 2013,
available at, http://chinadigitaltimes.net/2013/08/
china-skirts-us-sanctions-on-iranian-oil/.

31. Cheryl K. Chumley, "Obama has 'head handed to him'
in secret Iran sanction deal amid nuclear talks," *The
Washington Times,* November 8, 2013, available at,
http://www.washingtontimes.com/news/2013/nov/8/
obama-has-head-handed-him-secret-iran-sanction-dea/.

32. No Author, "Rouhani: Iran will not give up nuclear rights,"
Aljazeera, November 10, 2013, available at, http://www.
aljazeera.com/news/middleeast/2013/11/rouhani-iran-will-not-
give-up-nuclear-rights-201311107178166380.html.

33. Karl Vick, "Israel Remains Suspicious As Iran
Nuclear Talks Stall," Time World, November 11,
2013, available at, http://world.time.com/2013/11/11/
israel-remains-suspicious-as-iran-nuclear-talks-stall/.

34. Joseph S. Nye, "What China and Russia Don't Get About Soft
Power," *Foreign Policy Magazine,* April 29, 2013, available

at, http://www.foreignpolicy.com/articles/2013/04/29/what_china_and_russia_don_t_get_about_soft_power.

35. Wikipedia The Free Encyclopedia, 'War on Terror,'' February 11, 2014: http://en.wikipedia.org/wiki/War_on_Terror.

36. Peter G. Peterson, "The U.S. spend more on defense in 2012 than did the countries with the next 10 highest defense spending budgets combined." Peter G. Peterson Foundation, April 12, 2013, available at, http://pgpf.org/Chart-Archive/0053_defense-comparison.

37. John Lewis Gaddis, "Mutual Assured Destruction," Nuclearfile. org, February 6, 2014, available at, http://www.nuclearfiles.org/menu/key-issues/nuclear-weapons/history/cold-war/strategy/strategy-mutual-assured-destruction.htm.

38. Maayana Miskin, "Report: Israel has 80 Nuclear Warheads; Production Frozen," Israel National News, September 15, 2013, available at, http://www.israelnationalnews.com/News/News.aspx/171906.

39. Wikipedia The Free Encyclopedia, "Germany and Weapons of Mass Destruction," February 10, 2014, available at, http://en.wikipedia.org/wiki/Germany_and_weapons_of_mass_destruction.

40. Daniel Halper, "Harry Reid Blocks Iran Sanctions Vote," *The Weekly Standard,* January 13, 2014, available at, http://www.weeklystandard.com/blogs/harry-reid-blocks-iran-sanctions-vote_774165.html.

41. Tova Dvorin, "Obama Refuses to Speak to Netanyahu," Arutz Sheva Israel National News, November 19, 2013, available at, http://www.israelnationalnews.com/News/News.aspx/174090.

42. Michael Wilner, Geneva deal begins Jan. 20, allows Iran to continue centrifuge research," *The Jerusalem Post,* January 12, 2014, available at, http://www.jpost.com/International/Geneva-deal-begins-Jan-20-allows-Iran-to-continue-centrifuge-research-337940.

43. Batsheva Sobelman, "Kerry back in Middle East for talks with Israel, Palestinian leaders," *Los Angeles Times,* December 12, 2013, available at, http://articles.latimes.com/2013/dec/12/world/la-fg-wn-israel-palestinian-authority-talks-kerry-20131212.

44. Tova Dvorin, "Obama Refuses to Speak to Netanyahu," Arutz Sheva Israel National News, November 19, 2013, available at, http://www.israelnationalnews.com/News/News.aspx/174090.

45. No Author, "John Kerry cancels trip to Israel at last minute," UPI, January 13, 2014, available at, http://www.upi.com/Top_News/World-News/2014/01/13/John-Kerry-cancels-trip-to-Israel-at-last-minute/UPI-30071389620313/.

46. Sayyid Ali Khamenei, "Supreme Leader's Speech in Meeting with Basij Commanders," The Supreme Leader, November 20, 2013, available at, http://www.leader.ir/langs/en/index.php?p=contentShow&id=11328.

47. Keith Johnson, "Kerry Makes It Official: 'Era of Monroe Doctrine IS Over.'" *The Wall Street Journal,* November 18, 2013, available at, http://blogs.wsj.com/washwire/2013/11/18/kerry-makes-it-official-era-of-monroe-doctrine-is-over/.

48. No Author, "The Monroe Doctrine," UShistory.org, February 1, 2014, available at, http://www.ushistory.org/documents/monroe.htm.

49. Wikipedia The Free Encyclopedia, 'Roosevelt Corollary," February 9, 2014, available at, http://en.wikipedia.org/wiki/Roosevelt_Corollary.

50. Harry Kreisler, 'Through the Realist Lens: Conversation with John Mearsheimer," Institute of International Studies, UC Berkeley, (2002), available at, http://globetrotter.berkeley.edu/people2/Mearsheimer/mearsheimer-con2.html.

51. Kenneth Rapoza, "After a Decade Long Wait China And Russia Ink 'Super jet' Military Deal," *Forbes Magazine,* March 25, 2013, available at, http://www.forbes.com/sites/kenrapoza/2013/03/25/after-a-decade-long-wait-china-and-russia-ink-super-jet-military-deal/.

52. Calum MacLeod and Oren Dorell, "Chinese navy makes waves in South China Sea, *USA Today,* March 27, 2013, available at, http://www.usatoday.com/story/news/world/2013/03/27/china-military-south-china-sea/2023947/?utm_

source=Newsletter&utm_medium=Email&utm_campaign=Heritage%2BHotsheet.

53. Patrick J. Buchanan, 'China wins competition because US regulations don't apply," On the Issues, February 8, 2014, available at, http://www.ontheissues.org/celeb/Pat_Buchanan_Foreign_Policy.htm.

54. Ted Galen Carpenter, "President Bush's Taiwan Policy Immoral and Dangerous," CATO Institute, March 31, 2004, available at, http://www.cato.org/publications/commentary/president-bushs-taiwan-policy-immoral-dangerous.

55. Bonnie Glaser, "A Check sheet for Obama's Taiwan test," World Security Network, January 8, 2009, available at, http://www.worldsecuritynetwork.com/United-States/Glaser-Bonnie/A-check-sheet-for-Obamas-Taiwan-test.

About the Author

My name is Kevin C. Caffrey and I have a Master's Degree in Political Science from the University of Colorado at Denver. My undergraduate work began in my youth chiefly at Central Connecticut State University and this is where I received a majority of my political science credits. Because of the location of the school many of my professors held doctor's degrees from either Harvard University or Yale University. I finished my undergraduate work at Metropolitan State University of Denver. Most of my credits went well beyond the necessary amount of credits needed to graduate. The reason why I needed to continue on in the undergraduate program was so that I could receive a Secondary Education License in Social Studies.

In order to get my Secondary Education License I taught American History and United States Government at one of the local high schools in a poor section of Denver, Colorado. I learned a lot about the students that I taught. However, it was my hands-on teaching experience that drew me to one conclusion. I decided that teaching high school students' was not for me. In order to move forward in teaching I decided to get a Master's Degree so that I could teach at the college level.

I was born in Hartford Connecticut and grew up in West Hartford Connecticut. West Hartford offers one of the best high school educations in the country. I was raised Roman Catholic and went to weekly classes at the church and also went to church every Sunday. While living in Tampa, Florida a girl I was dating introduced me to the Methodist Church. It was at that point that I became a born again Christian filled with the Holy Spirit. It is my Christian ideological thinking that guides my moral and ethical positions on various political social issues.